GW01368384

THE WOLVES REVIEW 1995

Published by Sports Projects Ltd

ACKNOWLEDGEMENTS

The Wolves Review 1995
First published in Great Britain in June 1995.
by Sports Projects Limited.

© 1995 Sports Projects Limited
188 Lightwoods Hill, Smethwick, Warley,
West Midlands B67 5EH.

ISBN 0 946866 25 2

Printed and bound in Great Britain
by The Bath Press, Avon.

All rights reserved.
No part of this publication may be reproduced, stored in any retrieval system or transmitted, in any form or by any means, without the written consent of the publisher.

Editor: Tony Leighton

Statistics: Tony Matthews

Photographs: Empics

Design, layout and graphics: Nadine Goldingay

Special thanks to: Reg Thacker;
Tommy Leighton;
Ray Spiller (Association of Football Statisticians).

KEY

❑	Player booked
■	Player sent off
32	Figure in goals column indicates time of goal
†56	First substitute and time of substitution
†	First player substituted
‡56	Second substitute and time of substitution
‡	Second player substituted

Notes:

● *In friendly games, where several substitutes may have appeared, additional symbols are used in the following order:* #, §, ††, ‡‡, ##, §§, ≠.

The Wolves Review 1995

FOREWORD

Taylor-made for a season of high excitement

It ended in disappointment, but what a season 1994-95 was for Wolves and their supporters.

The excitement never let up - from the high anticipation born of big-name pre-season signings, through fluctuating League fortunes and nerve-jangling FA Cup ties, to the final devastation of defeat in the promotion play-offs.

The highs and lows, the dramas and traumas are all recorded here in the first of what is to become an annual Wolves Review.

This is much more than just another club yearbook - it takes the reader on a highly eventful journey, from the first kick of the season to the last.

Re-live great moments such as the early season thrashing of Albion, David Kelly's hat-trick against Bristol City, the dramatic FA Cup penalty shoot-out with Sheffield Wednesday and Steve Bull's 250th Wolves goal which clinched a place in the play-offs.

Gnash your teeth too, at the memory of a last gasp Coca-Cola Cup defeat by Nottingham Forest, the chronic injury problems which were the main reason for missing promotion, and that last-match double knock-out by John McGinlay - a punch which floored David Kelly but did not earn the Bolton striker a red card, followed by the goal which brought Wolves' campaign to its bitter end.

As well as recalling all the on-field first team action, the Review gives Reserve and Youth team statistics, notes the on-going hive of transfer activity, looks at Graham Taylor's management team and reflects on the death of Billy Wright in September.

It was the passing away of the greatest player ever to wear a Wolves shirt, not the failure to win promotion, which was the real cause for sadness during the 1994-95 season.

The great man is gone, but hopefully his memory can serve to inspire an era of Wolves achievement to match the glory years in which he played such a prominent part.

Tony Leighton
June 1995.

CONTENTS

Foreword   *Page 3*

FIRST TEAM MATCHES

Date	H/A	Opponent	Score	Scorers	Page
Aug 13	H	Reading	1-0	Froggatt	6
Aug 21	A	Notts County	1-1	Thompson (pen)	8
Aug 24	A	Lecce (Ang-Ital Grp A)	1-0	Kelly	10
Aug 28	H	West Bromwich Albion	2-0	Thompson (pen), Kelly	12
Aug 30	A	Watford	1-2	Emblen	14
Sep 3	A	Sunderland	1-1	Venus	16
Sep 6	H	Ascoli (Ang-Ital Grp A)	0-1		18
Sep 10	H	Tranmere Rovers	2-0	Stewart, Emblen	20
Sep 13	H	Southend United	5-0	Emblen, Kelly, Froggatt, Walters, Bull	22
Sep 17	A	Burnley	1-0	Bull	24
Sep 20	A	Chesterfield (CCC 1/1)	3-1	Bull 2, Kelly	26
Sep 24	A	Portsmouth	2-1	Walters, Kelly	28
Sep 27	H	Chesterfield (CCC 1/2)	1-1	Froggatt	30
Oct 1	H	Port Vale	2-1	Thompson 2 (pens)	32
Oct 5	A	Venezia (Ang-Ital Grp A)	1-2	Venus	34
Oct 8	A	Swindon Town	2-3	Kelly 2	36
Oct 15	H	Grimsby Town	2-1	Thompson (pen), Venus	38
Oct 22	H	Millwall	3-3	Bull 2, Venus	40
Oct 26	H	Nottingham F. (CCC 3)	2-3	Birch, Kelly	42
Oct 30	A	Stoke City	1-1	Bull	44
Nov 1	A	Bristol City	5-1	Walters, Thompson (pen), Kelly 3	46
Nov 5	H	Luton Town	2-3	Stewart, Johnson (og)	48
Nov 15	H	Atalanta (Ang-Ital Grp A)	1-1	Mills	50
Nov 20	A	Middlesbrough	0-1		52
Nov 23	H	Bolton Wanderers	3-1	Thompson (pen), Coleman (og), Birch	54
Nov 27	H	Derby County	0-2		56
Dec 4	A	Millwall	0-1		58
Dec 10	H	Notts County	1-0	Bull	60
Dec 18	A	Reading	2-4	Bull, Quinn (og)	62
Dec 26	A	Oldham Athletic	1-4	Dennison	64
Dec 28	H	Charlton Athletic	2-0	Bull, Chapple (og)	66
Dec 31	A	Barnsley	3-1	Dennison, Mills, Emblen	68
Jan 2	H	Sheffield United	2-2	De Wolf (pen), Emblen	70
Jan 7	A	Mansfield Town (FAC 3)	3-2	Kelly, Dennison, Mills	72
Jan 14	H	Stoke City	2-0	Kelly, Dennison	74
Jan 30	A	Sheffield Wed. (FAC 4)	0-0		76
Feb 4	A	Bolton Wanderers	1-5	Goodman	78
Feb 8	H	Sheffield Wed. (FAC 4R)	1-1	Kelly (Won 4-3 on penalties)	80
Feb 11	H	Bristol City	2-0	Dennison, Kelly	82
Feb 18	H	Leicester City (FAC 5)	1-0	Kelly	84

The Wolves Review 1995

CONTENTS

Feb	21	H	Middlesbrough	0-2		86
Feb	25	A	Port Vale	4-2	De Wolf 3 (1 pen), Bull	88
Mar	5	H	Portsmouth	1-0	Bull	90
Mar	8	H	Sunderland	1-0	Thompson (pen)	92
Mar	11	A	Crystal Palace (FAC 6)	1-1	Cowans	94
Mar	15	A	West Bromwich Albion	0-2		96
Mar	18	H	Watford	1-1	Thomas	98
Mar	22	H	Crystal Palace (FAC 6R)	1-4	Kelly	100
Mar	24	H	Burnley	2-0	Bull, Emblen	102
Apr	1	A	Southend United	1-0	Bull	104
Apr	4	A	Luton Town	3-3	Kelly 2, Emblen	106
Apr	8	H	Barnsley	0-0		108
Apr	12	A	Derby County	3-3	Goodman, Richards 2	110
Apr	15	A	Charlton Athletic	2-3	Bull 2	112
Apr	17	H	Oldham Athletic	2-1	Kelly 2	114
Apr	22	A	Sheffield United	3-3	Goodman, Bull, Kelly	116
Apr	29	A	Grimsby Town	0-0		118
May	3	A	Tranmere Rovers	1-1	Bull	120
May	7	H	Swindon Town	1-1	Thompson (pen)	122
May	14	H	Bolton W. (Play-off 1/1)	2-1	Bull, Venus	124
May	17	A	Bolton W. (Play-off 1/2)	0-2	(aet, 90 minutes: 1-0)	126

BILLY WRIGHT – A tribute   128

FRIENDLY MATCHES

July	19	A	Hvidovre	2-1	Bull 2	128
July	20	A	Solve	6-1	Daley 2, Mills, Froggatt, Dennison 2	129
July	23	A	Smedby Boik	9-1	Mills 3, Bull 5, Thompson	129
July	25	A	Kristianstads FF	2-0	Bull, Daley	130
July	27	A	Asarums IF FK	3-1	Mills 3	130
Aug	3	H	Manchester United	1-2	Bull	131
Aug	6	H	Coventry City	2-1	Bull, Kelly	132
Aug	8	A	Dundee	4-1	Blake (og), Kelly, Cook, Froggatt	133
Oct	10	A	Kidderminster Harriers	2-2	Bull 2	134
May	9	A	Shrewsbury Town	3-1	Bull, Goodman, Kelly	135

APPENDIX

MANAGEMENT AND PLAYERS	Pen pictures and statistics	137
ENDSLEIGH LEAGUE	Final table, play-off results and first team statistics	152
STATISTICS OF THE SEASON	Wolves facts and figures from 1994-95	154
RESERVE & YOUTH	Results, appearances and goalscorers	155
SUBSCRIBERS	Fans' roll call	159

The Wolves Review 1995   5

MATCH 1 • ENDSLEIGH LEAGUE DIVISION 1

Saturday 13th August 1994 • Molineux • 3.00pm

WOLVES 1 READING 0

Half-time 1-0 • Attendance 27,012

Referee Jim PARKER (Preston)

Linesmen J.B. GOULDING and K.J. NIND

Gold Shirts with Black Trim, Black Shorts	Goals	Blue and White Hooped Shirts, White Shorts	Goals
1 Mike STOWELL		1 Shaka HISLOP	
2 James SMITH		2 Andy BERNAL	
3 Andy THOMPSON		3 Dylan KERR	
4 Darren FERGUSON		4 Dariusz WDOWCZYK ‡	
5 Neil EMBLEN		5 Adrian WILLIAMS	
6 Peter SHIRTLIFF		6 Phil PARKINSON	
7 Kevin KEEN		7 Scott TAYLOR †	
8 Geoff THOMAS		8 Mick GOODING	
9 Steve BULL †		9 Jimmy QUINN	
10 David KELLY		10 Stuart LOVELL	
11 Steve FROGGATT	11	11 Simon OSBORN	
Substitutes		*Substitutes*	
12 Mark VENUS		12 Michael GILKES †65	
14 Lee MILLS †12		14 Geoff HOPKINS ‡72	
gk Paul JONES		gk None	

BEFORE	P	W	D	L	F	A	pts	AFTER	P	W	D	L	F	A	pts
Wolves	0	0	0	0	0	0	0	Wolves	1	1	0	0	1	0	3
Reading	0	0	0	0	0	0	0	Reading	1	0	0	1	0	1	0

Steve Froggatt, Neil Emblen and James Smith all make their competitive debuts... Geoff Thomas returns to first team action after missing 11 months through injury... Froggy caps his first appearance with a goal... Bully substituted after only 12 minutes through hamstring trouble... Jimmy Quinn misses a late sitter to leave Wolves with three points.

The Wolves Review 1995

MOLINEUX DRAWS DAY'S TOP CROWD

Dream start for Froggy

Anticipation and high expectation are in the air as the season kicks off with Wolves 9-2 favourites to win Division One and so gain promotion to the Premiership in Graham Taylor's first full season as manager.

The biggest opening day crowd in the country is at Molineux to watch Wolves entertain newly promoted Reading with three players making their competitive debuts.

Two of them, winger Steve Froggatt and central defender Neil Emblen, are big money signings – Froggatt a £1 million capture from Aston Villa and Emblen costing £600,000 from Millwall.

The third, former YTS full back Jamie Smith, has earned his call up after a splendid pre-season which included a fine performance against Ryan Giggs in the friendly against Manchester United.

It is also a big day for midfielder Geoff Thomas, making his first senior appearance since sustaining a dreadful knee injury during the 2-0 win at Sunderland last September.

On a sunny Molineux afternoon the only disappointing note is the absence of record signing Tony Daley. The England winger's £1.3m close season move from Villa sent a surge of excitement through Wolves supporters, but a knee injury sustained on the last day of the pre–season Scandinavian tour has sidelined him for a possible four months.

Even without Daley's electrifying speed the game starts at a cracking pace, the tempo of the game perhaps contributing to an unhappy debut for Emblen.

Two early mistakes by the tall, blond-haired defender present Reading with good goal-scoring opportunities, but Jimmy Quinn fluffs the first and Stuart Lovell the second.

Sandwiched between the two errors, however, is a great moment for Froggatt in the 11th minute. Steve Bull threads the ball into the penalty area and when Darren Ferguson gets in a 15-yard shot which goalkeeper Shaka Hislop can only parry, Froggatt pounces on the rebound to drive home Wolves' first goal of the season.

Molineux celebrates, but a minute later joy turns to despair as Bull hobbles off with a recurrence of the hamstring injury which forced him out of the action after just 22 minutes of last week's friendly against Coventry City.

Substitute Lee Mills works tirelessly but, without Bull, Wolves lose their cutting edge and Reading begin to enjoy more of the possession.

After the interval Mike Stowell becomes the Wolves hero, first diving to stop a 20-yard shot from Molineux old boy Mick Gooding, then acrobatically turning aside goalbound efforts from Simon Osborn and Lovell.

The biggest let–off arrives just two minutes from time when the unmarked Quinn – scorer of 40 goals in Reading's promotion season – scoops the easiest chance of the game over the bar from only eight yards.

"You would put your mortgage on Quinn scoring from that situation," says a relieved Graham Taylor after the game.

"I have to be pleased with the result," adds the manager, "but there is a lot of work still to be done and we know we will have to play better than that."

Steve Froggatt – winning goal

The Wolves Review 1995

MATCH 2 • ENDSLEIGH LEAGUE DIVISION 1

Sunday 21st August 1994 • Meadow Lane • 2.55pm

NOTTS COUNTY 1 WOLVES 1

Half-time 1-0 • *Attendance* 8,569

Referee Ian CRUIKSHANKS (Hartlepool)

Linesmen D.W. MANSFIELD and S.J. GRIFFITHS

Black and White Striped Shirts with Yellow Trim, White Shorts — Goals

1	Steve CHERRY	
2	Colin HOYLE	
3	Michael EMENALO ❏	
4	Phil TURNER	
5	Shaun MURPHY ❏	
6	Dean YATES	
7	Tony AGANA	
8	Andy LEGG	
9	Gary LUND	
10	Gary McSWEGAN	
11	Michael SIMPSON †	36

Substitutes

12	Paul COX	
14	Rob MATTHEWS †76	
gk	Paul REECE	

Gold Shirts with Black Trim, Gold Shorts — Goals

1	Mike STOWELL	
2	James SMITH	
3	Andy THOMPSON	71 pen
4	Darren FERGUSON ❏	
5	Paul BLADES	
6	Peter SHIRTLIFF	
7	Mark VENUS	
8	Geoff THOMAS ❏	
9	Mark RANKINE	
10	David KELLY	
11	Steve FROGGATT	

Substitutes

12	Paul BIRCH	
14	Neil EMBLEN	
gk	Paul JONES	

BEFORE	P	W	D	L	F	A	pts	AFTER	P	W	D	L	F	A	pts
12 Wolves	1	1	0	0	1	0	3	6 Wolves	2	1	1	0	2	1	4
23 Notts Co.	1	0	0	1	1	2	0	18 Notts Co.	2	0	1	1	2	3	1

FACTFILE

Bully's hamstrung - could be out for 10 days or 10 weeks says disappointed Graham Taylor... Neil Emblen left out after shaky debut... Kevin Keen dropped to make way for three-man central defence... Nigerian World Cup star Emenalo booked on debut... Andy Thompson salvages a point with a second half penalty.

The Wolves Review 1995

A SPIRITED SECOND-HALF TV SHOW

Handy Andy's a point-saver

The first of two successive televised Sunday matches takes Wolves to Meadow Lane, scene of a 2-0 victory back in April when a promotion play-off place was still in the offing for both clubs.

Neither made it but County, now without Mark Draper following his £1.25m move to promoted Leicester City, are as determined as Wolves that this will be their year.

Earlier in the week Wolves had been dealt a serious blow with the news that Steve Bull, substituted in each of his last two outings, has no chance of lining up against County.

Manager Graham Taylor confirmed: "A scan has revealed what we thought – Steve has a deep-seated hamstring injury which is the result of previous injuries.

"When he is right to come back he will, but I haven't a clue when that will be. It could be 10 days – it could be 10 weeks."

Ruling out a quick dip into the transfer market to find a replacement for Bull, Taylor also decides against using rookie striker Lee Mills at Meadow Lane.

James Smith shows some determined form at Notts County

The 23-year-old former non-League player was Bull's substitute last week against Reading, but the manager instead decides to play utility player Mark Rankine alongside striker David Kelly after a good performance up front in Monday's 3-1 reserve team victory over Albion at Molineux.

"Mark has good experience of playing up front," points out the manager. "In one season he scored 15 goals for Doncaster Rovers."

Taylor also makes changes in midfield and defence, dropping Kevin Keen from the middle line in order to introduce a three-man central defensive formation – which does not include Neil Emblen.

After a nervy debut against Reading, Emblen is dropped to the substitutes' bench and captain Peter Shirtliff is partnered by Mark Venus and Paul Blades in the centre of the back line.

Nigerian World Cup defender Michael Emenalo makes his debut for County, who take the lead after 36 minutes through a superbly struck 20 yard effort by Michael Simpson.

Wolves have had an earlier goal by Steve Froggatt disallowed for offside – unluckily so, according to the evidence of the TV cameras.

But the home side's lead is deserved and would have been greater but for Darren Ferguson's brilliant goal line clearance from Gary Lund and a bad miss on the hour by Tony Agana.

Wolves are having more of the game in the second half, however, and when Rankine is fouled in the penalty area after 71 minutes Andy Thompson strikes the equaliser from the resultant spot-kick.

Froggatt brings three fine second half saves from County goalkeeper Steve Cherry and also has claims for a last minute penalty turned down after being held back by Colin Hoyle.

A draw was the most Wolves deserved though, from a game they started poorly but pulled out of the fire with a spirited second half display.

The Wolves Review 1995

MATCH 3 • ANGLO-ITALIAN CUP (GROUP A, MATCH 1)

Wednesday 24th August 1994 • Stadio Via del Mare • 8.00pm (local time)

LECCE 0 WOLVES 1

Half-time 0-0 • Attendance 1,795

Referee P. L. FOAKES (Clacton-on-Sea)

Linesmen M. A. HAIR and R. M. DANES

Red and Yellow Striped Shirts, Red Shorts	Goals	White Shirts, with Gold and Black Trim, White Shorts	Goals
1 Davide TORCHIA		1 Paul JONES	
2 Rosario BIONDO		2 James SMITH	
3 Andrea FATTIZZO		3 Andy THOMPSON	
4 Giampaolo CERAMICOLA		4 Darren FERGUSON	
5 Stefano RICCI		5 Paul BLADES	
6 Fabio MACELLARI		6 Peter SHIRTLIFF	
7 Claudio D'ONOFRIO †		7 Mark VENUS †	
8 Renato OLIVE		8 Geoff THOMAS	
9 Walter MONACO		9 Mark RANKINE ‡	
10 Stefano MELCHIORI		10 David KELLY	81
11 Kwame AYEW		11 Steve FROGGATT	
Substitutes		*Substitutes*	
12 Giuseppe GATTA		12 Neil EMBLEN †46	
14 André GUMPRECHT		14 Kevin KEEN	
15 Umberto DE FILIPPI		15 Paul BIRCH ‡73	
16 Giampaolo CAZZELLA †		16 Lee MILLS	
gk Stefano TRINCHERA		gk Mike STOWELL	

BEFORE	P	W	D	L	F	A	pts
Lecce	0	0	0	0	0	0	0
Wolves	0	0	0	0	0	0	0

AFTER	P	W	D	L	F	A	pts
(Eng A) Wolves	1	1	0	0	1	0	3
(Ita A) Lecce	1	0	0	1	0	1	0

FACTFILE *Wolves' first competitive match in Europe for 14 years... "We're in the tournament to win it!" manager Taylor tells the doubters... Paul 'The Judge' Jones at last comes off the bench ... seven bookings for the Italians... David Kelly hits a late winner... victory puts Wolves at the top of Group A's English section.*

BACK INTO EUROPE

Good start to Anglo-Italian Cup

A Wembley final is the eventual aim as Wolves set out for Southern Italy and their first competitive match in Europe since a 1980 UEFA Cup tie against PSV Eindhoven in Holland.

Placed in *Group A* of the Anglo-Italian Cup along with English rivals Notts County, Swindon Town and Tranmere Rovers, Wolves' opening game is against *Serie B* side Lecce.

An early morning charter flight from Birmingham Airport has brought 19 players, plus club officials and supporters, to this most southerly of venues in the competition.

Doubts have been cast on the wisdom of entering a tournament which in the last couple of seasons has earned a degree of notoriety through incidents of violent on-pitch behaviour and a high quota of sendings-off.

But manager Graham Taylor, having been involved in the discussions at board level which led to the decision to take part, is very positive in his approach.

"We are in it to win it," he said. "If we pick up injuries in the tournament, I'm sure people won't be slow to tell us we should not be competing.

"But we have entered because we thought it would be good experience for the players and because we thought Wolves supporters would be excited at the prospect of a Wembley final."

One player who is looking forward to the experience more than most is goalkeeper Paul Jones, who gets his first senior outing since the last game of the 92-93 season.

After being substitute on 45 successive occasions – on none of which he set foot on the pitch – it's no wonder his seemingly permanent place on the bench has earned him the nickname 'The Judge' from his colleagues.

Jones for Stowell is the only team change from Sunday's match at Notts County, though with five substitutes allowed in Anglo-Italian games it is a larger than usual squad which steps out into the impressive Stadio Via del Mare – 'the stadium on the road to the sea'.

The 55,000 capacity ground is sparsely populated, but the 35 Wolves fans in attendance make their presence felt as Taylor's men settle quickly in the searing, strength-sapping heat.

In the opening seconds David Kelly shoots just wide, then Steve Froggatt forces goalkeeper Torchia into a reflex save before Mark Rankine twice misses out on good scoring opportunities.

Wolves almost pay the penalty for failing to take their early chances when Jones has to make a brilliant save to keep out a thunderous shot from Walter Monaco.

Jones pulls off another great stop, this time from substitute Giampaolo Cazzella, as Wolves come under pressure in the second half.

But the game is won nine minutes from time, when Froggatt swings over a deep cross which Kelly meets with a first time shot that flies spectacularly into the top corner of the net.

The goal rounds off a satisfying night, Wolves having produced their most fluent performance of the season to date and given themselves an excellent start in the competition.

With Notts County drawing 1-1 in Ascoli, Tranmere held 2-2 by Venezia at Prenton Park and Swindon losing 2-0 at home to Atalanta, Wolves are top of the English section of *Group A*.

Graham Taylor says: "I thought we would have to win one of our away games and possibly both home matches to go through, so this is a good start."

It is also good to fly home with no injuries having been suffered by the players. Actually, that is not strictly true...

Darren Simkin, who was not involved in the match, nevertheless returns to England with his arm in a sling – he had slipped off the arm of an hotel chair and smashed the door of a glass cabinet, in the process sustaining a gashed elbow which required 13 stitches. You can't take these lads from Bloxwich anywhere!

The Wolves Review 1995

MATCH 4 • ENDSLEIGH LEAGUE DIVISION 1

Sunday 28th August 1994 • Molineux • 2.55pm

WOLVES 2 WEST BROMWICH ALBION 0

Half-time 1-0 • Attendance 27,764

Referee P.E. ALCOCK (Surrey)

Linesmen B.J. RUDKIN and G.A. STONES

Gold Shirts with Black Trim, Black Shorts	Goals	Blue and White Striped Shirts, White Shorts	Goals
1 Mike STOWELL		1 Stuart NAYLOR	
2 James SMITH		2 Neil PARSLEY	
3 Andy THOMPSON ❑	22 pen	3 Scott DARTON	
4 Darren FERGUSON		4 Mike PHELAN	
5 Paul BLADES		5 Craig HERBERT	
6 Peter SHIRTLIFF		6 Daryl BURGESS ❑	
7 Neil EMBLEN †		7 Bernard McNALLY †	
8 Geoff THOMAS		8 Ian HAMILTON	
9 Paul BIRCH		9 Bob TAYLOR	
10 David KELLY	69	10 Carl HEGGS ‡	
11 Steve FROGGATT		11 Kevin DONOVAN	
Substitutes		Substitutes	
12 Mark RANKINE		12 Micky MELLON †75	
14 Mark VENUS †84		14 Lee ASHCROFT ‡75	
gk Paul JONES		gk Tony LANGE	

BEFORE	P	W	D	L	F	A	pts	AFTER	P	W	D	L	F	A	pts
6 Wolves	2	1	1	0	2	1	4	3 Wolves	3	2	1	0	4	1	7
22 Albion	1	0	1	0	1	1	1	22 Albion	2	0	1	1	1	1	1

FACTFILE *123rd League version of the Black Country derby... live TV plus the first division's biggest crowd of the season to date... Thompson's second penalty in successive League games... Emblen stars in new midfield role... revenge for last season's double defeat by the Baggies*

12 *The Wolves Review 1995*

REVENGE FOR THE BAGGIES' DOUBLE

One-sided derby win

Revenge is on the agenda as Wolves prepare for today's local derby. Last season's double by Albion effectively cost Graham Taylor's team a place in the promotion play-offs, though both defeats by the old enemy came under previous manager Graham Turner.

Today's 123rd League meeting between the two clubs will come under close media scrutiny - and not just because the game is due for live transmission by Central TV. After the ugly crowd scenes which marred February's match at Molineux, any repeat will be monitored by the cameras and notebooks of both local and national newsmen.

Pleas for a more peaceful atmosphere at today's game have been made by the chairmen and managers of both clubs. Thankfully, their words are heeded as an afternoon of delight for Wolves - but woe for the Baggies - unfolds in front of the season's biggest first division attendance to date.

Both sides go into the game weakened through injuries to key players, particularly up front where Albion are minus Andy Hunt while Wolves are once more missing ex-Baggie Steve Bull.

In the absence of his main striker, manager Graham Taylor decides to use David Kelly as a lone front runner with support coming from a five-man midfield. Pinpointing midfield as Albion's main strength, Taylor brings back Neil Emblen to play just in front of the back four. Emblen, so unconvincing in his central defensive debut that he was dropped, proves a revelation in his new role - both in blocking out the threat of Albion's midfield runners and also with a series of dangerous forward runs.

Apart from an early scare, when Mike Stowell has to keep out a Daryl Burgess volley, Wolves are rarely troubled at the back as they take control in every area of the action.

A goal looks inevitable as the pressure mounts with Geoff Thomas, Peter Shirtliff and Paul Blades all going close in the early stages.

The breakthrough arrives from a 22nd minute penalty. Kelly is pushed over just inside the area by Burgess and Andy Thompson, with his second spot-kick in successive League games, puts the ball into the top corner of the net.

Wolves step up a gear after taking the lead and as half time approaches both Paul Birch - playing his first game of the season - and Geoff Thomas are denied by goalkeeper Stuart Naylor.

The first half corner count - 10-2 in Wolves favour - tells its own story and the theme continues after the break, Naylor having to make smart saves from Steve Froggatt and Darren Ferguson within six minutes of the restart.

A rare Albion break sees Bob Taylor dragging a 20 yard effort wide, but Wolves are soon back on the offensive and the lead is increased in the 69th minute.

Naylor brilliantly turns a Kelly shot round the post for a corner, but from Ferguson's flag-kick Paul Blades gets the flick-on and Kelly dives in to head the ball home.

A late Albion rally never looks like pulling them back into the game, though after Stowell saves a long range effort from Taylor a simple six-yard chance is squandered by Donovan two minutes from time.

According to TV summariser Ron Atkinson, Aston Villa's former Albion manager, the game has been the most one-sided Black Country derby for years. Few would argue, though Graham Taylor is not totally satisfied.

"I would like to see us finishing sides off more than we did today", he says, but adds "This was a good win for the players, especially after last season - they were very much aware of those two defeats."

The Wolves Review 1995

MATCH 5 • ENDSLEIGH LEAGUE DIVISION 1

Tuesday 30th August 1994 • Vicarage Road • 8.15pm

WATFORD 2 WOLVES 1

Half-time 1-0 • Attendance 10,108

Referee JOHN KIRKBY (Sheffield)

Linesmen D.C. MADGWICK and R.L. SAUNDERS

Yellow Shirts with Black and Red Trim, Black Shorts	Goals	White Shirts with Gold and Black Trim, White Shorts	Goals
1 Kevin MILLER		1 Mike STOWELL	
2 Darren BAZELEY		2 James SMITH ❏	
3 Richard JOHNSON	87	3 Andy THOMPSON	
4 Colin FOSTER	15	4 Darren FERGUSON †	
5 David HOLDSWORTH		5 Paul BLADES ❏	
6 Craig RAMAGE ❏		6 Peter SHIRTLIFF	
7 Andy HESSENTHALER ❏		7 Neil EMBLEN	85
8 Derek PAYNE		8 Geoff THOMAS	
9 Jamie MORALEE		9 Paul BIRCH	
10 Gary PORTER ❏		10 David KELLY ‡	
11 Tommy MOONEY		11 Steve FROGGATT	
Substitutes		*Substitutes*	
12 Keith MILLEN		12 Mark RANKINE ‡72	
14 Lee NOGAN		14 Mark VENUS †72	
gk Perry DIGWEED		gk Paul JONES	

BEFORE	P	W	D	L	F	A	pts	AFTER	P	W	D	L	F	A	pts
3 Wolves	3	2	1	0	4	1	7	6 Wolves	4	2	1	1	5	3	7
24 Watford	3	0	1	2	0	4	1	17 Watford	4	1	1	2	2	5	4

FACTFILE *Graham Taylor's first competitive return to Vicarage Road... Wolves unchanged for first time this season... Kick-off time delayed 30 minutes... Wolves stung by Hornets... Neil Emblen's first Wolves goal fails to save visitors... Mike Stowell performs heroics to keep score down*

STUNG BY THE STRUGGLING HORNETS

Not a happy return for Graham Taylor

A top of the table place beckons as Wolves travel to bottom club Watford, who have just one point and no goals to their name after their opening three League games.

It is a special return to Vicarage Road for manager Graham Taylor, who in the 1980's led the Hornets to the most successful period in their history.

Current Watford boss Glen Roeder says: "The game will have that little bit extra because of Graham. He is the manager who set standards at Vicarage Road which a succession of people have tried with difficulty to emulate."

This is Taylor's first competitive game back on his old stamping ground and along with coach Steve Harrison – also his coach in Watford's halcyon days – there are some memories to be relived before tonight's action gets underway.

As it turns out, it is in fact delayed action after the kick-off time is put back half an hour. This is to allow around 20 coachloads of Wolves supporters to reach the ground after being held up in an horrendous M1 traffic tailback.

When the fans finally arrive, swelling the attendance past the 10,000 mark, they settle down to watch a game in which the Wolves line-up is unchanged for the first time this season.

The Watford fans give Graham Taylor a rousing reception, but Taylor's team is given short shrift by the home side in a storming start to the game.

Bottom of the table they may be, but Watford show much more fire and aggression than Albion showed against Wolves on Sunday and deservedly take a 15th minute lead.

Darren Bazeley pumps a long ball forward, Jamie Moralee gets the flick-on beyond the Wolves central defenders and Colin Foster barges his way through to drive a 12-yard shot into the net.

An attempted Wolves fightback is thwarted by some uncompromising play from the home team, who have three players booked in the space of 10 minutes as the visitors begin to get on top.

The best chance for a first half equaliser is wasted nine minutes before the break, David Kelly shooting over the bar from 10 yards after Andy Thompson and Geoff Thomas have combined to create the opportunity.

Watford regain control after the interval and only a string of fine saves by man-of-the-match Mike Stowell prevents a second goal.

A 52nd minute double-stop is the pick of the bunch, Stowell tipping a Tommy Mooney shot on to the crossbar then beating away the follow-up effort from Craig Ramage.

Good saves follow from Moralee and Andy Hessenthaler and, when Wolves substitutes Mark Rankine and Mark Venus are sent on in the 72nd minute, it looks like no more than a damage-limitation excercise.

Five minutes from time, however, Wolves appear to have got themselves out of jail with an undeserved equaliser. Paul Birch sends in a near-post corner, Paul Blades flicks on and Neil Emblen dives in to bravely head home his first goal for the club.

Sadly, the Wolves relief is short-lived. Stowell comes to the rescue again with a brilliant 87th minute diving save from Hessenthaler, but when the resultant corner is only half cleared defender Richard Johnson hammers home a 25-yard screamer to win the match with the first goal of his career.

The super strike lifts the Hornets off the bottom, pushes Wolves down to sixth place and completes a less than happy return to his old club for Graham Taylor.

The Wolves Review 1995

MATCH 6 • ENDSLEIGH LEAGUE DIVISION 1

Saturday 3rd September 1994 • Roker Park • 3.00pm

SUNDERLAND 1 WOLVES 1

Half-time 1-1 • Attendance 15,111

Referee DAVID ALLISON (Lancaster)

Linesmen I. BILLINGHAM and J. DOUGLAS

Red and White Striped Shirts with Black Trim, Black Shorts	Goals	Gold Shirts with Black Trim, Gold Shorts	Goals
13 Tony NORMAN		1 Mike STOWELL	
7 Gary OWERS		2 James SMITH	
26 Dariusz KUBICKI		3 Andy THOMPSON	
6 Kevin BALL ❑		4 Neil EMBLEN	
3 Richard ORD		5 Paul BLADES	
11 Craig RUSSELL		6 Peter SHIRTLIFF ❑	
5 Derek FERGUSON		7 Paul BIRCH	
15 Brian ATKINSON		8 Mark VENUS	42
17 Michael GRAY		9 Paul STEWART	
8 Don GOODMAN		10 David KELLY †	
10 Phil GRAY	21	11 Darren FERGUSON	
Substitutes		*Substitutes*	
14 Shaun CUNNINGTON		12 Geoff THOMAS	
18 Lee HOWEY		13 Mark RANKINE †67	
1 Alec CHAMBERLAIN (gk)		gk Paul JONES	

BEFORE	P	W	D	L	F	A	pts	AFTER	P	W	D	L	F	A	pts
7 Wolves	4	2	1	1	5	3	7	7 Wolves	5	2	2	1	6	4	8
11 Sunderland	4	1	3	0	4	3	6	11 Sunderland	5	1	4	0	5	4	7

FACTFILE

Wolves legend Billy Wright dies at 70 on morning of match... tributes pour in from across the world... on-loan Liverpool striker Paul Stewart makes Wolves debut... Geoff Thomas dropped for Mark Venus – who bags the equaliser... superb display by Mike Stowell.

STERLING PERFORMANCE ON DAY BILLY DIES

Point salvaged at Sunderland

This morning's death of former Wolves and England captain Billy Wright is dominating both the sports and news headlines as a big test approaches for Graham Taylor's team at Roker Park.

Billy, who died from cancer at the age of 70, was indisputably Wolves' greatest ever player and – with 105 caps including 90 appearances as captain – was arguably England's finest too.

From 1990 he was a club director at the instigation of president Sir Jack Hayward, who before kick-off at Sunderland pays a fitting tribute: "He was just a wonderful person, England's finest player and gentleman," says Sir Jack, whose words are echoed by countless eulogies from around the world on this sad day.

A minute's silence is held in honour of Billy before the match, which is set to feature the Wolves debut of on-loan Liverpool striker Paul Stewart. Signed yesterday for a month, there is also the possibility of the move being made permanent – the former Blackpool, Manchester City and Tottenham Hotspur player is rated at £1m-plus by Liverpool.

In the continued absence of Steve Bull and with Steve Froggatt forced out through an injury sustained at Watford in midweek, Stewart partners David Kelly up front. Graham Taylor drops Geoff Thomas in favour of Mark Venus in midfield, thus denying Thomas the chance of appearing on the ground where – almost a year ago – he collected the leg injuries which were to cost him 11 months of first team action.

Unbeaten Sunderland make the more impressive start, striker Phil Gray looking dangerous with a couple of early efforts and ex-Albion striker Don Goodman also sending a powerful shot just wide.

But a Wolves breakaway leads to Stewart heading narrowly wide, then in the 19th minute the unmarked Kelly wastes a glorious chance when he scuffs a 12-yard shot straight at goalkeeper Tony Norman.

Two minutes later the home side take the lead, Phil Gray racing on to Goodman's flick-on and rifling a 15 yard drive into the bottom corner of the net.

More goals are threatened but Mike Stowell, in inspired form, pulls off superb saves in quick succession from Michael Gray and Phil Gray.

A tenacious effort to halt the tide of attacks is rewarded three minutes before the interval, Paul Blades heading on a Paul Birch corner and Venus sending a 15-yard shot through a ruck of players to bag the equaliser.

A second half battle for control sees Sunderland maintaining the upper hand, but gritty defending and more fine goalkeeping from Stowell keep the home side out.

A magnificent 80th minute save from Phil Gray confirms Stowell as man of the match, but major parts are also played by Peter Shirtliff at the centre of defence, Neil Emblen in midfield and – getting better as the pressure builds – young Jamie Smith at right back.

The draw has brought as hard-earned a point as Wolves are likely to collect all season. On a day when their late, great captain would have been proud of Wolves 94, it is no wonder that more than one newspaper comes up with the headline 'The Wright Stuff'.

Man-of-the-Match Mike Stowell

The Wolves Review 1995

MATCH 7 • ANGLO-ITALIAN CUP (GROUP A, MATCH 2)

Tuesday 6th September 1994 • Molineux • 7.45pm

WOLVES 0 ASCOLI 1

Half-time 0-0 • Attendance 9,599

Referee Marcello CARDONA (Milan)

Linesmen Carlo GAVIRAGHI and Eugenio RANGHETTI

White Shirts with Gold and Black Trim, White Shorts — Goals

1	Paul JONES	
2	James SMITH ❑	
3	Andy THOMPSON	
4	Darren FERGUSON ❑	
5	Paul BLADES	
6	Peter SHIRTLIFF	
7	Neil EMBLEN	
8	Paul BIRCH ‡	
9	Paul STEWART	
10	Kevin KEEN †	
11	Mark VENUS	

Substitutes

12	Mark RANKINE ‡74	
14	Robbie DENNISON †46 ❑	
15	Tom BENNETT	
16	Lee MILLS	
gk	Mike STOWELL	

Red Shirts with White Trim, Red Shorts — Goals

1	Marco BIZZARRI	
2	Salvatore FUSCO	
3	Massimiliano FIONDELLA †	
4	Francesco ZANONCELLI	
5	Paolo BENETTI ■	
6	Luca MARCATO	57
7	Manuel MILANA	
8	Giovanni BOSI	
9	Oliver BIERHOFF ‡	
10	Michele MENOLASCINA	
11	Rubens PASINO	

Substitutes

12	Andrea IVAN	
14	Carmelo MANCUSO †36	
15	Giovanni SPINELLI ‡64	
gk	Gionata PAZZI	

BEFORE	P	W	D	L	F	A	pts
1 (Eng A) Wolves	1	1	0	0	1	0	3
3 (Ita A) Ascoli	1	0	1	0	1	1	1

AFTER	P	W	D	L	F	A	pts
2 (Eng A) Wolves	2	1	0	1	1	1	3
3 (Ita A) Ascoli	2	1	1	0	2	1	4

FACTFILE *Fans' shrine to Billy Wright outside main stand... David Kelly named today in Eire squad for next week's international – but replaced by Kevin Keen for tonight's game... Paul Stewart's home debut... Marcato's rocket the matchwinner... red card for Benetti.*

ITALIANS TAKE THE POINTS – AND THE JEERS

Wolves first home defeat

Arriving at Molineux for tonight's Anglo Italian match is a moving experience. An impromptu shrine to Billy Wright, following his death on Saturday, has been created through the laying of hundreds of tributes around the entrance to the stand which bears his name.

From flowers to flags and from replica team shirts to a myriad of scarves, supporters have laid tokens of homage to the great man. Wolves fans have not been alone in paying their respects – the colours of clubs such as Arsenal, Manchester United, Liverpool and Villa among others, demonstrate the universal respect in which Billy Wright was held.

An official pre-match tribute to Billy is set for Saturday's visit of Tranmere Rovers. In the meantime, the on-field business is about collecting a second successive Anglo-Italian Cup victory to take a step nearer to a Wembley final appearance.

While Wolves were winning their first match in the competition at Lecce, tonight's opponents Ascoli were being held to a 1-1 home draw (collecting seven bookings in the process) by Notts County.

They have played just one *Serie B* league game to date, Sunday's opening fixture in which they beat Lucchese 2-0.

This evening they face a Wolves team which has continuing injury problems. Geoff Thomas, who had apparently recovered from last season's knee problems, has been told he now needs a 'tidying-up' operation which will keep him out of action for several games.

Steve Froggatt is still missing with the injury which forced him out of Saturday's match at Sunderland, while a slight toe injury to goalkeeper Mike Stowell lets in Paul Jones for his second game in the competition.

Of greatest interest to Wolves supporters this evening is the home debut of on-loan Liverpool striker Paul Stewart, who impressed on his first appearance for the club in the match at Sunderland. And he makes an early impression here too, linking well with Neil Emblen to provide a 12th minute shooting chance which is struck just over the bar.

Despite the rain-sodden, greasy surface Wolves settle to play some neat football. In the 23rd minute, however, the Italians produce a quickfire move which ends with striker Oliver Bierhoff hitting a crisp 15-yard shot just wide of the post.

But Wolves immediately get back on top and are unlucky not to take the lead in the 38th minute, when Mark Venus meets a Paul Birch cross to loop a header over goalkeeper Marco Bizzarri – only to see his effort bounce off the upright.

Birch has a goal disallowed for offside just before the interval then, seven minutes into the second half, the midfielder drives a low cross shot into the side netting.

But when the deadlock is broken, the goal comes at the other end. The Wolves defence can only half clear a throw-in by substitute Carmelo Mancuso and, from 25 yards, pony-tailed midfielder Luca Marcato rockets a rising drive into the top corner of the net.

For a spell the visitors threaten a second goal, but in the closing stages Wolves mount a rally in which Venus sends a 20-yard free kick just wide and Stewart heads a 77th minute effort narrowly over the bar.

Four minutes later a relatively trouble free match is marred by an ugly incident which follows a challenge on Bizzarri by substitute Robbie Dennison.

The Wolves man is booked for his lunge at the goalkeeper, but not before defender Paolo Benetti is sent off for his retaliatory kick in the back of Dennison.

At the final whistle the Italians leave the field to jeers from the Wolves fans, who have witnessed their team's first home defeat of the season.

They are also knocked off the top of *Group A*, Notts County taking over the leadership through a 1-0 win against Lecce. In the other two *Group A* matches Atalanta beat Tranmere Rovers 2-0 and Swindon go down 1-0 at Venezia.

The Wolves Review 1995

MATCH 8 • ENDSLEIGH LEAGUE DIVISION 1

Saturday 10th September 1994 • Molineux • 3.00pm

WOLVES 2 TRANMERE ROVERS 0

Half-time 1-0 • Attendance 27,030

Referee Ian HEMLEY (Ampthill)

Linesmen J.J. ASHMAN and P. DOWD

Gold Shirts with Black Trim, Black Shorts	Goals	White Shirts with Blue and Green Trim, White Shorts	Goals
1 Mike STOWELL		1 Eric NIXON	
2 James SMITH		2 John McGREAL	
3 Andy THOMPSON		3 Ged BRANNAN	
4 Neil EMBLEN	52	4 Kenny IRONS	
5 Mark VENUS		5 Shaun GARNETT ❑	
6 Peter SHIRTLIFF ❑		6 Liam O'BRIEN	
7 Mark WALTERS		7 John MORRISSEY †	
8 Darren FERGUSON		8 John ALDRIDGE	
9 Steve BULL		9 Chris MALKIN	
10 Paul STEWART †	37	10 Pat NEVIN	
11 Steve FROGGATT ❑		11 Tony THOMAS	
Substitutes		Substitutes	
12 David KELLY †40		12 Ian MUIR †81	
14 Paul BIRCH		14 Steve MUNGALL	
gk Paul JONES		gk Danny COYNE	

BEFORE	P	W	D	L	F	A	pts	AFTER	P	W	D	L	F	A	pts
5 Tranmere	5	3	0	2	10	9		3 Wolves	6	3	2	1	8	4	11
7 Wolves	5	2	2	1	6	4	8	9 Tranmere	6	3	0	3	10	11	9

FACTFILE

Old favourites back at Molineux for pre-match Billy Wright tribute... debut for on-loan Mark Walters... Bully back after four week absence... Paul Stewart injured scoring his first Wolves goal... thrill-a-minute win puts Wolves back in top three.

PULSATING MATCH STIRS 50'S MEMORIES

Fitting tribute for Billy

A pre-match tribute to the late Billy Wright sets the tone for a memorable Molineux afternoon. Older Wolves fans in a packed stadium are given a trip down memory lane as many of Wright's playing colleagues from the 1950's step silently on to the pitch to pay homage to their former captain.

Players from more recent times also take part in the moving tribute, eloquently led by Central TV's Bob Hall and also including floral displays in the shape of Wolves and England shirts plus, poignantly, a bugler playing *The Last Post*.

As the old crowd-favourites walk back off the pitch, however, it is to the refrain of *The Happy Wanderer* – another reminder of Billy Wright's great days, when the tune was played to welcome Wolves on to the pitch at all home games.

And to follow, on this special day of sad remembrance for a footballing icon, Wolves 94 fittingly produce a thrill-a-minute match which also evokes memories of stirring battles from those halcyon Molineux days of the 1950's.

For a start – and unusually for modern day football – both sides have two out-and-out wingers in their line-ups. Tranmere boast Pat Nevin and ex-Wolves player John Morrissey, while the home side field fit-again Steve Froggatt and latest on-loan recruit Mark Walters.

Liverpool's one-time Aston Villa and Rangers winger Walters, signed yesterday on a month's loan, lines up in an exciting front four which includes Anfield colleague Paul Stewart plus Steve Bull, who is back from a hamstring injury which has kept him out since aggravating the problem on the opening day of the season.

The pace and passion of the match is signalled in the first 10 minutes, when Shaun Garnett and Peter Shirtliff are both booked for over-aggressive tackles and Mike Stowell makes superb saves from Chris Malkin and John Aldridge.

As play switches to the other end Mark Venus sends a header over the bar, then Neil Emblen has a shot blocked by Eric Nixon.

Wolves take the lead in the 37th minute, Stewart cleverly losing marker Garnett to collect an Andy Thompson through-ball and slide it past the advancing Nixon from 20 yards.

Sadly for Stewart and Wolves, however, Nixon follows through with a dreadful two-footed challenge which leads to the striker's substitution but not, amazingly, to a caution for the goalkeeper.

Bull sees a close range shot brilliantly saved by Nixon in first half injury time, Stowell then producing an equally fine stop from Nevin's 20-yard drive two minutes into the second half.

A 52nd minute throw-in by Froggatt sets up Wolves' second goal, blasted in from 20 yards by Neil Emblen after Bull's penalty area persistence has created the opening.

Bull shoots wide from an angle as Wolves look for the killer goal, but at the other end Morrissey skies a 10-yard shot over the bar, then Liam O'Brien somehow misses an open goal from eight yards.

Two minutes from time Emblen ends a fine run with a low shot which is superbly saved by Nixon, the late action summing up an excellent afternoon's football. It has been a throw-back to Wolves' greatest era but also, hopefully, a pointer to good times ahead for the boys in gold and black.

Paul Stewart – scored his first Wolves goal

The Wolves Review 1995 21

MATCH 9 • ENDSLEIGH LEAGUE DIVISION 1

Tuesday 13th September 1994 • Molineux • 7.45pm

WOLVES 5   SOUTHEND UNITED 0

Half-time 3-0 • Attendance 23,608

Referee Richard POULAIN (Huddersfield)

Linesmen E. J. WALSH and J. D. WESSON

Gold Shirts with Black Trim, Black Shorts	Goals	Blue Shirts, Blue Shorts	Goals
1 Mike STOWELL		1 Paul SANSOME	
2 James SMITH		2 Mark HONE	
3 Andy THOMPSON		3 Chris POWELL	
4 Neil EMBLEN	7	4 Keith JONES ▫	
5 Mark VENUS		5 Keith DUBLIN ▫	
6 Peter SHIRTLIFF		6 Graham BRESSINGTON ‡	
7 Mark WALTERS	63	7 Jonathan HUNT	
8 Darren FERGUSON		8 Ronnie WHELAN	
9 Steve BULL	67	9 Andy THOMSON	
10 David KELLY	10	10 Ricky OTTO	
11 Steve FROGGATT	38	11 Jamie FORRESTER †	
Substitutes		Substitutes	
12 Paul BLADES		12 Andy EDWARDS ‡70	
14 Paul BIRCH		14 Gary POOLE †60	
gk Paul JONES		gk Simon ROYCE	

BEFORE	P	W	D	L	F	A	pts	AFTER	P	W	D	L	F	A	pts
3 Wolves	6	3	2	1	8	4	11	1 Wolves	7	4	2	1	13	4	14
23 Southend	6	1	1	4	6	13	4	23 Southend	7	1	1	5	6	18	4

FACTFILE

Spectacular end to 13-match goal drought... Early Emblen strike... Mark Walters' first Wolves goal... Bully breaks his duck... first nap-hand in two years.... Taylor's Terriers top the table... Baggies can do Wolves a favour by beating Middlesbrough tomorrow

22   The Wolves Review 1995

GOAL-RUSH EARNS TOP SPOT

Bully bags first goal of season

With divisional leaders Middlesbrough not due to play Albion until tomorrow night, a victory over Southend this evening will take Wolves to the top of the table as long as they score at least two goals in the process.

Lowly Southend, who are second from bottom with only one win to their credit so far this season, should be there for the taking. But that also seemed the case last February, when the Shrimpers came to Molineux on the back of five successive League defeats and Wolves were unbeaten in nine. Result – a 1-0 win to Southend.

Nothing should therefore be taken for granted this evening, particularly in the goalscoring stakes as far as Wolves are concerned. Since a 2-0 victory over Notts County on April 16th, Graham Taylor's team have scored only 12 goals in 13 League and Cup matches.

And Taylor warns that Southend should not be underestimated despite their poor run of results, which have included a 4-1 hammering at Stoke City on Saturday.

"People might assume this is going to be an easy game," says the manager, "but any side in this division can damage you and we have to respect Southend."

Taylor's words are probably still echoing in the players' ears when the visitors win a second minute corner and Ricky Otto heads just wide from Ronnie Whelan's flag kick.

But the early scare is soon forgotten as Wolves sweep into a two goal lead. Neil Emblen registers his third goal of the campaign with a seventh minute shot into the roof of the net, then three minutes later David Kelly also notches his third of the season when an attempted clearance bounces off his shins and into the net.

Kelly, whose return to the team in place of the injured Paul Stewart is the only change from Saturday's line-up, is having a lively game as Wolves go all out to press home their advantage.

They do so in the 38th minute with Kelly this time the provider, crossing for Steve Froggatt to side-foot the ball home.

Towards half time Wolves ease the pressure and almost pay the price, Mike Stowell having to make good saves from Andy Thomson and Jamie Forrester as Southend show they can attack rather more effectively than they are able to defend.

But the heat is back on after the break and the game is put completely out of Southend's reach in the 63rd minute, when Mark Walters curls a glorious shot from the right hand edge of the penalty area into the far corner of the net.

Rapturous applause meets the Liverpool man's exquisite goal, but four minutes later the crowd erupts into an even more joyous roar as Steve Bull clips a shot in off the post to chalk up his first goal of the season.

It is too late for Southend to save the match, but they nevertheless attack when given the chance and after Thomson forces Stowell into a smart stop Jamie Smith has to clear a Graham Bressington header off the line.

But Emblen and Kelly both go close to piling on more agony for the visitors as Wolves run out easy winners. It is their first nap-hand since a 5-1 victory over Bristol Rovers in November 1992 – and they are back on the top of the division for the first time in over two years.

Neil Emblen – began the goal rush

The Wolves Review 1995

MATCH 10 • ENDSLEIGH LEAGUE DIVISION 1

Saturday 17th September 1994 • Turf Moor • 3.00pm

BURNLEY 0 WOLVES 1

Half-time 0-0 • Attendance 17,766

Referee Terry HEILBRON (Newton Aycliffe)
Linesmen G. BRADBURY and D. ENTWHISTLE

Claret and Blue Shirts, White Shorts	Goals	Gold Shirts with Black Trim, Black Shorts	Goals
1 Marlon BERESFORD		1 Mike STOWELL	
2 Gary PARKINSON		2 James SMITH ❏	
3 Chris VINNICOMBE		3 Andy THOMPSON	
4 Steve DAVIS ❏		4 Neil EMBLEN ❏	
5 Mark WINSTANLEY		5 Mark VENUS	
6 John DEARY		6 Peter SHIRTLIFF	
7 Alan HARPER		7 Mark WALTERS ❏	
8 Gerry HARRISON ❏†		8 Darren FERGUSON	
9 Adrian HEATH		9 Steve BULL ❏	59
10 Liam ROBINSON ❏		10 David KELLY	
11 Ted McMINN		11 Steve FROGGATT	
Substitutes		*Substitutes*	
12 Tony PHILLISKIRK		12 Paul BIRCH	
14 David EYRES †68		14 Paul BLADES	
gk Wayne RUSSELL		gk Paul JONES	

BEFORE	P	W	D	L	F	A	pts	AFTER	P	W	D	L	F	A	pts
2 Wolves	7	4	2	1	13	4	14	1 Wolves	8	5	2	1	14	4	17
20 Burnley	7	2	2	3	6	10	8	21 Burnley	8	2	2	4	6	11	8

FACTFILE

Wolves 99th League meeting with Burnley... newly promoted Clarets still searching for a home win... Bulls Eye for Steve again... first away win of season takes Wolves back to the top – and sends Burnley into the relegation zone... late flurry fails to rescue Burnley

BACK TO THE TOP WITH FIRST AWAY WIN

Kelly impresses, Bully hits winner

Not surprisingly unchanged from Tuesday's 5-0 trouncing of Southend, Wolves travel to Burnley hoping to win back the top spot which Middlesbrough reclaimed by beating bottom of the table Albion on Wednesday.

The newly promoted Clarets have yet to win a home match in the new League campaign, but they go into today's game boosted by successive away victories over Luton Town and Millwall.

Graham Taylor, who watched them beat Millwall on Wednesday, says: "They are a well organised, hard working team who will be high on confidence and determined to get that first home win. We will have to be prepared both mentally and physically".

So it proves, with Burnley having the better of the early exchanges and Chris Vinnicombe, Gerry Harrison and Adrian Heath all going close to opening the scoring.

But in their first meaningful attack Wolves almost take the lead, David Kelly firing a first time effort against the post from a Steve Froggatt cross.

Froggatt takes centre stage as Wolves, encouraged by the near miss, begin to get on top.

A lively contest is developing but the flow is halted by a rash of cautions, several of them for no more than minor offences which, nevertheless, lead to referee Heilbron brandishing his yellow card.

As both sides look to break the deadlock, Neil Emblen fails to take a half chance when he swivels to turn a close range shot over the bar; but at the other end Mike Stowell has to make a spectacular save from a Steve Davis 20-yard free kick just before half time.

Wolves' enjoy their best spell of the match in the opening period of the second half, signalled by Froggatt's accurate right wing cross which unfortunately Steve Bull fails to make the most of from a good position 12 yards out.

The impressive Kelly is unlucky with a long range shot which flashes just wide, but in the 59th minute Bull makes amends for his earlier miss by giving Wolves the lead.

Darren Ferguson's corner is flicked on by Kelly and Bull is left with the simplest of chances, nodding the ball into the empty net to record his second goal in successive matches.

Six minutes later Emblen heads over the bar, then Bull and Peter Shirtliff go close as Wolves look for a second goal.

But in the closing stages Burnley come back strongly and Adrian Heath, Mark Winstanley and John Deary all miss good chances before substitute David Eyres twice goes close to equalising in the last few minutes.

The final whistle leaves Burnley defeated, still without a home win and down in the relegation zone. For Wolves, however, a battling performance has not only brought them their first away win of the season but also – thanks to Port Vale beating Middlesbrough 2-1 at Vale Park – taken them back to the top of the table.

Steve Bull – on target for the winner

The Wolves Review 1995

MATCH 11 • COCA-COLA CUP ROUND 2, FIRST LEG

Tuesday 20th September 1994 • Saltergate • 7.30pm

CHESTERFIELD 1 WOLVES 3

Half-time 1-0 • Attendance 5,895

Referee P. DANSON (Blaby)

Linesmen P.J. JOSLIN and B. LOWE

Blue Shirts with White Trim, White Shorts — Goals

1	Chris MARPLES	
2	Jamie HEWITT ■	
3	Lee ROGERS	
4	Lawrie MADDEN	
5	Darren CARR ❑	
6	Nicky LAW ❑	
7	Tommy CURTIS	
8	Darren ROBERTS ‡	
9	Kevin DAVIES †	
10	Dave MOSS	11
11	Steve SPOONER	

Substitutes

12	Mark JULES ‡90	
14	Steve NORRIS †70	
gk	Andy BEASLEY	

Gold Shirts with Black Trim, Black Shorts — Goals

1	Mike STOWELL	
2	James SMITH	
3	Andy THOMPSON	
4	Neil EMBLEN †	
5	Mark VENUS	
6	Peter SHIRTLIFF	
7	Paul BIRCH	
8	Darren FERGUSON	
9	Steve BULL	63, 86
10	David KELLY	77
11	Steve FROGGATT	

Substitutes

12	Paul BLADES †20	
14	Kevin KEEN	
gk	Paul JONES	

FACTFILE

Graham Taylor's first domestic Cup tie as Wolves manager... it's the Jinx Cup!... ex-Wanderers Madden and Roberts in the Spirites line-up... first goal conceded in 314 minutes... Emblen stretchered off... Bully doubles up to extend marvellous Cup scoring record... Hewitt off in injury time

David Kelly – fired Wolves into a second-half lead

The Wolves Review 1995

CUP PROGRESS AFTER EARLY STUTTER

Bull brace extends great Cup record

Graham Taylor's first domestic Cup tie as Wolves manager sees his team as firm favourites against lowly opposition.

But this is the Jinx Cup, a competition in which Wolves have fared very badly since winning it for the second time when Andy Gray's goal gave them a 1-0 victory over Nottingham Forest in the 1980 Wembley final.

In the 14 years which have followed sponsorship has given the plain old League Cup a number of name changes, the latest of them by Coca-Cola.

What has not changed, however, is Wolves' lack of ability to make any kind of notable progress in the competition. They have gone out at the first hurdle on 10 occasions and, in the other four seasons, have lasted no longer than one further round.

So never mind that, Chesterfield are from the Third Division and Wolves are flying high in the First. Supporters, remembering two-leg defeats in recent years by the likes of Hull City and Notts County, travel to Saltergate with some trepidation.

The Wolves side shows just one change from Saturday, Paul Birch replacing Mark Walters after Liverpool have refused permission for their on-loan winger to play and thus become Cup-tied.

The Spirites' line-up features two former Wanderers, striker Darren Roberts and central defender Lawrie Madden.

The recent recall to the side of veteran Madden – 39 later this month – has co-incided with a revival which has seen Chesterfield win their last two matches without conceding a goal.

The confidence inspired by those results is clearly shown in the early stages, when the home side makes the running and takes the lead in the 11th minute. A good run by Kevin Davies sets up David Moss for a cracking drive which hits the net to record the first goal Wolves have conceded in 314 minutes of action.

The ill fortune continues when Neil Emblen has to be stretchered off with an ankle injury, Paul Blades replacing him but going into the centre of defence and Mark Venus moving up into midfield.

Wolves make little progress as Chesterfield continue to edge the first half. The balance of play switches dramatically after the break, however, and Steve Bull's 63rd minute goal signals victory for the visitors.

The goal is simple enough, a close range tap-in, but it has been cleverly created by Birch's through ball and Steve Froggatt's inch-perfect cross.

Bull turns provider 14 minutes later, crossing from the right for David Kelly to head home. And Bully wraps up an ultimately satisfying night for Wolves when, four minutes from time, he powers a 20-yard shot in off the post.

The goal extends the striker's remarkable Cup scoring record for Wolves – he has now bagged 48 goals in just 56 Cup matches for the club.

Chesterfield's night, which started so brightly, ends with more misery as Jamie Hewitt is sent off for a second bookable offence in injury time.

"It took us a while to get our act together," admits manager Taylor, "but once we did I thought we won well."

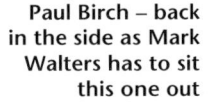

Paul Birch – back in the side as Mark Walters has to sit this one out

The Wolves Review 1995

MATCH 12 • ENDSLEIGH LEAGUE DIVISION 1

Saturday 24th September 1994 • Fratton Park • 3.15pm

PORTSMOUTH 1 WOLVES 2

Half-time 1-1 • Attendance 13,466
Referee Mike BAILEY (Cambridge)
Linesmen C. ROGERS and S. TOMLIN

Blue Shirts with White Trim, White Shorts	Goals	Gold Shirts with Black Trim, Black Shorts	Goals
1 Alan KNIGHT		1 Mike STOWELL	
2 Jon GITTENS		2 James SMITH	
3 Mark STIMSON		3 Andy THOMPSON ❑	
4 Alan McLOUGHLIN		4 Mark VENUS	
5 Kit SYMONS ❑		5 Paul BLADES	
6 Andy AWFORD †		6 Peter SHIRTLIFF ❑	
7 Ray DANIEL		7 Mark WALTERS	34
8 Bjorn KRISTENSEN ‡		8 Darren FERGUSON ❑	
9 Daryl POWELL ❑		9 Steve BULL	
10 Gerry CREANEY	11 pen	10 David KELLY	87
11 Paul HALL		11 Steve FROGGATT	
Substitutes		*Substitutes*	
12 Predrag RADOSAVLJEVIC †75		12 Kevin KEEN	
14 Robbie PETHICK ‡75		14 Paul BIRCH	
gk Mart POOM		gk Paul JONES	

BEFORE	P	W	D	L	F	A	pts	AFTER	P	W	D	L	F	A	pts
1 Wolves	8	5	2	1	14	4	17	1 Wolves	9	6	2	1	16	5	20
13 Portsmouth	7	2	4	1	7	7	10	19 Portsmouth	8	2	4	2	8	9	10

FACTFILE

Pompey still fizzing from Coca-Cola success... injured Neil Emblen misses out... another delayed start... another Mark Walters wonder goal!... Bully off target – but 'Ned' Kelly nabs the late winner... it's now five wins in a row for the table toppers.

WANDERERS WITH WINNING WAYS

Pompey chimes silenced by Ned

A third successive away game should hold no fears for Wolves after two straight wins on their travels. But, as Graham Taylor points out when viewing the visit to Fratton Park: "This will undoubtedly be the toughest of the three."

Though Portsmouth have not made the best of starts in the League, they go into this afternoon's game boosted by a fine 3-2 victory at Premier League Everton in the Coca-Cola Cup.

Pompey are unchanged from their midweek success, but Wolves, following their Coca-Cola win against less vaunted opposition at Saltergate, are forced to replace Neil Emblen due to the ankle injury he sustained during that game.

Mark Venus moves up from the centre of defence to take over from Emblen, while Paul Blades is drafted into the back four to play alongside Peter Shirtliff.

On the right wing on-loan Mark Walters, barred by Liverpool from playing in the Cup match, is brought back at the expense of Paul Birch.

Like the match at Watford three and a half weeks ago, traffic delays for the travelling hordes of Wolves fans cause the kick-off to be delayed.

When the action gets underway Wolves make a lightning start, winning a corner within seconds of the first whistle and keeping up the pressure with a stream of crosses into the penalty area.

No real early chances are created, however, and when a moment of midfield slackness allows Kit Symons to run at the Wolves defence an 11th minute penalty is the result.

Shirtliff fouls Symons and, from the spot-kick, Gerry Creaney sends Mike Stowell the wrong way to give the home side the lead.

Midway through the first half Stowell has to save brilliantly from an Alan McLoughlin shot which takes a wicked deflection off Mark Venus.

Pompey are on top at this stage but, from long balls out of defence, Steve Bull twice flashes shots wide of the post.

In the 34th minute though, Walters is bang on target with a goal reminiscent of his great effort against Southend 11 days ago. Receiving the ball from a Jamie Smith throw-in, Walters jinks inside to curl a magnificent shot into the far top corner of the net.

Lifted by the goal, Wolves begin to look far more dangerous and both Walters and Bull go close to scoring before the end of an entertaining first half.

The visitors make a bright start to the second, but Bull sends a chance high over the bar, then Venus puts a long range effort a yard wide.

Chances are hard to come by at either end as the play once more evens out, but Bull wastes a glorious opportunity when – with goalkeeper Alan Knight stranded – he once more misses the target.

It is proving a bad day for Bully in front of goal, but three minutes from time he makes amends by setting up the winner for David Kelly. Picking up a Darren Ferguson pass, Bull races past Symons to deliver a cross which 'Ned' turns into the net.

The goal gives Wolves their fifth successive win to keep them on top of the table, but manager Taylor keeps everyone's feet on the floor with a downbeat assessment of the performance.

"It was a good result," he says, "but after our equaliser I thought we would come out and have more of the play. It was a disappointment that we didn't."

MATCH 13 • COCA-COLA CUP ROUND 2, SECOND LEG

Tuesday 27th September 1994 • Molineux • 7.45pm

WOLVES 1 CHESTERFIELD 1

Aggregate 4-2 • Half-time 1-0 • Attendance 14,815

Referee Kelvin MORTON (Bury St Edmunds)

Linesmen P.A. ELWICK and A.D. MILLS

Gold Shirts with Black Trim, Black Shorts	Goals	Green and White Striped Shirts, White Shorts	Goals
1 Mike STOWELL		1 Andy BEASLEY	
2 James SMITH		2 Jamie HEWITT	
3 Andy THOMPSON		3 Lee ROGERS	
4 Mark VENUS		4 Steve SPOONER	
5 Paul BLADES		5 Darren CARR	
6 Peter SHIRTLIFF		6 Nicky LAW	
7 Paul BIRCH		7 Tommy CURTIS	
8 Darren FERGUSON		8 Darren ROBERTS	
9 Steve BULL †		9 Andy MORRIS	
10 David KELLY ‡		10 Wayne FAIRCLOUGH ❑	
11 Steve FROGGATT	3	11 Mark JULES	52
Substitutes		*Substitutes*	
12 Kevin KEEN ‡89		12 Dave MOSS	
14 Mark RANKINE †66		14 Steve NORRIS	
gk Paul JONES		gk Chris MARPLES	

FACTFILE

Club record on the horizon – a Walters signing too?... Birch back in for cup-tied winger... Lawrie Madden, commentator... Froggy's early strike... Spirites, playing only for pride, hit back to wreck record chance... Bull and Kelly injury blows... Wolves safely in draw for third round...

Steve Froggatt – gave Wolves an early lead

30   *The Wolves Review 1995*

THROUGH TO ROUND THREE WITH A STUTTER

An unconvincing performance

The club record of eight successive victories is tantalisingly close as Wolves go into tonight's Coca-Cola Cup second leg against Chesterfield.

With a 3-1 advantage from the away leg and in front of their own fans for the first time in a fortnight, Wolves are odds-on to make it six wins in a row and bring that record ever closer.

As in the first leg, Mark Walters is not allowed to play by Liverpool and so loses the chance to stake a further claim for a permanent move to Molineux.

After his tremendous goal against Portsmouth on Saturday, the on-loan winger – who has expressed an interest in joining Wolves – has received an unexpected boost from Graham Taylor.

While the manager was known to be keen to sign Walters' Liverpool colleague Paul Stewart on a permanent basis, it was thought his interest in Walters went only as far as short term cover for injured winger Tony Daley.

But Taylor has confirmed: "I would be prepared to go to my directors and talk about signing both of them if Liverpool were asking sensible money."

A combined fee of around £1.5m is thought to be the figure Liverpool would require for Walters and Stewart, the latter of whom is still out of action through injury.

Paul Birch again slots into the Wolves side in place of Walters, while one of Chesterfield's changes from the first leg sees ex-Wolves man Lawrie Madden out of tonight's game. But he is gainfully employed for the evening – commentating on the match for local radio!

In his first segment Madden has to report that Chesterfield are a goal down after just three minutes. Darren Ferguson's corner has been only half-cleared and Steve Froggatt, from the edge of the penalty area, has volleyed the ball into the corner of the net.

That effectively ends the tie as a contest, Chesterfield now needing to score four goals – and prevent Wolves from scoring again – for an aggregate win to the Third Division side.

But they make a brave attempt, pushing forward at every opportunity and going close to a goal when Nicky Law's 14th minute header glances off the crossbar.

The visitors continue to threaten but are almost undone just after half time, when goalkeeper Andy Beasley has to make a fine diving save from Andy Thompson's 30-yard free kick.

In the 52nd minute, however, Chesterfield get their equaliser when Darren Roberts – playing well on his return to his old stamping ground – crosses from the left for Mark Jules to score with a first time 18-yard shot.

Andy Morris hooks a shot over the bar as the visitors go for a second goal, but at the other end Beasley has to brilliantly save a Steve Froggatt header, then David Kelly puts a good chance over the bar.

In the closing stages Wolves are hit by injury problems, Bull having to be substituted due to a kick in the back, then Kelly meeting a similar fate after turning an ankle.

The after-match verdict from the treatment room is that Kelly's is the more serious injury, while the Taylor verdict is not too damning despite the victory run having been ended.

"The most important thing in a situation like this," says the team boss, "is to be in the draw for the next round." Which Wolves are, despite their unconvincing performance.

Graham Taylor – happy to be in the draw

The Wolves Review 1995

MATCH 14 • ENDSLEIGH LEAGUE DIVISION 1

Saturday 1st October 1994 • Molineux • 3.00pm

WOLVES 2 PORT VALE 1

Half-time 0-0 • Attendance 27,469

Referee Eddie WOLSTENHOLME (Blackburn)
Linesmen I.A. MADGE and M.A. WILLIAMS

Gold Shirts with Black Trim, Black Shorts	Goals	White Shirts with Black and Yellow Trim, White Shorts	Goals
1 Mike STOWELL		1 Paul MUSSELWHITE ❏	
2 James SMITH		2 Bradley SANDEMAN	
3 Andy THOMPSON	51, 79 pens	3 Allen TANKARD	
4 Mark VENUS		4 Andy PORTER	
5 Paul BLADES		5 Peter BILLING †	
6 Peter SHIRTLIFF		6 Dean GLOVER	
7 Mark WALTERS		7 Tony KELLY	
8 Darren FERGUSON		8 Neil ASPIN	
9 Steve BULL		9 Tony NAYLOR	
10 Mark RANKINE		10 Lee GLOVER	
11 Steve FROGGATT		11 Mark BURKE ‡	
Substitutes		*Substitutes*	
12 Paul BIRCH		12 Joe ALLON ‡75	82
14 Lee MILLS		14 Robin VAN DER LAAN †75	
gk Paul JONES		gk Arjen VAN HEUSDEN	

BEFORE	P	W	D	L	F	A	pts	AFTER	P	W	D	L	F	A	pts
1 Wolves	9	6	2	1	16	5	20	1 Wolves	10	7	2	1	18	6	23
8 Port Vale	9	4	1	4	10	12	13	12 Port Vale	10	4	1	5	11	14	13

FACTFILE *Graham Taylor named Manager of the Month... good news on the long-term injury front – but Kelly is out after midweek knock... penalty double for Thommo... fifth successive League win... Mark Burke back at Molineux – not happy at penalty decision.*

The Wolves Review 1995

FIFTH SUCCESSIVE LEAGUE WIN

Penalty double for Thompson

Graham Taylor has more to celebrate today than being named *Manager of the Month* for September. More importantly, as far as the manager is concerned, he is able to reveal that long term injury victims Tony Daley, Neil Masters and Chris Marsden are all expected to be back in action by the end of October.

Neil Emblen and Paul Stewart should also be back within a week or so after their recent knocks, while Steve Bull has recovered from his midweek injury against Chesterfield and lines up against Port Vale.

David Kelly's ankle problem from the Coca-Cola Cup match has not cleared up, however, so Mark Rankine comes into the side in the emergency striker role he fulfilled on a couple of occasions earlier in the season.

Former Wolves midfielder Mark Burke is in the Vale side and makes an impressive start, spraying around a number of neat passes as the visitors take a grip on the game.

Solid at the back with three central defenders and more inventive in midfield, Vale carve out several chances. But from the best of them Tony Naylor, Burke and Lee Glover all fail to find the net.

Vale goalkeeper Paul Musselwhite, after saving from Mark Walters in a rare threatening moment by Wolves, is booked just before the interval for dashing out to block Rankine's run at goal.

Vale have dominated the first half but, six minutes after the break, the turning point arrives when Peter Billing upends Darren Ferguson in the Vale penalty area and Andy Thompson steps up to score his third spot-kick of the season.

The goal inspires Wolves to their best spell of the game, but after Ferguson and Walters have gone close to scoring it takes another penalty to produce what proves to be the decisive goal.

When substitute Robin van der Laan is harshly adjudged to have handled a 79th minute Walters cross, Thommo-on-the-spot once again coolly slots home the resultant penalty.

It is the first time he has scored twice in a match for Wolves and, with four goals now to his name this season, it has also made him joint second-top scorer along with Bull.

A Wolves victory looks assured, but Vale produce a late rally which brings them a deserved goal in the 82nd minute.

Andy Porter's goalbound shot is parried by Mike Stowell, but substitute Joe Allon pounces on the loose ball to score the first opposition League goal on Wolves soil in the current campaign.

There are no further serious threats to Stowell's goal as Wolves run out somewhat fortuitous winners, much to the chagrin of Vale's Wolverhampton-born manager John Rudge and his players.

Ex-Wanderer Burke, bemoaning the penalty decisions, reckons: "When 27,000 fans are screaming for a penalty, it's not surprising when borderline decisions go in your favour."

In the days of Liverpool's pomp, that cry of frustration often came from opponents of the Reds after seeing penalties awarded in front of the Anfield Kop's baying thousands.

If the Anfield effect is shifting to Molineux, there are likely to be few complaints from anyone at Wolves.

Darren Ferguson – brought down in the box to earn Wolves first penalty

The Wolves Review 1995

MATCH 15 • ANGLO-ITALIAN CUP (GROUP A, MATCH 3)

Wednesday 5th October 1994 • Stadio Pierluigi Penzo • 8.00pm

VENEZIA 2 WOLVES 1

Half-time 1-1 • *Attendance* 750

Referee Alan DAWSON (Jarrow)

Linesmen B. INGRAM and A. P. MONKS

Black Shirts with Green Band, Black Shorts	Goals	White Shirts with Gold and Black Trim, White Shorts	Goals
1 Stefano VISI		1 Paul JONES	
2 Giancarlo FILIPPINI		2 Mark RANKINE	37 og
3 Paolo VANOLI		3 Andy THOMPSON	
4 Mauro NARDINI ❑		4 Mark VENUS	28
5 Cristiano SERVIDEI		5 Paul BLADES	
6 Fabiano BALLARIN		6 Tom BENNETT	
7 Alessandro MORELLO †		7 Paul BIRCH	
8 Pierluigi DI GIA		8 Darren FERGUSON	
9 Cristian VIERI	58 pen	9 Steve BULL	
10 Andrea BOTTAZZI		10 Lee MILLS	
11 Raffaele CERBONE ‡		11 Kevin KEEN	
Substitutes		*Substitutes*	
16 Enio BONALDI †54		12 Peter SHIRTLIFF	
15 Diego BORTOLUZZI ‡66		13 Mike STOWELL	
12 Pierantonio BOSAGLIA		14 James SMITH	
13 Roberto ROSSI		15 Mark WALTERS	
14 Roberto FOGLI		16 Robbie DENNISON	

BEFORE	P	W	D	L	F	A	pts	AFTER	P	W	D	L	F	A	pts
2 (Ita A) Venezia	2	1	1	0	3	2	4	2 (Ita A) Venezia	3	2	1	0	5	3	7
2 (Eng A) Wolves	2	1	0	1	1	1	3	3 (Eng A) Wolves	3	1	0	2	2	3	3

FACTFILE

Flying Potters share Wanderers journey... Jamie's England call-up... Venus rocks Venice with 25-yard bender... below par Wolves well beaten... Anglo-Italian adventure almost over...

The Wolves Review 1995

WOLVES SUNK IN VENICE

Venus special not enough

A tough match against in-form Venezia, lying just one point behind Italian *Serie B* leaders Verona, is in store for Wolves as they fly out for the third of their Anglo-Italian Cup games.

The plane from Birmingham Airport is shared with Stoke City players and officials heading for their game at Udinese, giving the Potters' former Wolves favourite Keith Downing the chance to renew acquaintances with his old Molineux colleagues.

There is good news from back home on the day of the match – Jamie Smith, just 10 games into his first team career, has been selected in the England Under 21 squad for next week's European Championship qualifier in Austria.

The 20-year-old full back will be joined in the 18-strong party by team mate Steve Froggatt, a regular member of England Under 21 squads from his days with Aston Villa.

A heavy cold has kept Froggatt out of the Wolves trip to Venice, where manager Taylor selects a much changed team to face a Venezia side which has beaten Swindon and drawn at Tranmere in its previous Anglo-Italian games.

A boat trip is the Wolves contingent's last leg of the journey to the Stadio Pierluigi Penzo, which is located on the thinly populated Sant Elena Island.

The 15,000 capacity stadium is hardly populated at all, the teams kicking off in front of a 750 crowd which contains around 200 Wolves fans who have made the long journey.

Sadly, the hardy travellers are provided with a below par performance by the weakened Wolves despite the fillip of going ahead with a spectacular 28th minute goal.

A challenge on Steve Bull is penalised 25 yards from goal and, from the resultant free kick, Mark Venus bends a glorious shot round the defensive wall and into the roof of the Venezia net.

Most of the action is coming at the other end, however, and eight minutes before the interval the Italians deservedly draw level.

The goal is nevertheless unfortunately conceded, Mark Rankine getting his boot to Andrea Bottazzi's angled shot and the ball looping over goalkeeper Paul Jones and into the net.

Jones, ably deputising for Mike Stowell, makes a number of good saves as the home side gets well on top. But the keeper also has luck on his side as three times the Italians strike the Wolves' woodwork.

Jones is finally beaten though, when Cristian Vieri scores from a 58th minute penalty after being brought down by Rankine.

The final half hour is Wolves' best spell of the match but, despite plenty of possession, they never threaten Stefano Visi's goal.

Three hours after the game the Wolves party is airbound and almost certainly out of the Anglo-Italian Cup, though travelling companions Stoke look certain to go through to the knock-out stages after beating Udinese 3-1 in their *Group B* match.

In the *Group A* matches which affect Wolves, Notts County have drawn 1-1 at Atalanta and Swindon Town have beaten Lecce 3-1 at the County Ground with ex-Wanderer Andy Mutch on target twice. Last night Tranmere Rovers lost 1-0 at home to Ascoli.

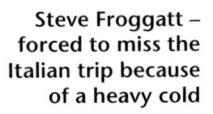

Steve Froggatt – forced to miss the Italian trip because of a heavy cold

The Wolves Review 1995

MATCH 16 • ENDSLEIGH LEAGUE DIVISION 1

Saturday 8th October 1994 • County Ground • 3.00pm

SWINDON TOWN 3 WOLVES 2

Half-time 2-2 • Attendance 14,036

Referee Peter FOAKES (Clacton)

Linesmen H. STOBBART and A.J. WEBB

Red Shirts with White Trim, Red Shorts	Goals	Gold Shirts with Black Trim, Black Shorts	Goals
1 Fraser DIGBY		1 Mike STOWELL	
2 Mark ROBINSON		2 James SMITH	
3 Paul BODIN	15	3 Andy THOMPSON	
4 Andy THOMSON		4 Mark VENUS	
5 Luc NIJHOLT		5 Paul BLADES ▢	
6 Shaun TAYLOR ▢		6 Peter SHIRTLIFF ▢	
7 Neil WEBB		7 Paul BIRCH	
8 Joey BEAUCHAMP	60	8 Darren FERGUSON	
9 Jan Aage FJORTOFT		9 Steve BULL	
10 Martin LING		10 David KELLY	13, 41
11 Keith SCOTT †	28	11 Mark WALTERS	
Substitutes		*Substitutes*	
12 Andy MUTCH †67		12 Mark RANKINE	
14 Kevin HORLOCK		14 Lee MILLS	
gk Nicky HAMMOND		gk Paul JONES	

BEFORE	P	W	D	L	F	A	pts	AFTER	P	W	D	L	F	A	pts
1 Wolves	10	7	2	1	18	7	23	1 Wolves	11	7	2	2	20	10	23
5 Swindon	10	5	2	3	12	9	17	5 Swindon	11	6	2	3	15	11	20

FACTFILE

Can the County Ground hoodoo be broken... Kelly and Walters back... goal line controversy so costly... Kelly double can't save the game... defeat, but Middlesbrough also lose to leave Wolves on top... only second league defeat of the season

The Wolves Review 1995

SWINDON HOODOO STRIKES AGAIN

Kelly back with double strike

If Wolves are to extend their sequence of League wins to six they have to break a significant hoodoo – all six of their previous visits to Swindon's County Ground have ended in defeat.

This afternoon would be a timely occasion to end the run of failures, particularly as second-in-the-table Middlesbrough start the day on equal points and Swindon, lying in fifth place, are only six points adrift.

Relegated from the Premiership after just one season in the top flight, Swindon have made a useful start to their First Division campaign and will be dangerous opponents, reckons manager Graham Taylor.

"They learned a lot in the Pemiership and have a much more physical presence about them these days," says the Wolves boss. "It's going to be a hard game."

Taylor's team is strengthened by the return of striker David Kelly after an injury-enforced two match absence, though winger Steve Froggatt is still missing, as are midfielder Neil Emblen and on-loan Liverpool striker Paul Stewart.

But the other on-loan import from Anfield, winger Mark Walters, is back along with Kelly to boost Wolves' attacking strength. This will be Walters' last match in his loan spell but, with the continuing injury problems of Tony Daley, manager Taylor is hoping to keep him for another month.

As the game gets underway Walters shows just why he is still wanted, producing some early moments of magic that have the home defence in a tangle.

It is from an excellent Darren Ferguson through-pass, however, that Wolves take a 13th minute lead when Kelly lashes the ball home.

Wolves' joy at going ahead turns to anger and frustration two minutes later, when Paul Blades appears to clear a Paul Bodin lob off the line only for a goal to be signalled.

Blades and skipper Peter Shirtliff are both booked for their lengthy protests to the linesman whose decision has cost them a goal, which – as TV replays later confirm – should not have been awarded.

Wolves are still cursing their luck when, 13 minutes after the controversial equaliser, Swindon move into the lead. Slack marking allows Keith Scott all the time and space he requires to turn and shoot past Mike Stowell.

But the reversal galvanises Wolves and four minutes before the interval they are back on level terms, Kelly heading his second goal of the game from Steve Bull's header across the goalmouth.

The second half starts evenly, but on the hour further defensive frailty costs Wolves another goal.

Paul Birch's poor header is compounded by Jamie Smith's scuffed clearance and Joey Beauchamp, the ball falling at his feet, smacks a 20 yard shot into the net.

The goal proves decisive. Wolves spend the last half hour pressing for another equaliser, but the home side defend well and, at times, in considerable depth.

So, Wolves suffer only their second League defeat of the season as the County Ground curse continues.

Consolation arrives with the news that Middlesbrough have lost at home to Tranmere, leaving Wolves in top spot.

But that controversial early decision which cost them a goal still rankles as Wolves begin the journey home.

It is left to manager Taylor to put the bad luck into perspective: "There have been games we have won which could have gone either way, and these things have a habit of levelling themselves out."

MATCH 17 • ENDSLEIGH LEAGUE DIVISION 1

Saturday 15th October 1994 • Molineux • 3.00pm

WOLVES 2 GRIMSBY TOWN 1

Half-time 1-1 • *Attendance* 24,447

Referee Mike PIERCE (Portsmouth)

Linesmen K.J. HAWKES and L. MARKMAN

Gold Shirts with Black Trim, Black Shorts		Goals	Black and White Striped Shirts, White Shorts		Goals
1	Mike STOWELL		1	Paul CRICHTON	
2	James SMITH		2	Gary CROFT	
3	Andy THOMPSON	12 pen	3	Kevin JOBLING ‡	
4	Mark VENUS	66	4	Peter HANDYSIDE	
5	Paul BLADES		5	Mark LEVER	
6	Peter SHIRTLIFF		6	Craig SHAKESPEARE	
7	Mark WALTERS ❑		7	Jim DOBBIN ❑	
8	Darren FERGUSON †		8	Tommy WATSON †	
9	Steve BULL		9	Neil WOODS	
10	David KELLY		10	Steve LIVINGSTONE	
11	Steve FROGGATT		11	Paul GROVES	43
	Substitutes			*Substitutes*	
12	Mark RANKINE †61		12	Paul FUTCHER ‡84	
14	Lee MILLS		14	Gary CHILDS †72	
gk	Paul JONES		gk	Nick COLGAN	

BEFORE	P	W	D	L	F	A	pts	AFTER	P	W	D	L	F	A	pts
1 Wolves	11	7	2	2	20	10	23	1 Wolves	12	8	2	2	22	11	26
14 Grimsby	11	3	5	3	18	14	14	17 Grimsby	12	3	5	4	19	16	14

FACTFILE *Wingers on the move... Froggatt back after illness... awards for Graham Taylor and Mike Stowell... Thommo's fifth penalty success of the season... poor performance but 100 per cent home League record maintained... two point gap opened at top of table.*

38

The Wolves Review 1995

WANDERERS OPEN GAP AT TOP

Victory despite poor display

As one Wolves winger returns to action, so another is set to depart Molineux.

Steve Froggatt, recovered from the illness that forced him out of two Wolves games plus the England Under 21 trip to Austria, replaces Paul Birch as the only team change from last week's defeat at Swindon.

Kevin Keen, meanwhile, is mulling over a £350,000 move to Stoke City. Signed by previous manager Graham Turner in August 1993, Keen has not started a League match since the opening day of the season and is clearly not part of Graham Taylor's plans.

Keen has told Stoke he will give them a decision after the weekend while a third winger, Robbie Dennison, has turned down a move to Second Division Wycombe Wanderers.

Grimsby come to Molineux without leading scorer Clive Mendonca, who earlier in the week sustained head injuries in a car crash.

Before the match Graham Taylor is presented with his September *Manager of the Month* award.

A less heralded but perhaps equally significant award has been made to goalkeeper Mike Stowell, named the Wilkinson Sword *'Protector of the Month'* as the holder of the First Division's best goalkeeping record during the month of September – just two goals against in five matches, which included three successive clean sheets.

Stowell is given an early chance to show his class against Grimsby, clinging on to a fiercely struck volley by Jim Dobbin.

But David Kelly and Mark Walters have already flashed shots just wide at the other end and, in the 12th minute, Wolves take the lead with Andy Thompson's fifth penalty of the season.

'Thommo' smacks home the spot kick after Mark Lever has been penalised for a shirt-tugging offence on Darren Ferguson.

Delight at the breakthrough is gradually tempered by Wolves' inability to produce an attacking blend to increase their lead.

Haplessly hit high balls contrast starkly with Grimsby's neat passing style and it is the visitors who take control of the match.

They lack a cutting edge without Mendonca but deservedly equalise two minutes before the interval. Steve Livingstone, deputising for Mendonca, flicks on Gary Croft's cross and former Burton Albion midfielder Paul Groves dives in to head the ball home.

Grimsby retain their grip after the break and Livingstone sends an overhead kick into the net, only for the goal to be ruled out through an infringement.

Against the run of play and in rather fortuitous circumstances, Wolves regain the lead in the 66rd minute.

A throw-in which should have gone Grimsby's way is instead awarded to Wolves, who take full advantage – Froggatt's long throw lands in the goalmouth via defender Peter Handyside's head and Mark Venus, dashing in at the back post, slams the ball over the line from close range.

Unlucky Grimsby hit back and twice go close to equalising, Dobbin having a goalbound effort brilliantly saved by Stowell and Livingstone missing the target with a header which should have been netted.

Wolves hang on to keep intact their 100 per cent home League record, but manager Taylor describes the performance as their worst at Molineux since he took charge seven months ago.

Three points are gratefully accepted, however, particularly as Middlesbrough have been hammered 5-1 at Luton to leave table topping Wolves two points clear of new second club Reading.

The Wolves Review 1995

MATCH 18 • ENDSLEIGH LEAGUE DIVISION 1

Saturday 22nd October 1994 • Molineux • 3.00pm

WOLVES 3   MILLWALL 3

Half-time 1-1 • Attendance 25,059

Referee John KIRBY (Sheffield)

Linesmen D.J. HINE and B.M. RICE

Gold Shirts with Black Trim, Black Shorts.   Goals

1	Mike STOWELL	
2	James SMITH	
3	Andy THOMPSON	
4	Mark VENUS	79
5	Paul BLADES	
6	Peter SHIRTLIFF	
7	Mark WALTERS †	
8	Darren FERGUSON ❑	
9	Steve BULL	27, 52
10	David KELLY	
11	Steve FROGGATT	

Substitutes

12	Tony DALEY †76	
14	Geoff THOMAS	
gk	Paul JONES	

Blue Shirts with White Sleeves, White Shorts.   Goals

1	Kasey KELLER	
2	Kenny CUNNINGHAM	
3	Ben THATCHER	
4	Pat VAN DEN HAUWE	
5	Tony WITTER ❑	
6	Andy ROBERTS ❑	
7	Dave SAVAGE ‡	
8	Ian DAWES	
9	Dave MITCHELL †	
10	Jon GOODMAN	39, 86
11	Mark KENNEDY	

Substitutes

12	Richard CADETTE †64	84
14	Mark BEARD ‡89	
gk	Tim CARTER	

BEFORE	P	W	D	L	F	A	pts
1 Wolves	12	8	2	2	22	10	26
21 Millwall	12	2	5	5	14	17	11

AFTER	P	W	D	L	F	A	pts
1 Wolves	13	8	3	2	25	13	27
22 Millwall	13	2	6	5	17	20	12

FACTFILE *Kevin Keen completes move to Stoke... First senior squad appearance for £1.3m Tony Daley... Bull double sets up Wolves for three points, but Lions make life difficult for Wolves... Venus on target – again!... late lapses so costly... 100 per cent home record ends...*

The Wolves Review 1995

HOME RECORD WRECKED

Daley's first Wolves outing

A reserve team appearance at Tranmere Rovers on Wednesday has set up winger Tony Daley for his first competitive senior outing since his record £1.3m move from Aston Villa in the close season.

It is a timely return to action as wing colleague Kevin Keen went through with his move to Stoke City early in the week.

Daley scored the final goal in the reserves' 4-1 win at Prenton Park, where fellow injury victims Geoff Thomas and Chris Marsden also played the full 90 minutes as they too took further steps on the road to recovery.

Marsden has to stay sidelined for the time being as far as the first team is concerned, but Thomas – out of the side since the end of August – comes back to join Daley on the substitutes' bench for the Millwall match.

With the Londoners struggling in the relegation zone after a quarter of the First Division campaign, the Wolves faithful who are once again packing Molineux are fully expecting Graham Taylor's team to keep up their perfect home League record.

It is the visitors who have the better of the early exchanges, however, Jon Goodman missing a 12-yard chance then Mark Kennedy having a 20-yard effort well saved by Mike Stowell.

But Wolves take the lead on 27 minutes, Mark Walters laying the ball back to Jamie Smith and from the full back's excellent cross Steve Bull directing a header into the corner of the net from 12 yards.

Despite the lift of a goal Wolves fail to raise their game and six minutes before half time Millwall deservedly draw level. Goodman forces the ball in from six yards after Kennedy's cross has been blocked.

Wolves are back in the lead straight after the interval, though, Bull notching his sixth goal of the season after Kasey Keller has parried a Steve Froggatt shot.

Wolves are sitting fairly comfortably on their lead as Walters is replaced by Daley 14 minutes from time, the winger receiving a great reception from the fans.

Disconcertingly, he pulls up when making his very first run. But he remains on the field in no apparent discomfort through the remarkable closing stages.

Wolves appear to have the match won 11 minutes from time, when Mark Venus drives in a 25-yard free kick to record his third goal in four games – after scoring only twice in his previous 86 appearances!

By the time Venus is able to ponder on his new found scoring prowess, however, Wolves have thrown away victory after allowing Millwall substitute Richard Cadette to run riot.

The on-loan striker races through to drill a low 84th minute shot past Stowell then, two minutes later, forces the keeper into a save – but as the ball breaks loose Dave Savage whips in a cross for Goodman to grab the equaliser with his second goal of the game.

It is a desperately disappointing end to the match and to Wolves 100 per cent home League record. Surprisingly though, Reading have lost at home to Sunderland so Wolves stretch their lead at the top of the table to three points.

James Smith – crossed perfectly for Steve Bull to head home the opener

The Wolves Review 1995

MATCH 19 • COCA-COLA CUP ROUND 3

Wednesday 26th October 1994 • Molineux • 8.00pm

WOLVES 2 NOTTINGHAM FOREST 3

Half-time 1-2 • Attendance 28,369
Referee Philip DON (Middlesex)
Linesmen P.M. ROBERTS and P.J. ROBINSON

Gold Shirts with Black Trim, Black Shorts.		Goals	Red Shirts with Black Trim, White Shorts.		Goals
1	Mike STOWELL		1	Mark CROSSLEY	
2	James SMITH		2	Des LYTTLE	
3	Andy THOMPSON		3	Stuart PEARCE ❏	5, 87
4	Darren FERGUSON †		4	Colin COOPER ❏	
5	Paul BLADES		5	Steve CHETTLE	
6	Mark VENUS		6	David PHILLIPS	
7	Paul BIRCH	41	9	Lars BOHINEN	
8	Geoff THOMAS		10	Stan COLLYMORE †	
9	Steve BULL		11	Steve STONE	
10	David KELLY	60	14	Ian WOAN	
11	Steve FROGGATT		22	Bryan ROY	21
	Substitutes			Substitutes	
12	Neil EMBLEN †76		8	Scott GEMMILL	
14	Mark RANKINE		14	Jason LEE †23	
gk	Paul JONES		gk	Tommy WRIGHT	

FACTFILE

Changes forced on Taylor for the big match... Forest unbeaten for 23 matches... record attendance for all-seater Molineux... fight back from two goal deficit... joy then heartbreak for Kelly... Disaster for 'Ned' as deflected Pearce free kick knocks Wolves out of the cup... 1980 cold comfort.

Mark Venus in action against Forest

42

The Wolves Review 1995

CRUEL LUCK FOR DAVID KELLY

Forest snatch last-gap win

Graham Taylor is in confident mood despite being forced into team changes for the most attractive match of his seven month Molineux reign.

Visitors Nottingham Forest, riding high in the Premiership's second spot after last season's promotion, are unbeaten for 23 matches in a sequence which stretches all the way back to March.

And with a devastating new strike partnership of Dutch international Bryan Roy and Cannock-born and former Wolves trainee Stan Collymore, Frank Clark's team are looking capable of taking apart any defence in the country.

The Wolves defence they have to face is minus captain Peter Shirtliff, out with an achilles problem.

Mark Venus drops back from midfield to occupy Shirtliff's central defensive position, while Geoff Thomas returns in midfield and also takes over as skipper.

On-loan Mark Walters is once more barred from playing by Liverpool so, with Tony Daley ruled out after being injured during his brief substitute appearance on Saturday, Paul Birch is brought in to play on the right side of midfield.

Forest are favourites but Wolves are sent out with a 'go get 'em' message from manager Taylor. "It's all there for us," he says. "Forest are on a roll but if our players are positive, confident and believe they can do it, this can be their night."

In front of a record crowd for the new-look Molineux, however, Taylor's words take on a hollow ring as Forest quickly sweep into a two goal lead.

Ex-England captain Stuart Pearce, booked in the opening exchanges for a wicked tackle on Paul Birch, forces home the first goal after Collymore has flicked on Ian Woan's fifth minute corner.

After their breakthrough Forest take total control and claim their second goal in the 21st minute. Collymore sends a neat pass into the path of Roy, who strides through to guide the ball past Mike Stowell from 20 yards.

Forest look irresistible at this stage but the turning point arrives just two minutes after Roy's goal, when the outstanding Collymore has to be substituted through a hamstring injury.

For a spell the visitors continue to dominate, but Wolves come more into the game and deservedly pull a goal back four minutes before half time.

Kelly crosses beyond the far post and Birch curls a first time effort back across the diving Mark Crossley and into the bottom far corner of the net.

The revival sparked, Wolves look much brighter after the break and on the hour Kelly gleefully heads the equaliser from Steve Froggatt's free kick.

With Wolves now looking the more likely winners substitute Neil Emblen goes agonisingly close to clinching victory in the 81st minute, flashing a cross-cum-shot just in front of Steve Bull and inches wide of the far post.

Three minutes from time though, the tie is decided in Forest's favour. Kelly, attempting to block Pearce's 25-yard free kick, instead diverts it unluckily past goalkeeper Mike Stowell and into the net.

The distraught look on the striker's face says everything about the cruel twist of fate which has despatched Wolves out of the Coca-Cola Cup.

And as supporters travel home cursing their team's luck, memories of that 1980 Wembley afternoon when Wolves beat Forest to win their last major knock-out trophy are no more than cold comfort.

The Wolves Review 1995

MATCH 20 • ENDSLEIGH LEAGUE DIVISION 1

Sunday 30th October 1994 • Victoria Ground • 2.55pm

STOKE CITY 1 WOLVES 1

Half-time 1-1 • Attendance 15,928
Referee John HOLBROOK (Ludlow)
Linesmen M.J. MOUNTAIN and A. STREETS

Red and White Striped Shirts, White Shorts	Goals	Gold Shirts with Black Trim, Black Shorts	Goals
1 Carl MUGGLETON		1 Mike STOWELL	
2 John BUTLER		2 James SMITH ‡	
3 Lee SANDFORD		3 Andy THOMPSON	
4 Ian CRANSON		4 Neil EMBLEN ❑ †	
5 Vince OVERSON		5 Paul BLADES	
6 Toddy ORLYGSSON		6 Mark VENUS	
7 Kevin KEEN	17	7 Mark WALTERS	
8 Carl BEESTON ❑		8 Geoff THOMAS	
9 Martin CARRUTHERS		9 Steve BULL	41
10 Paul PESCHISOLIDO †		10 David KELLY	
11 Nigel GLEGHORN		11 Steve FROGGATT	
Substitutes		*Substitutes*	
12 Wayne BIGGINS †75		12 Darren FERGUSON †80	
14 Larus SIGURDSSON		14 Paul STEWART ‡89	
gk Ronnie SINCLAIR		gk Paul JONES	

BEFORE	P	W	D	L	F	A	pts	AFTER	P	W	D	L	F	A	pts
1 Wolves	13	8	3	2	25	13	27	1 Wolves	14	8	4	2	26	14	28
15 Stoke City	13	5	3	5	17	20	18	11 Stoke City	14	5	4	5	18	21	19

FACTFILE

TV chance for return to winning ways... Keen keen to pile up Wolves' 'goals against' column... Emblen back – and booked... story book opener... Bully bites back... Stowell (and the woodwork) to the rescue... its a point gained rather than lost in a physical game.

44

The Wolves Review 1995

BULLY'S A POINT SAVER

Winger Keen fires the Potters

After two successive Molineux disappointments, Wolves make the short trip up the M6 to Stoke looking for a return to winning ways in front of the Central TV cameras.

While collecting three points is the top priority, however, there is also the important problem of the 'Goals Against' column to be addressed.

Three goals conceded in each of the last two matches have taken the recent tally to 16 against in nine outings – and this after leaking only five in the previous 10 games.

Manager Taylor insists the reason has not been so much a deterioration in Wolves' defensive standards as an improvement in the ability of opponents to punish defensive mistakes.

"I can remember easy chances being missed against us by Reading, Albion and Tranmere," says Taylor, "but suddenly similar chances are being taken and our results have started to suffer."

One man determined to increase the suffering today is winger Kevin Keen, set to make his home debut for the Potters following his recent move from Molineux. Keen scored his first Wolves goal against Stoke 14 months ago and would love to reverse the situation.

Wolves make two team changes from Wednesday's agonising Coca-Cola Cup exit, winger Mark Walters returning in place of Paul Birch and Neil Emblen taking over from Darren Ferguson in the centre of midfield.

Despite not being fully fit, Emblen's greater height and physical presence get him the nod ahead of Ferguson for a match in which strength and power will be the watchwords.

Stoke are reputed for their physical approach, particularly under recently returned manager Lou Macari, but in a bruising opening to the game Emblen is the first player to receive a caution. Just 11 minutes into his first senior start for almost six weeks, the Wolves midfield man is booked for a challenge on Carl Beeston.

Six minutes later Beeston belies Stoke's 'power game' image with an exquisite through-ball which cuts out three defenders and enables Keen to score his story-book goal with a low shot past Mike Stowell.

David Kelly and Steve Froggatt both go close with long range efforts before Wolves get their equaliser four minutes before half time. Geoff Thomas heads on an Andy Thompson cross and Steve Bull, dashing in front of marker Vince Overson, controls the ball with his chest before lashing a 12-yard shot into the roof of the net.

Stowell has to save well from an Ian Cranson header just before the interval, then minutes after the break the Wolves keeper is forced into a reflex save to keep out Paul Peschisolido's header.

In driving rain the home side now have the upper hand and Stowell is once more the Wolves saviour with a save just under the bar from Martin Carruthers.

When Stowell is well beaten by a Keen header the far post comes to the rescue. But the keeper has the final word, saving substitute Wayne Biggins' 12-yard shot in Stoke's last effective attack.

The point gained from a hard fought game has not been totally deserved but is welcome nevertheless. It keeps Wolves on top of the table, though Keen's goal means that the sequence of matches since the last clean sheet now stretches into double figures.

Andy Thompson comes under pressure from ex-Wolves man Kevin Keen

The Wolves Review 1995

45

MATCH 21 • ENDSLEIGH LEAGUE DIVISION 1

Tuesday 1st November 1994 • Ashton Gate • 7.45pm

BRISTOL CITY 1 WOLVES 5

Half-time 1-2 • Attendance 10,401

Referee Clive WILKES (Gloucester)

Linesmen K. BULLER and P. GRIGGS

Red Shirts with White Trim, White Shorts — Goals

1	Keith WELCH	
2	Stuart MUNRO	
3	Mark HUMPHRIES	
4	Mark SHAIL ■	
5	Matt BRYANT ❑	
6	Brian TINNION ❑	
7	Junior BENT †	
8	David SEAL	
9	Ian BAIRD	31
10	Scott PATTERSON ❑	
11	Rob EDWARDS	

Substitutes

12	Jason FOWLER †46	
14	Scott PARTRIDGE	
gk	Phil KITE	

Gold Shirts with Black Trim, Black Shorts — Goals

1	Mike STOWELL	
2	James SMITH	
3	Andy THOMPSON	36 pen
4	Darren FERGUSON	
5	Paul BLADES ❑	
6	Mark VENUS	
7	Mark WALTERS	12
8	Geoff THOMAS	
9	Steve BULL ❑ †	
10	David KELLY	63, 65, 88
11	Steve FROGGATT	

Substitutes

12	Paul STEWART †78	
14	Mark RANKINE	
gk	Paul JONES	

BEFORE	P	W	D	L	F	A	pts
1 Wolves	14	8	4	2	26	14	28
21 Bristol City	14	4	4	6	11	13	16

AFTER	P	W	D	L	F	A	pts
1 Wolves	15	9	4	2	31	15	31
21 Bristol City	15	4	4	7	12	18	16

FACTFILE *Paul Jones gets Wales stand-by call... third loan month lined up for Stewart, in spite of his wretched injury luck... spot-kick number six for Thompson... Mark Shail sent off for professional foul... Kelly's first Wolves hat-trick... best away win for over six years.*

The Wolves Review 1995

TABLE-TOPPERS GO NAP

Kelly bags a hat-trick

Perennial reserve goalkeeper Paul Jones is cheered with a surprise international call-up before journeying to Bristol for tonight's match at Ashton Gate.

Jones, in his fourth Wolves season as understudy to Mike Stowell, has been named as stand-by keeper for Wales' European Championship qualifier in Georgia on November 16th.

"I didn't even know I was under consideration," admits Jones, whose parents are English but who was born across the border at hospital in Chirk.

Despite his international recognition Jones remains on the Wolves substitutes' bench, though Darren Ferguson makes a quick return to the starting line-up in place of Neil Emblen – the man who replaced him at Stoke but unluckily sustained an ankle injury.

Striker Paul Stewart, whose second month on loan from Liverpool is coming to an end, is on the subs' bench for the second game in succession after recovering from injury.

Despite the fact that Stewart has made only two full appearances due to his wretched injury luck, manager Taylor still seems keen to sign him on a permanent basis and looks set to extend his loan to a third month.

Wolves go into action against struggling City knowing that victory will probably be essential to keep them on top of the table. Second placed Middlesbrough are just one point behind and this evening entertain Oldham in a match they will be clear favourites to win.

Ashton Gate has not been a happy hunting ground for Wolves in recent seasons but tonight they start well, taking the lead after 12 minutes when Mark Walters side-foots home a Steve Froggatt cross.

Defensive frailties soon set in though, and when Rob Edwards' 31st minute cross leads to chaos in the Wolves goalmouth Ian Baird equalises with a shot which goes in off the bar.

Five minutes later the game's pivotal point arrives in dramatic fashion. Steve Bull is flattened by Mark Shail in a chase for a long Mike Stowell clearance, Shail receives his marching orders for the clumsy offence and Wolves controversially get a penalty when the challenge appeared to have taken place outside the area.

Andy Thompson chalks up his sixth penalty success of the season to restore Wolves lead and set up a super second half for the visitors.

City spark brightly for a few minutes but it becomes one-way traffic as first Walters then David Kelly are denied by fine saves from Keith Welch.

The keeper is well beaten in the 63rd minute, however, Kelly firing home a first time shot to round off a good Walters-Darren Ferguson move. Two minutes later Kelly puts the result beyond any doubt with another well taken goal, this time after a Froggatt cross has been only half cleared.

Stewart, sent on as substitute for Bull with 12 minutes left, misses an easy scoring chance, but then two minutes from time sets up Kelly's hat-trick goal with an angled shot which rebounds for a simple tap-in.

It is Kelly's first hat-trick for Wolves and takes his season's goal tally to 11 – only three short of his total for the whole of last season.

The result is also Wolves' biggest away win for six and a half years. But most importantly, it keeps their grip on the first division leadership as Middlesbrough have beaten Oldham.

David Kelly – hat-trick hero

The Wolves Review 1995

MATCH 22 • ENDSLEIGH LEAGUE DIVISION 1

Saturday 5th November 1994 • Molineux • 3.00pm

WOLVES 2 LUTON TOWN 3

Half-time 0-1 • Attendance 26,749

Referee Eddie WOLSTENHOLME (Blackburn)

Linesmen J.M.R. EVANS and R.A. SMITH

Gold Shirts with Black Trim, Black Shorts	Goals	Blue Shirts with Orange and White Stripes, White Shorts	Goals
1 Mike STOWELL		1 Juergen SOMMER	
2 James SMITH		2 Julian JAMES	
3 Andy THOMPSON		3 Marvin JOHNSON	84 og
4 Darren FERGUSON		4 Gary WADDOCK	
5 Paul BLADES		5 Mitchell THOMAS	
6 Mark VENUS		6 Trevor PEAKE	
7 Mark WALTERS ‡		7 Paul TELFER	
8 Geoff THOMAS		8 Scott OAKES	
9 Steve BULL †		9 Kerry DIXON †	54
10 David KELLY		10 David PREECE	37
11 Steve FROGGATT		11 Dwight MARSHALL	47
Substitutes		*Substitutes*	
12 Paul STEWART ‡60	81	12 John HARTSON †67	
14 Neil EMBLEN †45		14 Tony THORPE	
gk Paul JONES		gk Fred BARBER	

BEFORE	P	W	D	L	F	A	pts	AFTER	P	W	D	L	F	A	pts
1 Wolves	15	9	4	2	31	15	31	1 Wolves	16	9	4	3	33	18	31
13 Luton Town	15	5	4	6	21	20	19	8 Luton Town	16	6	4	6	24	22	22

FACTFILE Luton boss David Pleat lined up for Spurs?... cautionary message from Taylor... Walters' last loan appearance... Hatters bring best away record in Division One to Molineux... Luton take charge... Steve Bull substitution shock... three goals against – again

FIRST HOME LEAGUE DEFEAT

Shock as Bull gets subbed

Wolves are bubbling as they move into the second third of the season with a home game against troubled Luton, whose manager David Pleat looks set to join Tottenham Hotspur following the sacking of ex-Albion manager Ossie Ardiles.

The Kenilworth Road outfit, lying just below the halfway mark in the table, appear to be in disarray. But they have the best away record in Division One with 14 points from seven games. And with only one of those matches ending in defeat, Wolves boss Graham Taylor sends out his buoyant, unchanged team with a cautionary message.

"It's no good thinking Luton are in limbo because of what's been going on there," says Taylor. "Their away record speaks for itself and we must be on top of our game."

The warning is stark enough but is apparently unheeded by Taylor's men as the visitors take charge from the early stages.

Scott Oakes twice goes close to opening the scoring with long range shots, but against the run of play Steve Bull gets a couple of chances to give Wolves the lead – only to wildly miss the target on each occasion.

Mike Stowell makes a good stop from another Oakes shot before Luton deservedly take the lead in the 37th minute. Oakes touches a 20-yard free kick to former Walsall midfielder David Preece, who curls a low shot just inside the far post.

If Wolves' poor first half display has been a surprise, an even bigger shock is sprung at the start of the second half as the team runs out without Bull. The striker, who had suffered no apparent injury in the first half, has been substituted by Neil Emblen.

The supporters' murmurings of surprise turn to groans of despair two minutes after the interval, when Paul Telfer's cross bounces off Mark Walters for Dwight Marshall to head home Luton's second goal.

Worse is to follow in the 54th minute, when Mitchell Thomas is given yards of space for a run and cross which leads to ex-England centre forward Kerry Dixon heading the visitors into a three goal advantage.

It is the third successive home game in which Wolves have conceded three goals, and this time more look likely with Luton in total command.

But manager Taylor's second substitution pays belated dividends, Paul Stewart replacing Liverpool colleague Mark Walters in what proves to be the winger's last loan appearance for Wolves.

With 81 minutes on the clock Stewart runs into the penalty area before hitting a shot which deflects off Marvin Johnson into the Luton net.

And three minutes later the luckless Johnson gives Wolves hope of snatching a lucky draw when he turns a David Kelly cross into the net for an own goal.

Stewart almost does the trick with an 87th minute header which flashes wide; but a point is one more than Wolves deserve from a poor performance which has resulted in their first home League defeat of the season.

Taylor admits: "We were outplayed – the goals we scored were no more than a saving grace. We couldn't sort out a formation or a pattern.

"Now we have to assess where we went wrong, then put it right over the next few matches. I'll be looking for a positive reaction from the players."

The manager also confirms that Bull's substitution was nothing to do with injury. It is the first time in his eight years at the club that the legendary striker has been substituted for tactical reasons.

The Wolves Review 1995

MATCH 23 • ANGLO-ITALIAN CUP (GROUP A, MATCH 4)

Tuesday 15th November 1994 • Molineux • 7.45pm

WOLVES 1   ATALANTA 1

Half-time 1-1 • Attendance 7,285

Referee Fiorenzo TREOSSI (Forli)

Linesmen R. Picchio and M. Ricciardelli

Gold Shirts with Black Trim, Gold Shorts	Goals	Black and Blue Striped Shirts, White Shorts	Goals
1 Mike STOWELL		1 Davide PINATO	
2 Neil EMBLEN		2 Cristiano PAVONE ❑	
3 Andy THOMPSON		3 Emanuele TRESOLDI	
4 Darren FERGUSON †		4 Walter BONACINA	7
5 Paul BLADES ❑		5 Simone PAVAN	
6 Mark VENUS		6 Oscar MAGONI	
7 Paul BIRCH		7 Franco ROTELLA ‡	
8 Geoff THOMAS		8 Domenico MORFEO †	
9 Lee MILLS	38	9 Federico PISANI	
10 Paul STEWART ❑		10 Leonardo RODRIGUEZ	
11 Steve FROGGATT		11 Thomas LOCATELLI	
Substitutes		Substitutes	
12 Mark RANKINE †62		gk Fabrizio FERRON	
14 Robbie DENNISON		13 G.Luca GIBELLINI †82	
15 Tom BENNETT		14 Nicola BOSELLI	
16 Steven PIEARCE		15 Luciano ZAURI ‡86	
gk Paul JONES		16 Massimo MUTARELLI	

BEFORE	P	W	D	L	F	A	pts	AFTER	P	W	D	L	F	A	pts
1 (Ita A) Atalanta	3	2	1	0	5	1	7	2 (Ita A) Atalanta	4	2	2	0	6	2	8
3 (Eng A) Wolves	3	1	0	2	2	3	3	2 (Eng A) Wolves	4	1	1	2	3	4	4

FACTFILE *Kelly, Smith on international duty... Bull out through injury... Cup progress a tall order... first goal of season for Mills... Wolves go out... ex-Wanderer Marsden helps Notts County into English final...*

The Wolves Review 1995

ANGLO-ITALIAN JOURNEY ENDS

Weakened Wolves exit with a draw

Wolves go into tonight's final Anglo-Italian Cup qualifying round tie after a 10-day gap from match action.

Saturday's First Division game against Bolton Wanderers was postponed due to international calls on Bolton players, though this evening Wolves are missing both David Kelly and Jamie Smith for the same reason.

Kelly is on duty with Eire for their European Championships qualifying match against Northern Ireland, while Smith is with the England Under 21 squad for their meeting with the Eire Under 21's at Newcastle.

A more disturbing omission from the Wolves team is Steve Bull, who reported an achilles heel problem this morning and was immediately pulled out of both training and tonight's match.

With on-loan Mark Walters having returned to Liverpool four team changes are thus forced on manager Graham Taylor, who took advantage of Wolves' weekend inactivity by watching Grimsby Town – allegedly with possible transfer bids in mind for defenders Gary Croft and Peter Handyside.

Taylor brings Neil Emblen into the right back spot for Smith, Paul Birch takes over Walters' right wing berth and up front Paul Stewart replaces Kelly while Lee Mills covers for Bull.

Progress to the English final of the competition is a tall order for Wolves – they not only need to beat in-form Atalanta but also have to hope that the two clubs above them in the English section – Notts County and Swindon Town – lose their respective matches.

Wolves' prospects look even slimmer after just seven minutes of Molineux action, Walter Bonacina giving Atalanta the lead after Leonardo Rodriguez provides the chance with a superb through ball. But Wolves battle back and draw level with Mills' first senior goal of the season seven minutes before half time.

The stand-in striker collects a Birch cross to turn and send in a shot which goalkeeper Davide Pinato can only help into the net.

Atalanta go back on the offensive after the interval and Mike Stowell has to make three good saves in as many minutes.

But Wolves regain the upper hand and both Darren Ferguson and Emblen force Pinato into fine saves before a late penalty appeal is turned down when Emanuele Tresoldi appears to handle inside the area.

Wolves have to settle for a draw, though even if the spot kick had been awarded and a winning goal scored they would not have moved into the English final.

Top team Notts County's goal difference would still have been superior even if Wolves had won 2-1. County clinched their place in the final through a 3-3 draw with Venezia.

One of their goals came from midfielder Chris Marsden, signed last Friday in a surprise £150,000 move from Wolves.

At Molineux Marsden had quickly become a crowd favourite following his £160,000 move from Huddersfield Town in January, but after breaking his leg in only his 11th game for the club he never had the opportunity to re-establish himself in the first team.

In tonight's other games in *Group A* of the Anglo-Italian Cup, Ascoli have beaten Swindon 3-1 to win the Italian section while Tranmere have been beaten 3-0 at Lecce.

Ascoli will now meet Ancona in the Italian final, the winners to meet either Notts County or *Group B* English section winners Stoke City in the Wembley final of the competition.

Darren Ferguson – went close in the second half

The Wolves Review 1995

MATCH 24 • ENDSLEIGH LEAGUE DIVISION 1

Sunday 20th November 1994 • Ayresome Park • 2.55pm

MIDDLESBROUGH 1   WOLVES 0

Half-time 0-0 • Attendance 19,953

Referee Alan FLOOD (Cheshire)

Linesmen A.C. HARTEVELD and M.J. STODDART

Red Shirts with Black and White Trim, White Shorts	Goals	Gold Shirts with Black Trim, Black Shorts	Goals
1 Alan MILLER		1 Mike STOWELL	
2 Neil COX		2 Mark RANKINE	
3 Chris MORRIS		3 Andy THOMPSON	
4 Steve VICKERS		4 Darren FERGUSON †	
5 Derek WHYTE		5 Paul BLADES ❏	
6 Robbie MUSTOE		6 Mark VENUS	
7 Craig HIGNETT		7 Neil EMBLEN	
8 Jamie POLLOCK		8 Geoff THOMAS ❏	
9 Paul WILKINSON †		9 Paul STEWART	
10 John HENDRIE	67	10 David KELLY	
11 Alan MOORE		11 Steve FROGGATT	
Substitutes		*Substitutes*	
12 Clayton BLACKMORE †83		12 Paul BIRCH †76	
14 Andy TODD		14 James SMITH	
gk Ben ROBERTS		gk Paul JONES	

BEFORE		P	W	D	L	F	A	pts	AFTER		P	W	D	L	F	A	pts
1	Wolves	16	9	4	3	33	18	31	2	Wolves	17	9	4	4	33	19	31
2	M'boro	16	9	3	4	23	16	30	1	M'boro	17	10	3	4	24	16	33

FACTFILE

Two-month League leadership under threat... operation fear for absent-again Bull... Stewart transfer deal set to go through... Wolves steamrollered into submission... cruel goal, but hero Stowell keeps the scoreline respectable... Boro the new leaders.

The Wolves Review 1995

KNOCKED OFF THE TOP SPOT

Hero Stowell so unlucky

Wolves' lengthy grip on the First Division leadership faces its toughest test yet at Ayresome Park.

Victory for second placed Middlesbrough will leapfrog them over Graham Taylor's team into top spot, held by Wolves since the 5-0 demolition of Southend on September 13th.

As feared, Steve Bull misses the match through the heel injury which could eventually lead to an operation. David Kelly, back from international duty, slots back into the front line alongside Paul Stewart.

The on-loan Liverpool striker's permanent move to Molineux is set to go ahead after manager Taylor agreed a £1m fee (£750,000 plus 'add-ons') on Thursday.

Taylor has also stepped up his bid to bring Norwegian international central defender Ronny Johnsen to Molineux, though the deal looks unlikely to go ahead in the foreseeable future.

In the meantime the manager has all his attention fixed on this afternoon's televised top-of-the-table clash. It is the biggest game of the season to date in the Endsleigh League and Taylor warns: "We can't afford to have any shrinking violets."

The steely determination he is looking for is far more evident in Middlesbrough than Wolves, however, Bryan Robson's team roaring into the match with the fervour which was always a hallmark of the former Manchester United and England captain.

Wolves are on the wrack from the kick-off, Paul Wilkinson sending an early header over the bar then Craig Hignett racing through unchallenged to smack a 25-yard shot against the post.

The ever dangerous John Hendrie goes close on three occasions as Midlesbrough take a stranglehold on the game, but 10 minutes from half time Wolves almost snatch the lead when good work by David Kelly sets up Darren Ferguson for a 20-yard shot which bounces off the crossbar.

Mike Stowell makes a good stop from Hignett shortly before the interval then, in a 15 minute spell at the start of the second half, the Wolves goalkeeper pulls off tremendous saves from Wilkinson, Hignett and Alan Moore.

When Stowell is finally beaten it is in cruel fashion, Hendrie's 67th minute shot deflecting off Geoff Thomas to wrong-foot the keeper and streak into the net.

Hendrie's lucky but deserved goal is almost followed by another as the striker twice forces Stowell into further heroic saves.

The continual pressure on Stowell's goal is relieved for a short spell, opposition keeper Alan Miller making his first save of the match from a 77th minute Thomas shot, then Wolves having a strong penalty appeal turned down when Stewart appears to be tripped by Derek Whyte.

But the game ends as it started, with Boro well in control and Stowell keeping out goal-bound shots from Hendrie and Hignett in the last three minutes.

Wolves have been totally outplayed, as Taylor readily admits. "They got hold of the game with power and purpose," says the Wolves boss. "We had to defend – we just couldn't get them off our backs."

A delighted Bryan Robson beams: "That was our best performance of the season. We deserved more goals, but I'm very happy with the result and to see us back on top of the table."

Wolves are second and only two points behind, but – after two successive League defeats and only two wins in their last seven outings – question marks are suddenly being put against Wolves' potential to win the championship...

MATCH 25 • ENDSLEIGH LEAGUE DIVISION 1

Wednesday 23rd November 1994 • Molineux • 7.45pm

WOLVES 3 BOLTON WANDERERS 1

Half-time 0-1 • *Attendance* 25,903

Referee Keith COOPER (Swindon)

Linesmen B.P. ELLICOTT and N.E. GREEN

Gold Shirts with Black Trim, Black Shorts	Goals	Blue Shirts, Blue Shorts	Goals
1 Mike STOWELL		1 Keith BRANAGAN	
2 Mark RANKINE		2 Jason LYDIATE ❑	
3 Andy THOMPSON	53 pen	3 Jimmy PHILLIPS	
4 Darren FERGUSON ❑		4 Mark PATTERSON ❑	
5 Paul BLADES †		5 Alan THOMPSON	
6 Mark VENUS		6 Scott GREEN	
7 Paul BIRCH	75	7 Simon COLEMAN	68 og
8 Geoff THOMAS		8 Richard SNEEKES ‡	
9 Paul STEWART		9 Mixu PAATELAINEN	15
10 David KELLY		10 Fabian de FREITAS †	
11 Steve FROGGATT		11 David LEE	
Substitutes		*Substitutes*	
12 Neil EMBLEN †62		12 Owen COYLE †62	
14 James SMITH		14 Alan STUBBS ‡72	
gk Paul JONES		gk Mark WESTHEAD	

BEFORE	P	W	D	L	F	A	pts	AFTER	P	W	D	L	F	A	pts
2 Wolves	17	9	4	4	33	19	31	1 Wolves	18	10	4	4	36	20	34
3 Bolton	17	8	5	4	30	18	29	3 Bolton	18	8	5	5	31	21	29

FACTFILE

Major blow for Daley – out for rest of season... captain's rallying cry... form team Bolton take the initiative... penalty king Thompson nets spot-kick number seven... Ferguson flying, Froggy reaps the benefits... Paul Birch's first League goal of the season... top spot reclaimed.

FORM TEAM BOLTON ARE TOPPLED

Quick return to the top spot

Wolves go into their second crunch game in four days in the wake of yet more bad injury news.

Record signing Tony Daley, whose only appearance since his close season £1.3m move from Aston Villa lasted just 14 minutes, has learned he must have a cruciate knee ligaments operation which will force him to miss the rest of the season.

"It's a terrible blow for Tony," says manager Graham Taylor, "but he accepts that it has to be done. We signed an exciting 26 year old – now we have to hope we shall have an exciting, fully fit 27-year-old sometime next year."

With Peter Shirtliff still missing after an achilles operation and Steve Bull possibly set for the same fate, Wolves will seemingly be below full strength for some time to come.

But despite that captain Geoff Thomas, following Sunday's surrender at Middlesbrough, is determined to lead his side back to the top of the table against another of Wolves' main promotion rivals.

Thomas says: "We let everybody down at Ayresome Park, including ourselves. When you lose a big game like that, it's inevitable questions will be asked.

"A few of us would admit we haven't played well enough for several games now. But we've got to be positive – a win over Bolton will take us back to the top and give everybody a lift."

Tonight's match brings just one team change from Sunday's defeat, Paul Birch replacing Neil Emblen in midfield as Wolves take on third placed Bolton Wanderers.

Bruce Rioch's side are the First Division's current form team, with their 10-match unbeaten run including five straight wins leading into this evening's big game.

And it is the visitors who take the early initiative. Good play brings them a 15th minute breakthrough, Mixu Paatelainen shooting into the empty net after Alan Thompson's effort has rebounded off a post.

As the first half progresses Wolves find it difficult to establish any kind of rhythm against well organised opponents, though David Kelly twice frees Paul Stewart for shots which fail to bring an equaliser.

At the other end Fabian de Freitas then Paatelainen both misdirect headers as Bolton continue to create chances. But Wolves improve towards half time and take control after the interval.

The equaliser arrives after 53 minutes, Andy Thompson striking in his seventh penalty of the season following a handling offence by Jason Lydiate.

And 15 minutes later Wolves move ahead as Simon Coleman attempts to cut out Steve Froggatt's low cross, only to turn the ball into the net for an own goal.

The architect of the goal was Darren Ferguson, who is having his most influential game of the season and keeping Froggatt in particular supplied with a flow of excellent passes.

The 75th minute killer goal comes from the other flank, however. Stewart and Kelly combine to produce a chance for Birch, who drills home a diagonal shot to record his first League goal of the season.

It ensures that Wolves collect only their third win in eight first division outings, also taking them back to the top after their best home League performance since beating Southend 10 weeks ago.

Tony Daley – another operation

MATCH 26 • ENDSLEIGH LEAGUE DIVISION 1

Sunday 27th November 1994 • Molineux • 2.55pm

WOLVES 0 DERBY COUNTY 2

Half-time 0-1 • Attendance 22,768

Referee John LLOYD (Wrexham)

Linesmen T.A. ATKINSON and M.J. JOY

Gold Shirts with Black Trim, Black Shorts	Goals	White Shirts with Black Trim, White Shorts	Goals
1 Mike STOWELL		1 Steve SUTTON	
2 Mark RANKINE		2 Jason KAVANAGH	
3 Andy THOMPSON ‡		3 Shane NICHOLSON	
4 Darren FERGUSON		4 Martin KUHL	
5 Paul BLADES ❏		5 Craig SHORT	
6 Mark VENUS		6 Paul WILLIAMS	
7 Paul BIRCH		7 John HARKES	
8 Geoff THOMAS		8 Lee CARSLEY	
9 Paul STEWART †		9 Tommy JOHNSON	14
10 David KELLY		10 Mark STALLARD	62
11 Steve FROGGATT		11 Paul SIMPSON	
Substitutes		Substitutes	
12 Neil EMBLEN †67		12 Dean STURRIDGE	
14 James SMITH ‡71		14 Darren WASSALL	
gk Paul JONES		gk Andrew QUY	

BEFORE	P	W	D	L	F	A	pts	AFTER	P	W	D	L	F	A	pts
2 Wolves	18	10	4	4	36	20	34	2 Wolves	19	10	4	5	36	22	34
18 Derby	18	6	5	7	20	19	23	11 Derby	19	7	5	7	22	19	26

FACTFILE

Pursuit of Ronny Johnsen goes on... Wolves aim to reclaim top spot for the second time in five days... smallest League gate of the season to date... bright start quickly disintegrates... Paul Stewart booed off... angry Graham Taylor words follow another TV flop.

The Wolves Review 1995

CAMERA-SHY SHAMBLES

Taylor blasts his TV flops

The stakes are high for Wolves as they appear on live TV for the second successive Sunday – and with two more Sunday TV dates to follow before Christmas.

Middlesbrough's win at Charlton yesterday has put them back on top, meaning Graham Taylor's team must beat Roy McFarland's misfiring outfit to become leaders for the fourth time this season.

A sign of the Molineux times is provided by the gate of 22,768 – the smallest League crowd so far this season, though it is still higher than any other First Division club's biggest League attendance and more than the turn-out to watch Blackburn go top of the Premiership yesterday.

With Wolves' resources stretched, the good news is that central defender Paul Blades has surprisingly recovered from a neck injury that was threatening to rule him out against his first club.

Off the field though, manager Taylor has failed in his efforts to sign much needed defensive replacements.

Norwegian Ronny Johnsen remains elusive despite a faxed bid to his club Lillestrom, who may come up with an alternative deal in the next few days.

In the meantime, Wolves go into their West v. East Midlands clash with the same side which saw off Bolton in midweek.

They start promisingly enough, supporters clearing their throats after only three minutes to scream for a penalty as Derby midfielder Lee Carsley clears a Geoff Thomas shot off the line. TV replays show Carsley had blatantly handled the ball but, for once, Wolves' luck with spot-kick decisions is out.

The incident proves a rare fright in the visitors' goalmouth, however, for they quickly put the squeeze on David Kelly and Paul Stewart and begin to look dangerous on the break.

The game is only 14 minutes old when poor defending by Mark Venus and Mark Rankine allows Tommy Johnson in, the striker driving home a left-footed shot to put Derby County ahead.

Darren Ferguson and Steve Froggatt occasionally threaten to manufacture a reply but Derby, like Luton and Middlesbrough before them, are powerful opponents.

Visiting goalkeeper Steve Sutton stops Wolves' best equalising attempt, a close range header from Stewart.

It heralds an unhappy sequence of events for the on-loan striker, who becomes the butt of the fans' frustration and is roundly booed when he is substituted midway through the second half. Will his permanent move from Liverpool, already agreed by the two clubs, now be in jeopardy?

By the time of Stewart's exit from the action Wolves are a further goal behind, Mark Stallard having scored in the 62nd minute with a perfectly placed header from Johnson's left wing cross.

The final half hour is sheer misery for Wolves. An increasingly critical crowd, plus injuries to Andy Thompson and Kelly – the latter's a head injury which leads to him being stretchered off – add to the gloom as Derby finish emphatic winners.

It has been the unhappiest afternoon of Taylor's reign, the manager ending it with an angry broadside at his players.

"They let themselves and everyone around them down," he fumes.

"This is a big club, desperate to get into the Premiership, and you have to have players with bottle and the will-to-win. We fell terribly, terribly short. We needed leaders out there – but we had 11 players who were looking down at the grass."

The Wolves Review 1995

MATCH 27 • ENDSLEIGH LEAGUE DIVISION 1

Sunday 4th December 1994 • The New Den • 2.55pm

MILLWALL 1 WOLVES 0

Half-time 0-0 • *Attendance* 8,025

Referee Ian HEMLEY (Bedfordshire)
Linesmen W.M. JORDAN and K.R. TORRANCE

Blue Shirts with White Sleeves, Blue Shorts — Goals

1 Kasey KELLER
2 Mark BEARD
3 Ben THATCHER
4 Andy ROBERTS
5 Tony WITTER
6 Keith STEVENS
7 Ian DAWES
8 Alex RAE
9 Greg BERRY †
10 Dave MITCHELL — 67
11 Mark KENNEDY

Substitutes

12 Richard CADETTE †81
14 Dave SAVAGE
gk Tim CARTER

Gold Shirts with Black Trim, Black Shorts — Goals

1 Mike STOWELL
2 James SMITH
3 Tom BENNETT
4 Darren FERGUSON ❑ †
5 Paul BLADES
6 Mark VENUS
7 Neil EMBLEN
8 Geoff THOMAS
9 Steve BULL ❑
10 David KELLY ■
11 Steve FROGGATT

Substitutes

12 Mark RANKINE
14 Lee MILLS †70
gk Paul JONES

BEFORE	P	W	D	L	F	A	pts
3 Wolves	19	10	4	5	36	22	34
21 Millwall	19	4	7	8	24	28	19

AFTER	P	W	D	L	F	A	pts
3 Wolves	20	10	4	6	36	23	34
20 Millwall	20	5	7	8	25	28	22

FACTFILE

Paul Stewart sent back to Liverpool... ex-Baggie Don Goodman the new striker target... Johnsen deal off so Taylor goes Dutch to lure defender John de Wolf... Andy Thompson out for two months – but Bull returns after injury... New Den, same old story... David Kelly sent off...

58   The Wolves Review 1995

NEW DEN – SAME OLD STORY

Another sorry afternoon

Wolves arrive at Millwall's well-appointed New Den at the end of another incident-packed Molineux week.

Graham Taylor has sent striker Paul Stewart back to Liverpool at the end of his three-month loan; and now the manager is on the brink of a near £2 million splash on Sunderland's former Albion striker Don Goodman and Dutch international central defender John de Wolf.

Stewart has returned unhappily to Anfield, insisting he still wanted to join Wolves permanently despite becoming the target of restless fans.

But he was substituted in the match against Derby due to a groin injury and Taylor said on the striker's departure: "I couldn't go ahead with the deal.

"We persevered with Paul when he missed 11 matches with an ankle injury, but I couldn't spend big money on him now he is injured again."

Taylor wasted no time in switching his attentions to Goodman, setting up a £1.1m deal and holding discussions with the player he now hopes will join on Monday – in a double signing with de Wolf.

Having missed out on capturing Norwegian Ronny Johnsen, Taylor moved smartly to rubber stamp a £600,000 deal for the popular Feyenoord captain.

After watching de Wolf in his last match in Holland, a Dutch Cup tie against Willem II in Tilborg, Taylor has allowed the bearded hero to stay and bid farewell to his home crowd in Rotterdam.

He is then due in England to become Wolves' first major signing from overseas since New Zealander Ricky Herbert joined the club in 1984.

The transfer activity has produced a buzz of excitement among the Wolves fans who have made the journey to South London, their anticipation heightened by the fact that Steve Bull is back in the side today following an injury enforced month-long absence.

On the debit side, however, full back Andy Thompson has been ruled out for three months following a hernia operation so Steve Froggatt is set to face Millwall in an emergency left back role.

With Paul Birch also out injured, Neil Emblen returns to the starting line-up against his former club. And there is a surprise recall for Tom Bennett, who will operate just in front of the back four in his first League game of the season.

Millwall start the match in the relegation zone thanks to Albion's 2-1 win against Barnsley yesterday, but the Londoners are oozing confidence after their midweek Coca-Cola Cup win at Nottingham Forest.

It is nevertheless Wolves who make the better start, Bull firing narrowly off-target as Taylor's team tries to get it right for once in front of the TV cameras.

Millwall eventually gain the upper hand though, forcing Mike Stowell into a couple of fine saves before the game's two major incidents condemn Wolves to defeat.

Another sorry afternoon is summed up in four second half minutes. David Kelly becomes the first Wolves player to be sent off since Taylor's arrival, the Eire international getting his marching orders for a reckless studs-up lunge at right back Mark Beard; then Mark Kennedy sends in a 67th minute cross for Aussie Dave Mitchell – who scored the winner in the corresponding game last season – to head the only goal of the game.

Wolves consequent defeat is their fourth in five League games. They are now down to third place – and in need of inspiration from their impending new signings.

The Wolves Review 1995

MATCH 28 • ENDSLEIGH LEAGUE DIVISION 1

Saturday 10th December 1994 • Molineux • 3.00pm

WOLVES 1 NOTTS COUNTY 0

Half-time 0-0 • Attendance 25,786

Referee Jim PARKER (Preston)

Linesmen A.C. HOWELLS and A.P. MONKS

Gold Shirts with Black Trim, Black Shorts	Goals	Black and White Striped Shirts, White Shorts	Goals
1 Mike STOWELL		1 Steve CHERRY	
2 James SMITH		2 Gary MILLS	
3 Mark VENUS		3 Andy LEGG	
4 Darren FERGUSON		4 Phil TURNER †	
5 John DE WOLF		5 Dean YATES	
6 Neil EMBLEN		6 Michael JOHNSON	
7 Mark RANKINE ‡		7 Paul DEVLIN	
8 Don GOODMAN		8 Peter BUTLER	
9 Steve BULL	46	9 Gary LUND ‡	
10 Tom BENNETT †		10 Chris MARSDEN	
11 Steve FROGGATT		11 Tony AGANA	
Substitutes		Substitutes	
12 Paul BLADES †46		12 Nigel JEMSON †75	
14 David KELLY ‡69		14 Shaun MURPHY ‡75	
gk Paul JONES		gk Paul REECE	

BEFORE	P	W	D	L	F	A	pts	AFTER	P	W	D	L	F	A	pts
3 Wolves	20	10	4	6	36	23	34	2 Wolves	21	11	4	6	37	23	37
24 Notts Co.	19	3	6	10	20	30	15	24 Notts Co.	20	3	6	11	20	31	15

FACTFILE

Double debut day... birthday boy de Wolf the new skipper – and an instant hit with the fans... Dutch press come to town in force... all eyes on the new boys – Goodman goes close, but Bully bags the points... first clean sheet for 18 matches... second spot reclaimed.

NEW BOYS INSPIRE VICTORY

De Wolf an instant hero

Molineux is awash with fresh hope and anticipation as Notts County arrive in town for one of the most momentous days in Wolves' recent history.

John de Wolf, capped 11 times by Holland and 32 today, is in line for his debut – as captain in place of the dropped Geoff Thomas. Don Goodman is named as well for the visit of the First Division's bottom club, with Steve Bull as his partner in an exciting new-look attack.

De Wolf, recruited for £600,000, has signed a two-and-a-half year deal. Goodman, 28, has put pen to paper on a three-and-a-half year contract.

And the signs are that Taylor's mid-season recruitment drive is not over. He has two more central defenders on trial in the reserves – former Welsh international Brian Law and a Swede of Croatian parents, Jozo Matovac.

A host of Dutch journalists and cameramen are watching as de Wolf makes a powerful start, brushing aside County's forwards and quickly revealing a huge throw-in that takes even his team-mates by surprise.

But the early pressure fails to bring a breakthrough and Wolves' hearts are in their mouths as Neil Emblen – alongside de Wolf at centre-half with Paul Blades omitted and Mark Venus switched to left-back – escapes unpunished from a borderline penalty area challenge.

After a goalless first half, Wolves need only a minute of the second period to go ahead with Bull's first goal since the end of October.

The record-breaking striker is still appealing for hands against County defender Michael Johnson when Jamie Smith swings the ball back into the goalmouth, Bull sweeping a first-time shot into the far corner of the net.

Goodman also goes close in a promising debut, but the game belongs to de Wolf. The Dutchman is named Man of the Match despite some late scares, Dean Yates heading off target from the best of several County chances.

An exhausted de Wolf speaks of his relief at a winning end to a big personal week, but says: "The English game is very fast. In Holland there were periods when I could ease up, but over here it's go, go, go."

Taylor praises his new boys but reckons: "I'm plugging one gap and another is appearing." His midfield has again been outplayed, this time by a County side containing former Wolves favourite Chris Marsden. The manager adds: "We are having difficulty sustaining our attacks."

It has not been a convincing performance, but Wolves have scrambled back above Tranmere into second place and have an unusual feeling of defensive satisfaction. They have kept a clean sheet for the first time in 18 games stretching back to the win at Burnley in September.

Above all, de Wolf has become an instant hero and the sound of the crowd chanting his name must have been music to Taylor's ears – especially as Peter Shirtliff has suffered a serious reaction to his heel injury and needs an operation that will keep him out for another two months.

John de Wolf – impressive debut

The Wolves Review 1995

MATCH 29 • ENDSLEIGH LEAGUE DIVISION 1

Sunday 18th December 1994 • Elm Park • 2.55pm

READING 4 WOLVES 2

Half-time 2-1 • *Attendance* 10,136

Referee Paul ALCOCK (Redhill)

Linesmen C.N. BREAKSPEAR and R. WARD

Blue and White Hooped Shirts, White Shorts	Goals	Gold Shirts with Black Trim, Black Shorts	Goals
1 Shaka HISLOP		1 Mike STOWELL	
2 Andy BERNAL ❑		2 James SMITH	
3 Dylan KERR		3 Mark VENUS ❑	
4 Scott TAYLOR ❑		4 Neil EMBLEN	
5 Keith McPHERSON		5 John DE WOLF ❑	
6 Phil PARKINSON ❑		6 Paul BLADES	
7 Michael GILKES	62, 88	7 Mark RANKINE	
8 Mick GOODING		8 Don GOODMAN	
9 Jimmy QUINN	38, 58(og)	9 Steve BULL	9
10 Stuart LOVELL ❑ †		10 Darren FERGUSON	
11 Simon OSBORN	23	11 Steve FROGGATT †	
Substitutes		*Substitutes*	
12 Tommy JONES		12 Paul BIRCH †5 ❑ ‡	
14 Uwe HARTENBERGER †84		14 Lee MILLS ‡45	
gk Simon SHEPPARD		gk Paul JONES	

BEFORE	P	W	D	L	F	A	pts	AFTER	P	W	D	L	F	A	pts
2 Wolves	21	11	4	6	37	23	37	2 Wolves	22	11	4	7	39	27	37
9 Reading	21	9	6	6	24	20	33	5 Reading	22	10	6	6	28	22	36

FACTFILE

Wolves "no" to David Kelly bid... it's Darren Simkin out, Gordon Cowans in and goodbye to Matovac... Taylor in outburst over Bull story "fabrication"... Froggatt stretchered off in latest injury gloom – but there's no break... leaky defence gifts the points in TV spectacular.

GOOD GAME – BAD RESULT

Steve Froggatt stretchered off

Wolves write another catalogue of headlines before setting off in search of their first double of the season.

Having rejected a £450,000 offer from Stoke City for striker David Kelly, manager Graham Taylor has angrily hit out at reports linking Steve Bull with a move to Leeds United.

He describes the stories, which suggest that Chris Fairclough is on his way to Molineux in part-exchange, as "pure and absolute fabrication."

But Taylor has been his usual busy self in the transfer market, selling reserve defender Darren Simkin to Shrewsbury for £35,000 and investing £20,000 to bring Derby's former Villa and England midfielder Gordon Cowans back to the West Midlands. The manager has, however, ended his interest in Swedish triallist Jozo Matovac.

Cowans – to whom Taylor gave a tenth and final England cap in 1990 – is 36, but the manager says: "He will bring a lot of know-how and, in the absence of Geoff Thomas, we don't have an experienced central midfielder."

Cowans is signed too late to play in the televised match at Elm Park, where Wolves' only change in their starting line-up sees Paul Blades returning in place of Tom Bennett.

Steve Bull plays despite the near certainty that he will soon need heel surgery that could keep him out for six weeks. And Wolves suffer another crushing injury blow just a couple of minutes into the match.

Steve Froggatt is caught by a late challenge from behind by Scott Taylor and, following a seven minute delay while treatment is administered on the pitch, the winger is stretchered off.

His replacement Paul Birch is soon injured himself and lasts only until the interval. By then Wolves are trailing, though not before Bull has headed home Darren Ferguson's right-wing corner to give them a ninth minute lead.

Unfortunately, with John de Wolf being given a troublesome insight into the demands of English football, Wolves are pegged back by Simon Osborn's flashing 23rd minute header then sent into arrears by a far-post header from Northern Ireland inernational, Jimmy Quinn seven minutes before the break.

Reading are super-charged despite the controversial loss of manager Mark McGhee to Leicester City in midweek.

But striker Quinn – in caretaker control along with former Wolves midfielder Mick Gooding – has the misfortune to glance Ferguson's free-kick into his own net for the equaliser just before the hour.

Chances continue to come thick and fast in a breathtaking contest described by Central TV's Gary Newbon as "our best game of the season."

But despite the introduction of substitute Lee Mills as a third striker, the afternoon turns sour for Wolves as Reading winger Michael Gilkes pops up with match-winning goals in the 62nd and 88th minutes.

It is the first time Wolves have conceded four goals in a game this season and manager Taylor, quietly seething at the tackle which put Froggatt out of the game but which failed to earn its perpetrator a booking, refuses to attend his customary post-match press conference.

Reading had scored only 10 goals in 10 home league games before today and Wolves, although still second in the table, are suddenly only two points clear of sixth place with their injury situation getting increasingly worse.

The limited good news on the injury front is that Froggatt has not broken his leg. But he has suffered damaged ligaments and severe bruising – and he is set to miss quite a number of matches.

MATCH 30 • ENDSLEIGH LEAGUE DIVISION 1

Monday 26th December 1994 • Boundary Park • 3.15pm

OLDHAM ATHLETIC 4 WOLVES 1

Half-time 1-0 • *Attendance* 11,962

Referee John WATSON (Whitley Bay)

Linesmen B. BELLO and A.B. OLDHAM

Blue Shirts, White Shorts	Goals	Gold Shirts with Black Trim, Black Shorts	Goals
1 Paul GERRARD		1 Paul JONES	
2 Chris MAKIN		2 James SMITH	
3 Neil POINTON		3 Mark VENUS	
4 Nick HENRY ❏		4 Neil EMBLEN	
5 Richard GRAHAM ❏		5 John DE WOLF	
6 Steve REDMOND		6 Brian LAW ❏	
7 Gunne HALLE		7 Mark RANKINE	
8 Andy RITCHIE †	3,58,68	8 Gordon COWANS	
9 Sean McCARTHY	81	9 Lee MILLS	
10 Lee RICHARDSON		10 Darren FERGUSON ❏ †	
11 Mark BRENNAN ❏		11 Robbie DENNISON	59
Substitutes		*Substitutes*	
12 Darren BECKFORD †85		12 Tom BENNETT	
14 Rick HOLDEN		14 Neil MASTERS †77	
gk John HALLWORTH		gk Mike STOWELL	

BEFORE	P	W	D	L	F	A	pts	AFTER	P	W	D	L	F	A	pts
2 Wolves	22	11	4	7	39	27	37	4 Wolves	23	11	4	8	40	31	37
15 Oldham	22	8	5	9	28	29	29	11 Oldham	23	9	5	9	32	30	32

FACTFILE *Brian Law's round-the-world trek ends at Molineux... Teenage winger signs up as well... it's all change for the Boxing Day trip to Boundary Park... Paul Jones, Lee Mills, Robbie Dennison come in from the cold... debuts for Law and Gordon Cowans fail to stop the rot.*

64   The Wolves Review 1995

WOEFUL WOLVES HAMMERED AGAIN

Changes can't stop the rot

In a month packed with new signings, Graham Taylor's spending spree has continued during the week between Wolves' nightmare on Elm Park and the Boxing Day trip to Boundary Park.

Welshman Brian Law, impressive in defence during his month's trial in the reserves, has been secured on a permanent basis after Taylor negotiated a £100,000 fee with QPR. The Londoners had held the player's registration from before he quit the game with ligament damage in his feet. Wolves have also had to pay back around £34,000 in insurance money which Law received at the time of his enforced retirement.

On the same day as Law's signing, Taylor reveals he has agreed a £50,000 fee with Millwall for 19-year-old winger Jermaine Wright, a player the manager describes as "one for the future." Wright will not be considered immediately for first-team duty but Law, who realised his injuries had cured naturally while he backpacked round the world, receives the perfect festive gift – confirmation that he'll go straight into the first team for a Boxing Day debut.

Sadly, it turns out to be a far from pleasant experience in a desperately poor team performance that prompts bitterly disappointed fans to head for the exits long before the final whistle.

Wolves play like a bunch of strangers, which is perhaps no great surprise considering the wholesale changes made from the match at Reading.

In addition to the debuts given to Law and Gordon Cowans, three players – goalkeeper Paul Jones, striker Lee Mills and winger Robbie Dennison – are drafted in for their first League appearances of the season on a day when Wolves are without an entire forward line. David Kelly is still suspended while Steve Bull, Don Goodman and Steve Froggatt are all injured.

From the start of the match Wolves are particularly poor in defence, typified after just three minutes when John de Wolf's weak headed clearance sets up Andy Ritchie for the opening goal.

Though the interval arrives without further damage – and even with the odd hint of Wolves getting into the game against mediocre opponents – everything goes wrong in the second half.

The unmarked Ritchie heads his second goal from Mark Brennan's cross in the 58th minute. Sixty seconds later Wolves get a temporary reprieve when the persevering Dennison capitalises on a mistake by Chris Makin to pull a goal back.

But the beginning of the end arrives in the 68th minute, when Ritchie sidefoots home a Sean McCarthy cross to complete his second hat-trick in successive home matches.

And 12 minutes later Wolves are wiped out as McCarthy gets his name on the scoresheet after Nick Henry has been allowed to run unchallenged into the penalty area.

Neil Masters makes a welcome first senior appearance since March as substitute, but the full back can make no great impression on a dreadful Wolves display.

A concerned Graham Taylor, after seeing his side concede four goals for the second match in succession, observes: "There was some very bad play that led to the goals against us. But we must make sure we don't go too soft. I've got to get it right and make sure the players do too. If we keep our nerve, I'm sure we will do that."

Gordon Cowans – Wolves debut

The Wolves Review 1995

MATCH 31 • ENDSLEIGH LEAGUE DIVISION 1

Wednesday 28th December 1994 • Molineux • 7.45pm

WOLVES 2 CHARLTON ATHLETIC 0

Half-time 2-0 • Attendance 27,500

Referee P. HARRISON (Royston)

Linesmen R.M. DAVIS and J.R. HUCBARD

Gold Shirts with Black Trim, Black Shorts		Goals	Red Shirts with White Trim, White Shorts		Goals
1	Paul JONES		1	Mike SALMON	
2	Paul BLADES		2	Steve BROWN †	
3	Mark VENUS		3	Paul MORTIMER	
4	Neil EMBLEN		4	Keith JONES ❏	
5	John DE WOLF ❏		5	Phil CHAPPLE	42 og
6	Brian LAW		6	Alan McLEARY	
7	Don GOODMAN ❏ †		7	Mark ROBSON ‡	
8	Lee MILLS		8	Stuart BALMER ❏	
9	Steve BULL ‡	38	9	Carl LEABURN ❏	
10	Gordon COWANS		10	David WHYTE	
11	Robbie DENNISON		11	Colin WALSH	
	Substitutes			*Substitutes*	
12	Tom BENNETT ‡79		12	Garry NELSON ‡60	
14	Neil MASTERS †67		14	Micky BENNETT †60 ❏	
gk	Mike STOWELL		gk	Mike AMMANN	

BEFORE	P	W	D	L	F	A	pts	AFTER	P	W	D	L	F	A	pts
5 Wolves	23	11	4	8	40	31	37	2 Wolves	24	12	4	8	42	31	40
16 Charlton	22	7	8	7	35	33	29	16 Charlton	23	7	8	8	35	35	29

FACTFILE

Injured strikers back in action... a year of bumper Molineux gates... John Richards in the limelight again... milestone goal for Steve Bull... Paul Jones' penalty heroics... three good points and a welcome clean sheet... another injury blow for Bull – heel may need surgery.

TIMELY RETURN TO FORM FOR WOLVES

Penalty save sets up win

Despite Wolves' poor run there is no let-up in the level of support as Charlton arrive at Molineux for the second half of the Christmas programme.

The stadium is a sell-out in all but the visitors' area and Wolves, whose lowest First Division crowd of the season (22,768 v Derby in November) is still more than the highest of any of their rivals, have now had 24 consecutive league gates of more than 20,000 going back to December 28th last year.

With the fans still in festive mood, there is an extra buzz of anticipation as Steve Bull and Don Goodman both return after missing the Oldham game through injury.

Darren Ferguson is dropped as Graham Taylor reverts to a more orthodox system after the deployment of Lee Mills as a lone striker at Boundary Park; and Paul Blades is preferred to young Jamie Smith at right-back.

After conceding four goals in each of their last two matches, Wolves are immediately in danger of going one down following some rash work in defence by Mark Venus. With the ball running away from goal the full-back manhandles Charlton winger Mark Robson to gift the Londoners a penalty after just two minutes.

To the relief of Wolves' stunned fans, however, Paul Jones takes off to his right and blocks midfielder Steve Brown's spot-kick with his legs.

The keeper's first penalty save in league football spurs his side and Wolves' quickly-gained control is undermined only by two bad misses from Bull and two squandered half-chances by Mills.

But the breakthrough comes in the 38th minute, when Mills glances on Gordon Cowans' right wing corner for Bull to stoop low and head home from close range.

The goal means that Bull has now matched – in league games alone – the full league and cup tally of 194 with which John Richards had remained the club's all-time record scorer for a decade before Bull's overall aggregate gave him the record in 1992.

Appropriately, the popular Richards is at the game having just been elected to the Wolves board – and he is given a rousing half-time reception when he goes on to the pitch to be introduced to the crowd.

By then Wolves have increased their lead, Venus superbly sending Mills away on the right for a low centre which is rammed against his own post by Phil Chapple – who is unable to get out of the way as the ball cannons back against his legs and into the net.

The second half becomes a spirited search by the lively Goodman for his first Wolves goal. Having gone close with a blazing left-foot drive just before the interval, he sees four more efforts either saved by keeper Mike Salmon or whistle off target.

Wolves' performance is their best for many weeks and, against opponents who'd won their previous two games, there is the bonus of a second clean sheet in successive Molineux outings.

Charlton rarely threaten and the game is won and lost by the time Bull and Goodman go off in turn deep into the second half, to be replaced by substitutes Neil Masters and Tom Bennett respectively.

The down-side of the victory is the state of Bull's heel, which Graham Taylor later reveals is almost certain to require surgery within a week.

Steve Bull – back with a bang

The Wolves Review 1995

MATCH 32 • ENDSLEIGH LEAGUE DIVISION 1

Saturday 31st December 1994 • Oakwell • 3.00pm

BARNSLEY 1 WOLVES 3

Half-time 1-2 • Attendance 9,207

Referee Scott MATHIESON (Stockport)
Linesmen D.J. ADCOCK and R. INGHAM

Red Shirts, White Shorts		Goals
1	Lee BUTLER	
2	Nicky EADEN	
3	Gary FLEMING	
4	Martin BULLOCK	
5	Charlie BISHOP	
6	Steve DAVIS	
7	Brendan O'CONNELL ❑	
8	Neil REDFEARN	21 pen
9	Andy PAYTON	
10	Andy LIDDELL	
11	Darren SHERIDAN †	
Substitutes		
12	Andy RAMMELL †77	
14	Glynn SNODIN	
gk	David WATSON	

Gold Shirts with Black Trim, Black Shorts		Goals
1	Paul JONES ❑	
2	Paul BLADES	
3	Mark VENUS ❑	
4	Neil EMBLEN	75
5	John DE WOLF	
6	Brian LAW	
7	Don GOODMAN	
8	Tom BENNETT ❑	
9	Lee MILLS †	4
10	Gordon COWANS ❑	
11	Robbie DENNISON	1
Substitutes		
12	David KELLY †65	
14	Mark RANKINE	
gk	Mike STOWELL	

BEFORE	P	W	D	L	F	A	pts
2 Wolves	24	12	4	8	42	31	40
6 Barnsley	24	11	5	8	28	27	38

AFTER	P	W	D	L	F	A	pts
2 Wolves	25	13	4	8	45	32	43
7 Barnsley	25	11	5	9	29	30	38

FACTFILE True grit warning from manager Taylor... massive Wolves support at Oakwell... whirlwind start sets up victory... Mills scores on 'home' soil... under-fire defence finally gets it right... in-form Dennison told he's too good to be sold... Emblen goal seals a convincing win.

The Wolves Review 1995

WANDERERS END YEAR IN FINE STYLE

Mills – a boon back home

With their spirits raised by the impressive triumph over Charlton, Wolves are urged by their manager to produce more of the same as they go into a difficult New Year weekend.

Wednesday's victory at last achieved the standards required after a nightmare run of six defeats in eight league games and Graham Taylor, on the eve of the trip to Oakwell, says: "We were too strong for Charlton – now I want flat-out commitment from everyone in a gold shirt.

"There have been a few home truths recently and I have changed things about a lot. But the messing around has stopped and we must now produce the consistency we have failed to show so far."

The response, at the ground where Wolves virtually laid down their promotion arms last April, could not have been better. Barnsley have won their last six home games but find themselves two down in four minutes as Taylor's hyped-up side make a whirlwind start.

There are only 20 seconds on the clock when Robbie Dennison, after starting a lovely move involving Lee Mills and Don Goodman, scores with a toe-poked shot into the corner.

Mills powers home the second with his left foot after Goodman and Neil Emblen are shut out just outside the area.

Wolves' usual big following are in full cry as they occupy the old ground's main stand, but Barnsley quickly reveal the resolve and finesse that have made them surprise promotion candidates.

Gordon Cowans scrambles a shot from Brendan O'Connell off the line, then Paul Jones has to make a tremendous diving save from Andy Payton. The match is blown wide open again when Jones brings down Andy Liddell and, after escaping with only a yellow card, is beaten by Neil Redfearn's resulting 21st minute penalty.

Seeking their first away win for two months, Wolves are unconvincing at the back in the first half and are fortunate to reach the interval with their lead intact.

But it is a different story after the break as a steady build-up of Barnsley pressure cuts little ice with a tight-knit rearguard.

Despite the wave of red shirts pouring forward there is only one real scare, Steve Davis heading against the bar after Jones' hesitancy has given him the chance.

Manager Taylor later admits: "If that had gone in, I think we might have been struggling to hang on even for a draw. It was the turning point of the game."

Mills, watched by several members of his family in the town where he used to work in local government, limps off midway through the second half to be replaced by David Kelly.

But Wolves make sure of maximum points when Emblen pops up to head home a Mark Venus centre 15 minutes from time.

Ultimately, it is a convincing and impressive win to sign off from 1994 on a high note. With Middlesbrough only drawing at Stoke, Wolves are five points off top spot and back in the form worthy of title challengers.

One player in particular who has impressed manager Taylor is the re-instated Dennison, still transfer listed but not – in the short term at least – about to leave Molineux.

"We can't afford to lose him while he is playing so well and while we have our other wingers out injured", the manager says. "I can't speak too highly of how he has come back into the side and played. He has been first-class."

Robbie Dennison – quick strike

The Wolves Review 1995

MATCH 33 • ENDSLEIGH LEAGUE DIVISION 1

Monday 2nd January 1995 • Molineux • 3.00pm

WOLVES 2 SHEFFIELD UNITED 2

Half-time 0-0 • Attendance 27,809

Referee Pip WRIGHT (Northwich)

Linesmen M. CARRINGTON and P.D. HARDING

Gold Shirts with Black Trim, Black Shorts		Goals	Red and White Striped Shirts, White Shorts		Goals
1	Paul JONES		1	Alan KELLY	
2	Paul BLADES		2	Kevin GAGE	
3	Mark VENUS ▫		3	Roger NILSEN	
4	Neil EMBLEN	90	4	Charlie HARTFIELD	
5	John DE WOLF ▫	89 pen	5	Brian GAYLE	
6	Brian LAW		6	Dane WHITEHOUSE	
7	Don GOODMAN		7	Paul ROGERS ▫	
8	David KELLY		8	Carl VEART	
9	Lee MILLS		9	Phil STARBUCK	
10	Gordon COWANS		10	Glyn HODGES	
11	Robbie DENNISON		11	Andy SCOTT †	
Substitutes			*Substitutes*		
12	Tom BENNETT		12	Nathan BLAKE †53	60, 68
14	Mark RANKINE		14	Jostein FLO	
gk	Mike STOWELL		gk	Billy MERCER	

BEFORE		P	W	D	L	F	A	pts	AFTER		P	W	D	L	F	A	pts
2	Wolves	25	13	4	8	45	32	43	2	Wolves	26	13	5	8	47	34	44
5	Sheff Utd	25	11	7	7	40	26	40	5	Sheff Utd	26	11	8	7	42	28	41

FACTFILE

Worst fears confirmed for Bully – but Kelly returns... highest First Division gate of the season... Blake double has Wolves on the rack... De Wolf's first revives flagging challenge... grandstand finish rescues amazing draw... Taylor: "How did we do that?" – Bassett: speechless!

DE WOLF AND EMBLEN STAR IN THE GREAT ESCAPE

Blades blunted by late show

Having ended the old year with an impressive victory against Barnsley at Oakwell, Wolves launch 1995 with another tough match against Yorkshire opponents.

It is a meeting of two in-form sides, reflected in the highest First Division gate of the season – a full-house 27,805.

But the Wolves masses have no Steve Bull to cheer, the striker having failed to recover from his heel injury and being booked into a Birmingham hospital for surgery tomorrow.

Astonishingly, he is the club's seventh player this season to require an operation. But at least the team's striking strength has been boosted by the availability of David Kelly after suspension.

After the Eire international's comeback as substitute on Saturday, he is in the starting line-up this afternoon with Tom Bennett sacrificed in the interests of a more attack-minded system.

For the opening half hour the game is in danger of dying on it's feet, two evenly-matched sides playing out an uncompromising, unattractive battle for supremacy.

It might have been different had Don Goodman's snap-shot curled a few inches the other side of Alan Kelly's post, or if Wolves had not narrowly survived one or two hair-raising defensive moments.

But the final stages of the half bring sustained Wolves pressure with Robbie Dennison once more highly impressive. One glorious run by the winger ends with Neil Emblen having a shot blocked, then Lee Mills sees a 25-yard drive scrambled round the post before Emblen sends a shot just wide.

Sadly the half-time whistle interrupts Wolves' momentum and, when the game restarts, they find themselves on the back foot.

They are lucky to escape when substitute Nathan Blake (on the bench despite his two goals against Portsmouth on Saturday) miscues as Kevin Gage's cross falls to him off Don Goodman.

But Blake gets it right on the hour, when Charlie Hartfield superbly volleys back his own half-cleared corner for the unmarked Welsh striker to head home from close range.

And the game looks up for Wolves when Gage's huge pass out of defence leaves a limping John De Wolf for dead in the 68th minute, sending Blake away for a lob he executes brilliantly at the expense of the advancing Paul Jones.

There seems no way back for the home side, who have shots from Emblen and Gordon Cowans blocked before Don Goodman sees a point-blank effort saved by Alan Kelly, following a pull-back by his namesake in the Wolves attack.

Sheffield even threaten a third goal as Carl Veart drives over the bar following sloppy defending.

But Wolves, not for the first time, stage a sensational recovery when all appears lost. Several thousand fans are on their way home when Gage's poor last minute back-pass allows Goodman to sprint into the area and win the penalty - off keeper Kelly - from which De Wolf sidefoots home his first English goal.

Even more remarkably, there's another shock in store for Dave Bassett's men when Dennison scoops over a cross from the left and Emblen rises highest to loop a header over Kelly for the equaliser.

"Managers are expected to explain comebacks like that, but how can you?" Graham Taylor asks. "I haven't a clue. These things just happen."

Bassett refers to the customary Christmas TV listings to describe Wolves' *Great Escape* and inquires: "Did they slip Steve McQueen on there?"

The Wolves Review 1995 71

MATCH 34 • FA CUP THIRD ROUND

Saturday 7th January 1995 • Field Mill • 3.00pm

MANSFIELD TOWN 2   WOLVES 3

Half-time 2-0 • Attendance 6,701
Referee Eddie WOLSTENHOLME (Blackburn)
Linesmen R.M. DAVIS and S.E. WILLIAMS

Blue and Yellow Striped Shirts, Blue Shorts	Goals	White Shirts, White Shorts	Goals
1 Darren WARD		1 Paul JONES	
2 Adrian BOOTHROYD		2 Paul BLADES	
3 Ian BARACLOUGH		3 Mark VENUS	
4 Paul HOLLAND		4 Neil EMBLEN	
5 Lee HOWARTH		5 John DE WOLF †	
6 Mark PETERS ❏		6 Brian LAW	
7 Simon IRELAND †	10	7 Don GOODMAN	
8 O'Neill DONALDSON	8	8 David KELLY	52
9 Steve WILKINSON ‡		9 Lee MILLS	71
10 Stewart HADLEY		10 Gordon COWANS	
11 Kevin LAMPKIN		11 Robbie DENNISON ❏	60
Substitutes		*Substitutes*	
12 Steve PARKIN †75		12 Tom BENNETT	
14 John PEARSON ‡75		14 Mark RANKINE †	
gk Jason TRINDER		gk Mike STOWELL	

FACTFILE: De Wolf fit for FA Cup debut – but criticised for playing on while injured... Wolves sized up for a giant-killing... two goal deficit again repaired... poor defending once more to blame... David Kelly, Robbie Dennison and Lee Mills the goal heroes of astonishing second-half fightback.

John De Wolf's first English cup-tie

COMEBACK CAPERS CONTINUE

Classic 'game of two halves'

The wind of change effected by Graham Taylor is clearly highlighted by the make-up of his side for the awkward FA Cup third-round visit to third division Mansfield.

As well as being his own first tie as Wolves' boss in the competition, it also provides five of his players with Cup debuts for the club.

Only three members of today's team – Paul Blades, Mark Venus and David Kelly – remain from the side beaten by Chelsea in last season's quarter-final.

But, with John de Wolf eagerly anticipating his first taste of English cup football, Wolves are unchanged from Monday's draw with Sheffield United.

"I had never heard of Mansfield until we were drawn against them," admits the big Dutchman before the game. "But all week I have heard about the FA Cup.

"In Holland a First Division side will beat a Second Division side 19 times out of 20, but in the FA Cup it seems anybody can beat anybody else." After just 10 astonishing minutes at Field Mill, de Wolf must be pondering on those words.

On a heavily sanded pitch, his own eighth minute mistake has left O'Neill Donaldson free to race clear and open the scoring. And three minutes later more poor defending has led to Simon Ireland making it 2-0 with a shot that deflected in off Robbie Dennison.

Against a side that has hit 23 goals in it's previous six games, Wolves find themselves on the rack in an opening half display that manager Taylor later describes as "one of the most disgraceful I have ever seen from a professional side."

Though Wolves eventually get to grips with their fired-up hosts, there is barely a shot or header to trouble home goalkeeper Darren Ward before the interval.

But a half-time roasting from Taylor – whose Aston Villa side hit back to win 3-2 at Crewe in similar circumstances six years ago to the day – does the trick.

His chastened players come out fighting and are back in contention when David Kelly drives home his 12th goal of the season – and his first for two months – from a 52nd minute free-kick by Gordon Cowans (a member of the aforementioned 1989 Villa side).

Eight minutes later Dennison curls in a spectacular 25-yarder to make it 2-2. Then, after a crucial goalline clearance by Blades at the other end, the fightback is completed when Lee Mills drills an unstoppable 71st minute shot just inside the near post.

For the second time in six days, Wolves have managed to salvage a result from an apparently hopeless position and are rewarded with an attractive fourth round tie at Sheffield Wednesday.

But not before Taylor redresses the balance. "As strongly as I would condemn our first-half performance, I would praise our second-half display" he says. "We have ended with a good result when it looked like we would get nothing. We were sadly lacking and badly short in the first half, but the players responded in a way that has rescued their reputations."

De Wolf, who was substituted midway through the second half, is criticised by Taylor for staying on as long as he did with a rib injury that was clearly restricting him. The manager says he wants to see common-sense as well as courage and leadership.

And before leaving for home Taylor has a word of sympathy for Mansfield boss Andy King, the ex-Wolves midfielder, who says with no fear of contradiction: "We gave them a hell of a fright."

MATCH 35 • ENDSLEIGH LEAGUE DIVISION 1

Saturday 14th January 1995 • Molineux • 3.00pm

WOLVES 2 STOKE CITY 0

Half-time 1-0 • Attendance 28,298

Referee Jeff WINTER (Stockton-On-Tees)

Linesmen A.J. GREEN and K.J. NIND

Gold Shirts with Black Trim, Black Shorts		Goals	Red and White Striped Shirts, White Shorts		Goals
1	Paul JONES		1	Ronnie SINCLAIR	
2	Paul BLADES		2	Ian CLARKSON	
3	Mark VENUS		3	Lee SANDFORD	
4	Neil EMBLEN		4	Ian CRANSON	
5	John DE WOLF		5	Vince OVERSON ▫	
6	Brian LAW		6	Toddy ORLYGSSON	
7	Paul BIRCH		7	John BUTLER	
8	David KELLY	16	8	John DREYER †	
9	Lee MILLS		9	Keith SCOTT ‡	
10	Gordon COWANS		10	Paul PESCHISOLIDO	
11	Robbie DENNISON	86	11	Nigel GLEGHORN	
	Substitutes			*Substitutes*	
12	Tom BENNETT		12	Wayne BIGGINS ‡79	
14	Mark RANKINE		14	John WILLIAMS †60	
gk	Mike STOWELL		gk	Mark PRUDHOE	

BEFORE	P	W	D	L	F	A	pts	AFTER	P	W	D	L	F	A	pts
2 Wolves	26	13	5	8	47	34	44	2 Wolves	27	14	5	8	49	34	47
12 Stoke City	25	9	8	8	28	29	35	14 Stoke City	26	9	8	9	28	31	35

FACTFILE *Taylor's call for Cup tie spirit... Don Goodman adds to injury woes... Manager reflects on 'unbelievable' injury list... biggest Endsleigh League crowd of the season... Kelly's 13th unlucky for Stoke... more Dennison delight, but he's still on the list... Middlesbrough's lead cut to one point.*

The Wolves Review 1995

GAP CLOSED ON THE LEADERS

Robbie's rocket stuns the Potters

After last week's FA Cup comeback success at Mansfield, Graham Taylor calls for the same spirit from his players as they step back into their challenge for promotion with a difficult home game against Stoke.

"People are already talking about the fourth round Cup game at Sheffield Wednesday," says the manager, "but to my mind we have got another 20 'cup' games in the League. It is our job to give it all we've got because Wembley for this club has to be the Premiership."

The manager also has a moan about the club's continuing injury problems, exacerbated yesterday when Don Goodman sustained a calf strain which has forced him out of today's match.

While refusing to offer injuries as an excuse for what Taylor admits has so far been an inconsistent season from his team, he is nevertheless able to reel off a list of 15 players who between them have missed an average of 12 games apiece – more than a third of the matches played to date.

One of the unlucky 15, Paul Birch, has recovered from his latest knock and slots into the right hand side of midfield in place of Goodman.

Birch seemed almost certain for a return in any case, enabling Goodman to switch to the centre of the attack with David Kelly a surprise candidate for the Taylor axe.

The Republic of Ireland striker makes the most of his reprieve, giving Wolves the lead when he volleys home Robbie Dennison's 16th minute corner. It is the leading scorer's 13th goal of the season and his third in three successive Molineux appearances against Stoke – who last month were rumoured to have made a £450,000 transfer bid for him.

A minute before Kelly's goal, Paul Jones had stopped a well struck 20 yard drive from Nigel Gleghorn – but that turns out to be the only save the goalkeeper has to make in a game where Wolves always have the upper hand.

It is not until after the interval, however, that they come close to scoring again.

Stoke keeper Ronnie Sinclair is kept busy by Kelly in particular – after stopping a goalbound header from the striker, Sinclair smothers a close range attempt then sees Kelly turn a shot just wide from Robbie Dennison's clever through-ball.

Paul Peschisolido fires Stoke's best effort of the second half wide from 20 yards before Dennison sends a rising drive narrowly over the Stoke bar.

But that proves to be just a sighter for the Wolves winger, who clinches victory four minutes from time with his fourth goal in six games.

The transfer listed Irishman treats the Endsleigh League's biggest crowd of the season to one of it's finest goals, cutting in from the right to curl a 20 yard shot into the top corner after Gordon Cowans has supplied a perfectly weighted pass.

Still a big crowd favourite, Dennison remains on Taylor's long-term 'not wanted' list despite his sparkling return to the first team limelight.

Though the manager concedes that he has been surprised by the 31-year-old's contribution, he seems certain to deem him surplus to requirements when Villa imports Steve Froggatt and Tony Daley are fit to resume their wing duties.

But Dennison's wing play and goals have been vital to a revival which has brought Wolves four wins in the last five games and closed the gap on divisional leaders Middlesbrough to just one point – though the Teesiders have two games in hand.

The Wolves Review 1995

MATCH 36 • FA CUP FOURTH ROUND

Monday 30th January 1995 • Hillsborough • 8.00pm

SHEFFIELD WEDNESDAY 0 WOLVES 0

Half-time 0-0 • Attendance 21,757

Referee Alan WILKIE (Chester-le-Street)

Linesmen P.J. JOSLIN and G.M. LEE

Blue and White Striped Shirts, Blue Shorts — Goals

13	Kevin PRESSMAN	
2	Peter ATHERTON	
17	Des WALKER	
12	Andy PEARCE	
3	Ian NOLAN	
8	Chris WADDLE	
16	Graham HYDE	
11	John SHERIDAN ‡	
14	Chris BART-WILLIAMS	
10	Mark BRIGHT	
19	Guy WHITTINGHAM †	

Substitutes

20	Gordon WATSON †67	
5	Dan PETRESCU ‡83	
gk	Chris WOODS	

Gold Shirts with Black Trim, Black Shorts — Goals

1	Paul JONES	
2	Paul BLADES ❑	
3	Andy THOMPSON	
4	Neil EMBLEN	
5	John DE WOLF ❑	
6	Brian LAW	
7	Paul BIRCH ‡	
8	David KELLY ❑	
9	Lee MILLS †	
10	Gordon COWANS	
11	Robbie DENNISON	

Substitutes

12	Mark VENUS ‡54	
14	Don GOODMAN †25	
gk	Mike STOWELL	

FACTFILE

Ring rusty Wolves head for TV showdown... in-form Wednesday the favourites... Thommo back after hernia op... Goodman on bench... bright start threatens the TV jinx... dubious decision, but Jones is the penalty save hero... and now its all to do again at Molineux.

Paul Jones – the penalty-save hero

The Wolves Review 1995

JONAH JUMPS TO IT

Penalty save earns replay

Wolves' preparations for tonight's big match have been far from ideal. Injuries have continued to be a major problem and, with last weekend's scheduled League fixture at Luton postponed due to rain, Graham Taylor's men have gone 16 days without match action before their stiff FA Cup test against the Premiership's form team.

Sheffield Wednesday have climbed from a relegation threatened position to European-place challengers with an excellent run since mid-December, making them favourites to win tonight's Hillsborough clash in front of the Sky TV cameras.

Wolves make just one team change from the Stoke match, Andy Thompson replacing Mark Venus at left back after being out for two months following his hernia operation. Don Goodman, who missed the win against Stoke due to a calf injury, is not yet 100 per cent fit but joins Venus on the substitutes' bench.

As well as beating in-form opponents Wolves have to overcome their TV jinx if they are to progress into Round Five, where a home tie awaits against Leicester City (the Premiership strugglers went through with a 1-0 win at Portsmouth on Saturday). Wolves live TV ratings so far this season read: Appearances 7, Defeats 4, Wins 1.

The statistics do not make good reading, but Wolves' early play makes good viewing as they take the game to Wednesday and create several dangerous situations.

Lee Mills has a second minute shot saved by Kevin Pressman, then both David Kelly and Mills send efforts over the bar with the visitors continuing to call the shots.

When Wednesday force their way into contention Guy Whittingham – on loan with Wolves last season and a recent signing from Aston Villa – heads over from a good position before having a second header blocked on the line by Gordon Cowans.

Mills, suffering from double vision after taking a knock on the head, is replaced by Goodman after 25 minutes. But Wolves regain control towards half time and Neil Emblen forces Pressman into a good save.

Emblen and Paul Birch both go close to opening the scoring just after the interval, Birch later becoming Wolves' second injury victim to be substituted.

The substitutes, Goodman and Venus, both miss chances to break the deadlock before disaster strikes three minutes from time. Chris Bart-Williams breaks into the Wolves' penalty area and though Emblen nicks the ball away from him, the Wednesday player goes down under the challenge and referee Alan Wilkie immediately awards a penalty.

With regular spot-kick taker John Sheridan having been substituted four minutes earlier, Bart-Williams picks himself up to take the most important shot of the night.

The midfield man strikes the ball towards the corner of the net – but Paul Jones flings himself to his right, shoots his left arm high into the air and punches the ball clear.

It is a stupendous save that stuns Hillsborough, but justice is done and the keeper has earned Wolves a Molineux replay.

"It was definitely not a penalty", Jones insists, "but from the position the referee was in he probably thought Neil had lunged into their player.

"I do my homework on penalty takers, but with John Sheridan and their back-up man Guy Whittingham both off the field it made my job a bit more difficult.

"Still, I have my own thoughts about which way the kicker will choose to put the ball – only I'm keeping those thoughts a secret!"

Wednesday manager Trevor Francis, having seen his side miss their third successive penalty, admits: "I'm very disappointed, but we didn't deserve to win the match."

The Wolves Review 1995

MATCH 37 • ENDSLEIGH LEAGUE DIVISION 1

Saturday 4th February 1995 • Burnden Park • 3.00pm

BOLTON WANDERERS 5 WOLVES 1

Half-time 2-1 • Attendance 16,964

Referee John KIRKBY (Sheffield)

Linesmen M. RYAN and M.A. WILLIAMS

	White Shirts with Black and Red Trim, Black Shorts	Goals		Gold Shirts with Black Trim, Gold Shorts	Goals
1	Keith BRANAGAN		1	Paul JONES	
2	Scott GREEN		2	Paul BLADES	
3	Jimmy PHILLIPS	60	3	Andy THOMPSON	
4	Jason McATEER		4	Neil EMBLEN ‡	
5	Simon COLEMAN	37	5	John DE WOLF	
6	Alan STUBBS		6	Brian LAW	
7	David LEE		7	Don GOODMAN	26
8	Richard SNEEKES	9	8	David KELLY	
9	Mixu PAATELAINEN		9	Lee MILLS †	
10	Owen COYLE	78	10	Gordon COWANS	
11	Alan THOMPSON	83	11	Robbie DENNISON	
	Substitutes			*Substitutes*	
12	Fabian de FREITAS		12	Tom BENNETT ‡75	
14	Jason LYDIATE		14	Geoff THOMAS †63	
gk	Aidan DAVISON		gk	Andy DE BONT	

BEFORE	P	W	D	L	F	A	pts	AFTER	P	W	D	L	F	A	pts
2 Wolves	27	14	5	8	49	34	47	4 Wolves	28	14	5	9	50	39	47
3 Bolton	28	13	8	7	44	30	47	1 Bolton	29	14	8	7	49	31	50

FACTFILE

Leadership beckons for the winners... happy Burnden memories... Don Goodman's first Wolves goal... Wolves unlucky to behind at the break, but its a second half disaster... Taylor unhappy with lack of direction... will Wolves still be Up For The Cup in midweek?

BURNDEN BLUES

Bolton batter leadership hopes

Victory at Burnden Park could take Wolves back to the top of the table for the first time since late November, when a 3-1 home win against today's hosts Bolton saw them snatch pole position from Middlesbrough.

The leadership again lies in Boro's hands at the start of today's fixtures, though Bryan Robson's team face a difficult home match against promotion chasing Reading. If the Royals and Wolves both win, it is the Molineux men who will be top dogs tonight.

But Bolton are on equal points with Wolves and thus have exactly the same incentive. So, for the fans in the away end, a repeat of the scoreline in the corresponding match last season would do nicely.

Wolves won 3-1 on what was a memorable March 29th – Graham Taylor's first game as the club's manager.

Today Taylor leads a team brimming with confidence after Monday's goalless Cup draw at Sheffield Wednesday extended their unbeaten run to six matches.

The manager has to make one team change, Paul Birch having been forced out with a hamstring injury he sustained at Hillsborough. Don Goodman, who started as substitute on Monday, takes over Birch's role wide on the right.

Geoff Thomas – out for the last two months – is given a place on the subs' bench after making his comeback in the reserves during midweek.

The match starts brightly with both sides looking for an early breakthrough, which arrives after just nine minutes. Sadly for the hordes of visiting fans it is Bolton who take the lead, Richard Snekes driving home a low shot from a well worked short corner.

Though Wolves produce a spirited rally Sneekes twice goes close to a second goal with long range shots, one narrowly missing the target and the other bringing a good save from Paul Jones.

But in the 26th minute the visitors draw level through Goodman's first Wolves goal. On what is his eighth appearance, the striker crashes the ball in from close range after a Mills header has been saved by goalkeeper Keith Branagan.

The Bolton keeper brilliantly keeps out a fine shot by Neil Emblen as Wolves look for a second goal, but eight minutes before half time the home side regains the lead. Jones can only parry an Owen Coyle effort and Simon Coleman heads in the loose ball.

A second half tactical move sees Goodman switching into the middle to partner Mills, with David Kelly taking over on the right flank.

A couple of promising moves result, but out of the blue Bolton stretch their lead when Jimmy Phillips drives home a spectacular 25 yard shot.

An hour has gone and suddenly Wolves are on the rack. Jones has to save from Alan Thompson and Alan Stubbs, but the goalkeeper can do nothing to prevent the killer blow – Coyle's 78th minute shot takes a deflection off Brian Law to wrong-foot Jones and slip into the net.

The misery is completed seven minutes from time, Thompson scoring from the edge of the penalty area to wrap up Wolves' heaviest defeat under Graham Taylor – some return to Burnden Park!

Though his team may not have been four goals worse than Bolton in terms of performance, manager Taylor moans: "We attempted to play football going nowhere, but they played with the recognition that there was a goal at the other end of the pitch. That was the difference."

Now what price FA Cup glory in next Wednesday's Molineux replay against Sheffield Wednesday?

The Wolves Review 1995

MATCH 38 • FA CUP ROUND 4 REPLAY

Wednesday 8th February 1995 • Molineux • 7.45pm

WOLVES 1 SHEFFIELD WEDNESDAY 1

AET; Wolves win 4-3 on penalties • Half-time 1-0 • Attendance 28,136

Referee Alan WILKIE (Chester-le-Street)
Linesmen P.D. HARDING and A.J. HILL

Gold Shirts with Black Trim, Black Shorts	Goals	Blue and White Striped Shirts, Blue Shorts	Goals
1 Paul JONES		13 Kevin PRESSMAN	
2 Paul BLADES †		2 Peter ATHERTON ❏	
3 Andy THOMPSON		17 Des WALKER	
4 Neil EMBLEN		12 Andy PEARCE	
5 John DE WOLF		3 Ian NOLAN	
6 Brian LAW		8 Chris WADDLE ❏	
7 Mark RANKINE ‡		16 Graham HYDE ‡	
8 David KELLY	13	14 Chris BART-WILLIAMS ❏	
9 Don GOODMAN		18 Klas INGESSON †	
10 Gordon COWANS		15 Andy SINTON	
11 Robbie DENNISON		10 Mark BRIGHT	56
Substitutes		*Substitutes*	
12 Tom BENNETT ‡117		11 John SHERIDAN †71	
14 Lee MILLS †90		19 Guy WHITTINGHAM ‡106	
gk Andy de BONT		gk Chris WOODS	

FACTFILE

Taylor stays calm after Bolton disaster... "cool heads" demanded by the manager... Bright cancels out Kelly opener... "cool heads" win dramatic penalty shoot-out – Jones, Cowans and Goodman the heroes in fantastic finale after disastrous start.

Paul Jones flies to stop Waddle's spot-kick

The Wolves Review 1995

SHOOT-OUT DRAMA

Sudden-death victory glee

Saturday's drubbing at Bolton has not affected Graham Taylor's resolve nor his team plans as he prepares for tonight's Cup replay.

But he warns his players that they must bounce back from their 5-1 League defeat with a good Cup performance and result – otherwise, he fears, there could be a slide back into the malaise that proved so costly a couple of months ago.

"The last thing we need is to return to the state of play we were in just before Christmas", says the manager.

"We are facing a very difficult Cup tie and the danger is that if we lose, heads will drop and the mood will go back to what it was.

"But our players are keen to put the Bolton result behind them and do themselves justice. I don't want any fanfares, just cool heads and a clear purpose."

Wolves go into the game with just one change from Saturday's disaster. Mark Rankine comes into the side on the right of midfield, with Don Goodman switching to the attack in place of Lee Mills.

Like the first contest at Hillsborough, the Sky TV cameras beam tonight's replay out live. And after just 13 minutes Wolves' armchair fans are celebrating along with the supporters at Molineux as David Kelly opens the scoring.

Robbie Dennison's left wing corner is inadvertently flicked on at the near post by defender Klas Ingesson and Kelly, dashing in, heads the ball home from only a yard off the line.

Goodman twice goes close to increasing the lead in a rip-roaring first half, but 11 minutes after the break Wednesday draw level through Mark Bright. A Graham Hyde shot is cleared off the line by Gordon Cowans, but Bright follows up to force the loose ball into the net.

As Wolves look to regain the lead Kelly misses two chances in quick succession. But Wednesday eventually take control and when the game goes into extra time, they seem odds-on to win the tie.

But they waste their goalscoring opportunities, the clearest of them right at the death when Bright scoops an easy chance over the bar from 10 yards.

And so to an incredible penalty shoot-out, with five players from each side to take part before – if necessary – 'sudden-death' comes into play.

The contest starts in despairing fashion for Wolves, spot-kick king Andy Thompson then Dennison both failing to find the net.

Bright and Guy Whittingham convert Wednesday's first two attempts and, when goalkeeper Kevin Pressman steps up to smash home their third spot-kick, Wednesday are surely home and dry with a 3-0 lead.

But after Gordon Cowans coolly slots the ball home and Andy Pearce hits the bar, Kelly scores to make it 3-2. That leaves the last Wednesday penalty to Chris Bart-Williams, whose late spot-kick in the first match was so dramatically saved by Paul Jones to set up the replay.

Bart-Williams shoots, Jones dives – and once again saves, leaving the Wednesday man distraught and the Wolves fans going wild. John de Wolf scores to level things up: now it's sudden-death.

Chris Waddle, whose last penalty was his fateful shoot-out miss for England in the 1990 World Cup semi-final against Germany, walks up to the ball, shoots – and it's another Jones save!

Waddle walks away disconsolately and the tension around Molineux is unbearable as Goodman – in his first-ever penalty shoot-out – gets the chance to win an impossible victory. Head down, he charges at the ball and whacks it – and yes, it's in the roof of the net!

The striker closes his eyes in relief, Molineux erupts – and Wolves are through to the next round after one of the most heart-stopping penalty shoot-outs witnessed anywhere in the world.

The Wolves Review

MATCH 39 • ENDSLEIGH LEAGUE DIVISION 1

Saturday 11th February 1995 • Molineux • 3.00pm

WOLVES 2 BRISTOL CITY 0

Half-time 1-0 • Attendance 25,451

Referee Mike RILEY (Leeds)

Linesmen S.J.Griffiths and P.J.Robinson

Gold Shirts with Black Trim, Black Shorts		Goals	Red Shirts with White Trim, White Shorts		Goals
1	Paul JONES		1	Keith WELCH	
2	Paul BLADES		2	Vergard HANSEN	
3	Andy THOMPSON		3	Stuart MUNRO	
4	Neil EMBLEN †		4	Mark SHAIL	
5	John DE WOLF		5	Matt BRYANT	
6	Brian LAW		6	Brian TINNION	
7	Mark RANKINE ‡		7	Martin KUHL	
8	David KELLY	61	8	Junior BENT	
9	Don GOODMAN		9	Robert FLECK	
10	Gordon COWANS		10	Wayne ALLISON †	
11	Robbie DENNISON	25	11	Gary OWERS	
	Substitutes			*Substitutes*	
12	Tom BENNETT †24 ▫		12	Ian BAIRD †75	
14	Lee MILLS ‡80		14	Richard DRYDEN	
gk	Mike STOWELL		gk	Phil KITE	

BEFORE		P	W	D	L	F	A	pts	AFTER		P	W	D	L	F	A	pts
4	Wolves	28	14	5	9	50	39	47	2	Wolves	29	15	5	9	52	39	50
22	Bristol City	29	8	6	15	25	39	30	22	Bristol City	30	8	6	16	25	41	30

FACTFILE

Pre-match video-tasty... Cup line-up takes on relegation battlers... Stowell back on bench... Molineux mudbath... Robbie's five-in-10... penalty let-off... Kelly's clincher, but Jonah's the hero... Bully, Shirtliff on the way back... triallist Maas allowed to leave.

The Wolves Review

UNCONVINCING VICTORY

Wolves ride their luck

The cheers are ringing round Molineux before a ball is kicked in this afternoon's match against relegation threatened Bristol City.

The reason – film of Wednesday's FA Cup penalty shoot-out drama is being screened on the video wall which sits between the Stan Cullis and Billy Wright stands. And fans are happy to re-live the thrilling moments that led to a place in the fifth round.

Today's action is unlikely to be as dramatic as the Cup replay against Sheffield Wednesday, but with promotion-boosting points at stake the outcome of the game is just as vital.

Graham Taylor sticks to Wolves' midweek line-up plus the two outfield substitutes, though goalkeeper Mike Stowell returns to the bench in place of Andy de Bont.

Stowell seems some way off regaining his first team jersey, however, with Paul Jones' continuing good form keeping him in the Number One spot and also increasing the likelihood that he will sign a new contract with the club.

On a mud-bath of a pitch which has had two inspections before being passed fit for play, Jones is kept busy in the early stages of the match as City make a bright start.

But the visitors, anxious to avenge their 5-1 thrashing by Wolves at Ashton Gate in November, spoil their approach play. Wayne Allison heads a fine chance over the bar from close range, then on-loan Robert Fleck shoots over the top after Brian Law has failed to cut out a through ball.

Wolves are dealt a blow when Neil Emblen is injured and has to be substituted in the 24th minute. But 60 seconds later it's celebration time as John de Wolf hurls in a long throw, Don Goodman heads the ball on – and Robbie Dennison stabs the ball home at the far post.

After Dennison's fifth goal in 10 starts Wolves get a lucky let-off in the 33rd minute – referee Mike Riley turns down City appeals for a penalty after Brian Law has blatantly pulled back Allison. Even Graham Taylor has to admit after the match that a spot-kick should have been awarded.

The incident proves a crucial turning point. Kelly has a header cleared off the line just before half-time, but his 15th goal of the season arrives in the 61st minute.

Seconds after Allison has wasted another good chance to grab a City goal, the ball is swept along the Wolves left and when Dennison crosses Kelly flicks a header over goalkeeper Keith Welch and into the net.

If the scoreline is somewhat flattering to Wolves at this stage, it becomes even more so as Junior Bent twice sees shots brilliantly saved by Jones while Allison – yet again – fails to score from an excellent position.

Wolves ride their luck to keep a clean sheet, collect maximum points and to celebrate a week of good results plus encouraging news off the pitch – Steve Bull has returned to training following his achilles operation and Peter Shirtliff is ready for match action after recovering from a similar op.

On the transfer front, manager Taylor has decided not to pursue his interest in de Wolf's former Feyenoord team-mate Robbie Maas, who has finished his Molineux trial spell.

But Taylor says he will keep tabs on Scunthorpe midfielder Christian Sansom, who like Maas has this week completed his trial and returned to his contracted club.

Neil Emblen – forced off through injury after only 24 minutes

The Wolves Review

83

MATCH 40 • FA CUP FIFTH ROUND

Saturday 18th February 1995 • Molineux • 3.00pm

WOLVES 1 LEICESTER CITY 0

Half-time 1-0 • Attendance 28,544

Referee Robbie HART (Darlington)

Linesmen B.M. RICE and D. PUGH

Gold Shirts with Black Trim, Black Shorts		Goals	Blue Shirts with White and Gold trim, Blue Shorts		Goals
1	Paul JONES		33	Kevin POOLE †	
2	Mark VENUS		34	Mike GALLOWAY ❏	
3	Andy THOMPSON		2	Simon GRAYSON ‡	
4	Tom BENNETT		19	Colin HILL ❏	
5	John DE WOLF		4	Jimmy WILLIS	
6	Brian LAW		3	Mike WHITLOW	
7	Mark RANKINE ❏		17	Steve THOMPSON	
8	David KELLY	34	18	Garry PARKER	
9	Don GOODMAN		6	Mark ROBINS	
10	Gordon COWANS		9	Iwan ROBERTS	
11	Robbie DENNISON		10	Mark DRAPER	
	Substitutes			*Substitutes*	
12	Geoff THOMAS		21	Lee PHILPOTT ‡67 ❏	
14	Lee MILLS		25	David LOWE	
gk	Mike STOWELL		1	Gavin WARD (Gk) †45	

FACTFILE

Another Premiership club bars Wolves Cup progress... Kelly back from Dublin nightmare... £600,000 Parker in Leicester debut... biggest crowd for 14 years... match receipts record broken for third time this season - £236,972 the new high... Kelly's great winner puts Wolves in quarter final

Andy Thompson – forced to switch flanks in a defensive re-shuffle

84   The Wolves Review

WEMBLEY JOURNEY CONTINUES

Kelly's great match-winner

Wolves go into another big FA Cup battle against Premiership opponents at the end of a week packed with media hype surrounding the game. There have also been mixed fortunes for the players hoping to take their side into the sixth round for the second successive year.

Two members of the 18-man squad named for today's match, David Kelly and Jamie Smith, have been on international duty this week. Full back Smith acquitted himself well in the Football League Under 21's 3-2 victory in Italy against the Serie B Under 21's.

Striker Kelly had a night of mixed emotions in Dublin, scoring the only goal of Eire's game against England before an orchestrated riot by so-called England supporters forced the abandonment of the match midway through the first half.

"It was scary and something I never want to see again", said a shell-shocked Kelly before returning to England to start preparations for today's match.

He will once more play alongside Don Goodman, Steve Bull's return from his achilles operation having been held up through 'flu. Further bad news on the player front is that Steve Froggatt – injured at Reading in December – may have to undergo surgery and miss the rest of the season.

Midfielder Neil Emblen, injured in last week's 2-0 win against Bristol City, misses today's game along with right back Paul Blades who is beginning a two-match suspension.

Tom Bennett replaces Emblen while Mark Venus comes in for Blades, though Venus slots in at left back with Andy Thompson switching to the right.

Leicester have Garry Parker making his debut in midfield alongside £3million rated Mark Draper. Parker has just been signed for £600,000 from Aston Villa, whose former Leicester manager, Brian Little, is keen to capture Draper.

Together with Molineux's biggest crowd of the season (yielding record receipts for the third time in seven months), BBC TV's 'Match of the Day' cameras are in place as manager Graham Taylor sends his team out saying: "This kind of Cup tie will show whether we have the players who can cope with the attention and expectancy."

And the Cup-hungry Wolves respond to the manager's challenge, having the better of an untidy opening half-hour then taking the lead with a glorious 34th minute goal.

Kelly dummies Mike Galloway inside the centre circle – leaving the on-loan Celtic player flat on his backside – then spreads the ball wide for Don Goodman to go haring along the right touchline. Somehow Kelly keeps pace with his flying partner, for when Goodman delivers a cross into the penalty area the Eire man is there to fling himself forward and send a superb header flashing into the net.

Though both Mark Robins and Jimmy Willis spurn chances to equalise just after half time, Wolves go close to a second goal three times in quick succession.

Two good efforts from Goodman and a Mark Rankine shot are all well saved by substitute goalkeeper Gavin Ward, on for Kevin Poole who was injured in a collision with Kelly.

Venus has to clear off the line from Iwan Roberts and Robins shoots straight at Paul Jones as the visitors try frantically to stay in the match.

But – after almost seven nail-biting minutes of injury time – Wolves run out deserving winners. Wembley is still on the 1995 agenda!

MATCH 41 • ENDSLEIGH LEAGUE DIVISION 1

Tuesday 21st February 1995 • Molineux • 7.45pm

WOLVES 0 MIDDLESBROUGH 2

Half-time 0-0 • Attendance 27,611

Referee Kevin BREEN (Liverpool)

Linesmen A. BLACK and G.A. STONES

Gold Shirts with Black Trim, Black Shorts	Goals	Red Shirts with Black and White Trim, White Shorts with Trim	Goals
1 Paul JONES		1 Alan MILLER	
2 Mark VENUS †		2 Chris MORRIS	
3 Andy THOMPSON		3 Derek WHYTE ❑	
4 Geoff THOMAS		4 Steve VICKERS	55
5 John DE WOLF		5 Nigel PEARSON	
6 Brian LAW ■		6 Clayton BLACKMORE	
7 Mark RANKINE		7 Bryan ROBSON	
8 David KELLY		8 Jamie POLLOCK	
9 Don GOODMAN		9 Uwe FUCHS ❑	81
10 Gordon COWANS		10 Robbie MUSTOE ❑	
11 Robbie DENNISON ‡		11 Alan MOORE	
Substitutes		*Substitutes*	
12 Peter SHIRTLIFF ‡86		12 Jamie MORENO	
14 Lee MILLS †74		14 Viv ANDERSON	
gk Mike STOWELL		gk Ben ROBERTS	

BEFORE	P	W	D	L	F	A	pts	AFTER	P	W	D	L	F	A	pts
3 Middlesboro'	29	15	7	7	42	26	52	2 Middlesboro'	30	16	7	7	44	26	55
4 Wolves	29	15	5	9	52	39	50	6 Wolves	30	15	5	10	52	41	50

FACTFILE

Wembley ambitions on the back-burner... League the priority, insists Cup hero Kelly... Thomas back as Wolves look for revenge victory over title rivals... missed chances and Jones' double blunder so costly... Law sent off... out of the play-off places - what a dreadful night!

86   The Wolves Review

BLACK NIGHT

Jones' gaffes, Law off

It's one big match after another as Wolves put their FA Cup ambitions on the back-burner and return to the task of pursuing promotion to the Premiership.

The Wembley dream is still very much alive after Saturday's victory over Leicester has set up a quarter final tie at either Watford or Crystal Palace, who replay at Selhurst Park next week following Saturday's goalless draw at Vicarage Road.

But Wolves' fifth round hero David Kelly insists that League success must be the priority. "I'd rather beat Middlesbrough and win the League than go to Wembley and win the Cup", he says.

"If we get promotion there will be plenty of games next season like last Saturday's – teams like Manchester United, Newcastle and Blackburn will be coming to Molineux.

"So it's vital we beat Middlesbrough and put ourselves ahead of them in the table. We played poorly and were well beaten up at their place – now we need to put the record straight."

With promotion rivals Tranmere, Reading and Sheffield United also in action tonight, Wolves must beat Boro to be certain of remaining in the play-off places when the revised table is published in the morning.

One team change has been forced on manager Graham Taylor due to a suspension for Tom Bennett. The Scotsman's midfield place is taken by Geoff Thomas, whose last appearance was as substitute in the ill-fated visit to Bolton Wanderers four games ago.

Thomas figures in a powerful start by Wolves, who create several early half-chances without finding a finishing touch.

Crucially, however, two clear-cut opportunities are wasted in quick succession. Thomas volleys wide of an open goal from Don Goodman's 25th minute header down, then 60 seconds later Kelly strikes the ball against Alan Miller's legs after the goalkeeper has miskicked an intended clearance straight to the Wolves striker.

Middlesbrough take full advantage of their let-offs, gaining control in midfield and gradually getting completely on top.

Paul Jones saves well from Jamie Pollock straight after the interval. But a 55th minute error by the keeper gifts Boro the lead, Jones pushing a Steve Vickers header into the roof of the net when trying to flip the ball over the bar.

The mistake is compounded in the 81st minute, when Jones cannons a hacked clearance off Uwe Fuchs' legs to release the German striker for a simple second goal.

Two minutes later the picture looks even blacker for Wolves as Brian Law is sent off for a penalty area tackle-from-behind on Pollock. Jones, the FA Cup fourth round penalty saving hero, does it again to keep out Alan Moore's resultant spot-kick.

But the unhappy keeper cannot repair the damage already done and Wolves, just as at Ayresome Park in November, end up well beaten by Bryan Robson's team.

With Bolton, Reading and Sheffield United all managing to win their games, the men from Molineux are out of the play-off places for the first time since early September. A disastrous evening!

Geoff Thomas – back in the starting line-up

The Wolves Review

MATCH 42 • ENDSLEIGH LEAGUE DIVISION 1

Saturday 25th February 1995 • Vale Park • 3.00pm

PORT VALE 2 WOLVES 4

Half-time 1-3 • Attendance 13,676

Referee John LLOYD (Wrexham)

Linesmen S.T. BAINES and R.R. RAWSON

White Shirts with Black Trim, Black Shorts — Goals

1 Paul MUSSELWHITE
2 Bradley SANDEMAN
3 Allen TANKARD
4 Ray WALKER †
5 Neil ASPIN
6 Kevin SCOTT
7 Steve GUPPY
8 Robin van der LAAN
9 Martin FOYLE ‡
10 Tony NAYLOR   18
11 Kevin KENT   56

Substitutes

12 Joe ALLON ‡83
14 Lee GLOVER †83
gk Arjen van HEUSDEN

Gold Shirts with Black Trim, Gold Shorts — Goals

1 Paul JONES
2 Paul BLADES
3 Andy THOMPSON
4 Mark RANKINE
5 John de WOLF   2, 42, 68 pen
6 Peter SHIRTLIFF
7 Don GOODMAN
8 David KELLY ▫
9 Steve BULL † ▫   45
10 Gordon COWANS
11 Robbie DENNISON

Substitutes

12 Mark VENUS †77
14 James SMITH
gk Mike STOWELL

BEFORE	P	W	D	L	F	A	pts
6 Wolves	30	15	5	10	52	41	50
15 Port Vale	29	10	8	11	35	36	38

AFTER	P	W	D	L	F	A	pts
5 Wolves	31	16	5	10	56	43	53
18 Port Vale	30	10	8	12	37	40	38

FACTFILE

Surprise return for Bully... Thomas stands down... Shirtliff back too – as captain... Vale the form team... de Wolf's first ever hat-trick – but no more pens warns Thommo... Steve Bull back with a bang... Dennison the creator... transferred Lee Mills does Wolves a goalden favour

The Wolves Review

DESTROYER DE WOLF

Historic hat-trick

There is a pleasant surprise in store for Wolves' fans as they make the short journey up the M6 to Vale Park. Any spirits still laid low from Tuesday's defeat by Middlesbrough are lifted with the news that Steve Bull is about to make his comeback this afternoon.

Out of action since the end of December due to his achilles operation, Bully was not expected to figure in today's match after a scheduled midweek outing for the reserves was rained off.

But manager Graham Taylor, feeling the need for an all-round morale booster after Tuesday, has gambled by bringing back his top striker a little earlier than he would probably have liked.

The manager has also brought back Peter Shirtliff, who like Bull has been out of action following achilles surgery. The central defender, whose inclusion ends a run of 12 consecutive matches for Brian Law, has not started a match since the 3-3 draw with Millwall on October 22nd.

Midfielder Geoff Thomas is the man to make way for Bull, though positional switches involving Don Goodman and Mark Rankine accommodate the return of the Tipton Terrier. At the back Paul Blades, his two-match suspension completed, takes over from Mark Venus.

The re-jigged Wolves side has a difficult job in store against Division One's team of the moment – Vale head the form table with 13 points from their last five matches.

But it takes just 85 seconds of action for Wolves to show they are up to the task. Robbie Dennison's corner is missed by goalkeeper Paul Musselwhite and, when David Kelly's header is cleared off the line by Steve Guppy, John de Wolf rams a 12 yard shot into the net.

Vale deservedly draw level when Paul Jones fails to hold Ray Walker's 18th minute drive and Tony Naylor forces home the rebound.

Determined Wolves regain the lead three minutes before the interval, however. Musselwhite again fails to deal with a Dennison inswinger and de Wolf takes advantage to head in his second goal.

The Dutchman then turns provider in first half injury time, guiding through the pass from which Bull scores with a delightful 20-yard lob.

The two goal lead is short lived, though. Vale come out fighting after the interval and reduce the deficit in the 56th minute, Foyle dummying Shirtliff to fire in a cross-cum-shot which Kevin Kent turns over the line.

An equaliser looks on the cards when Naylor beats the off-side trap, but Jones pulls off a tremendous save which proves the turning point. Wolves regain the initiative and after Shirtliff hits the post with a header, the all-important fourth goal arrives from a 68th minute penalty.

Kevin Scott handles a Bull flick and, when usual spot-kick merchant Andy Thompson gives the nod to de Wolf, the big defender slams the ball home to produce an historic moment.

The victory-clinching goal not only completes de Wolf's first ever hat-trick but also produces the first treble scored by a Wolves central defender since 1902, when skipper Ted Pheasant hit three against Newcastle.

De Wolf's afternoon started with the deflating news that he was losing the captaincy to fit-again Shirtliff; but it has ended in triumph. He beams: "Scoring my first hat-trick at any level more than made up for my disappointment. Mind you, Thommo has told me it was the first and last time he would let me take a penalty off him!"

In the East Midlands, meanwhile, another small slice of goal history has worked in Wolves' favour. Striker Lee Mills, transferred to Derby County yesterday in a shock £400,000 deal that started on a loan basis, has bagged a debut winner against third placed Bolton – who are now just one point ahead of Wolves.

MATCH 44 • ENDSLEIGH LEAGUE DIVISION 1

Wednesday 8th March 1995 • Molineux • 7.45pm

WOLVES 1 SUNDERLAND 0

Half-time 0-0 • Attendance 25,926

Referee Pip WRIGHT (Northwich)

Linesmen B.L. POLKEY and D. UNSWORTH

Gold Shirts with Black Trim, Black Shorts	Goals	Red and White Striped Shirts, Red Shorts	Goals
1 Mike STOWELL		13 Tony NORMAN	
2 James SMITH		26 Dariusz KUBICKI	
3 Andy THOMPSON	47 pen	3 Richard ORD	
4 Mark RANKINE		4 Gary BENNETT	
5 John de WOLF ‡		6 Kevin BALL ❏	
6 Peter SHIRTLIFF		25 Martin SCOTT ❏	
7 Don GOODMAN		5 Derek FERGUSON	
8 David KELLY		22 Martin SMITH †	
9 Steve BULL †		8 Steve AGNEW	
10 Gordon COWANS		11 Craig RUSSELL	
11 Robbie DENNISON		18 Lee HOWEY ❏	
Substitutes		*Substitutes*	
12 Tom BENNETT ‡58		23 Steve BRODIE †87	
14 Jermaine WRIGHT †36		9 Gordon ARMSTRONG	
gk Paul JONES		1 Alec CHAMBERLAIN (gk)	

BEFORE	P	W	D	L	F	A	pts	AFTER	P	W	D	L	F	A	pts
5 Wolves	32	17	5	10	57	43	56	3 Wolves	33	18	5	10	58	43	59
19 Sunderland	33	8	15	10	32	32	39	20 Sunderland	34	8	15	11	32	33	39

FACTFILE *Smith comes in from the cold... Wolves make the running – Sunderland do the spoiling... Bull limps off... de Wolf stretchered off... Goodman out of luck against old club... Thompson's penalty winner... victory – at a cost... victory puts Wolves within striking distance of leaders.*

VICTORY AT A COST

De Wolf injured – out for season

Wolves go into their encounter with relegation threatened Sunderland knowing that victory will take them up to third place in the table, just three points behind leaders Tranmere Rovers and with a game in hand.

Following Sunday's 1-0 win against Portsmouth, four players – John de Wolf, Steve Bull, Robbie Dennison and Andy Thompson – have recovered from knocks and are included in tonight's team.

But full back Paul Blades has been dropped to make way for Jamie Smith, the youngster returning to the starting line-up for the first time since the 4-1 Boxing Day defeat at Oldham.

Manager Graham Taylor explains: "Jamie did well at the start of the season then levelled off, but the time is right to bring him back. It's not a bad thing to get some fresh legs in the team with so many matches coming up.

"After Sunderland, we've got the Cup match at Crystal Palace then a run of tough League games. The programme is hard, but that's the price of success and the players are getting used to the pressure."

Sunderland are under their own pressure near the bottom of the table and, from the first whistle, make it clear their aim is to avoid defeat at all costs.

Wolves make the early running though, and almost take the lead from a Dennison corner. De Wolf heads for goal, but Tony Norman palms the ball on to the underside of the bar and the visitors' defence scramble away the danger.

An immediate riposte sees Mike Stowell having to beat out a Lee Howey effort, but this turns out to be Sunderland's only goal attempt of the first half.

As Wolves build up the pressure, so Sunderland build up their resistance with tackles which incense the crowd and leave several home players limping.

The almost inevitable happens when Bull, the victim of a crunching 22nd minute challenge by Kevin Ball, has to be taken off nine minutes before half time.

But Wolves continue to do all the pressing, goalkeeper Tony Norman rescuing the visitors again when he dives to push a goalbound Don Goodman header for a corner.

Goodman, playing against his former club for the first time since moving to Molineux, has more bad luck in front of goal during the second half.

But not before Andy Thompson – resuming penalty duties after handing over to de Wolf at Port Vale – has put Wolves ahead with a 47th minute spot-kick awarded for a foul on Goodman by Gary Bennett.

Joy at the breakthrough goal turns to despair just after the hour, when de Wolf is injured in a challenge with Howey and has to be stretchered off.

There is no blame attached on this occasion to Howey, the man who last season put Geoff Thomas on a stretcher. But later in the game the Sunderland player is lucky to escape with only a yellow card for a dreadful late tackle on Peter Shirtliff.

Goal chances are meanwhile coming and going for Wolves. David Kelly and Robbie Dennison have good shots blocked, but Goodman curses his luck as first he hits a post, then misses out in a one-on-one situation and, finally, heads over the bar from an excellent position.

Wolves run out deserving winners, but at a severe cost – Bull may have to miss Saturday's Cup tie and, even worse, de Wolf may be out for the rest of the season with ligament trouble.

MATCH 45 • FA CUP SIXTH ROUND

Saturday 11th March 1995 • Selhurst Park • 3.00pm

CRYSTAL PALACE 1 WOLVES 1

Half-time 0-0 • Attendance 14,604

Referee Gary WILLARD (Worthing)

Linesmen P. MARCH and P.A. VOSPER

Red Shirts with Blue Stripes, Red Shorts		Goals	Gold Shirts with Black Trim, Black Shorts		Goals
1	Nigel MARTYN ❑		1	Mike STOWELL	
12	Damian MATTHEW ❑ †		2	James SMITH	
5	Eric YOUNG		3	Andy THOMPSON	
6	Chris COLEMAN ❑		4	Mark RANKINE ❑	
14	Richard SHAW		5	Brian LAW	
4	Gareth SOUTHGATE		6	Peter SHIRTLIFF ❑	
16	Darren PITCHER		7	Don GOODMAN	
8	Iain DOWIE ❑ ‡	53	8	David KELLY	
18	Andy PREECE		9	Steve BULL	
11	John SALAKO		10	Gordon COWANS	66
23	Ricky NEWMAN		11	Robbie DENNISON †	
	Substitutes			*Substitutes*	
10	Bruce DYER ‡82		12	Tom BENNETT	
2	John HUMPHREY †75		14	Neil EMBLEN †60	
gk	Rhys WILMOT		gk	Paul JONES	

FACTFILE

De Wolf in despair... Brian Law steps in... Bully's OK... omens look good... Wolves aim to cash in on Palace's low morale... hypnotist called in at the Palace... Ref the star of the first half... Dowie delivers... Cowans' curler so crucial... Stowell's storming finish sets up a deserved replay.

Gareth Southgate and David Kelly battle for the ball at Selhurst Park

DETERMINED DISPLAY BRINGS PALACE TO MOLINEUX

Cowans' first earns a replay

Confirmation of John de Wolf's injury plight has soured the run-up to today's big match, victory in which will give Wolves their first FA Cup semi-final appearance since the 1981 meeting with Tottenham Hotspur.

De Wolf has flown home to Holland to see a specialist and almost certainly to undergo surgery which will force him to miss the rest of the season.

Before leaving Molineux, de Wolf re-lived his midweek agony in the match against Sunderland. He said: "As soon as I hit the ground I felt something tear in my knee – it was like a piece of cloth being ripped. I have never felt such pain in my life.

"This is the biggest disappointment of my career. I was confident I would help Wolves win the Cup and promotion, but now my dream is in ruins. I just hope the team go on and do it without me."

While de Wolf contemplates the premature end to his season, Steve Bull – the other injury victim of Wednesday night's bruising encounter – has happily recovered in time to take his place in Wolves' Selhurst Park line-up.

And that means the only team change from Wednesday is the forced one to replace de Wolf. Brian Law steps back into the side as Wolves go for glory.

After already beating two Premiership sides in the competition, the quarter final omens are good for Wolves – the only non-Premiership club in the last eight.

In the last 25 years they have lost just once to Palace in 20 meetings. In that sequence, two of Wolves 11 victories have come in the FA Cup – at Molineux last season, and at Selhurst Park in 1978-79's run which ended in a semi-final defeat by Arsenal.

This afternoon Wolves are aiming to make it a hat-trick of Cup wins against a team who are struggling to avoid relegation and on Wednesday were knocked out of the Coca-Cola Cup in their semi-final second leg at home to Liverpool.

Since then, and in a blaze of publicity, Palace have called on the help of star TV hypnotist Paul McKenna in an attempt to build up match-winning confidence.

But there is nothing mesmerising from Palace or Wolves in a first half whose main talking points are the questionable decisions of referee Gary Willard.

As well as booking four players, he rarely allows the game to flow and also disallows penalty claims at both ends – first when Law appears to handle a Chris Coleman cross, then when Bull is floored by Eric Young.

Though neither goal comes under severe pressure, Gordon Cowans has to clear Iain Dowie's 16th minute header off the Wolves line while David Kelly's 34th minute shot forces Nigel Martyn into a diving save at the other end.

By the closing stages of the first half Wolves are on top, but a poor opening to the second period hands the intitiative to the home side.

Eight minutes after the break Palace take the lead, Dowie sweeping the ball home after Coleman has headed on a Richard Shaw free kick.

But Wolves refuse to buckle and draw level through Cowans in the 66th minute. The veteran midfielder muscles Damian Matthew out of possession then, from the edge of the penalty area, brilliantly curls a low shot just inside the far post to record his first Wolves goal.

Wolves celebrate, but not for long, their energies quickly re-focussed on the action as Palace mount a late assault. Dowie sends a header just over the bar, then Mike Stowell makes superb last minute saves from Coleman and Young.

In his first FA Cup appearance of the season, Stowell is the last-gasp hero. But Wolves have deserved their replay – and with it, the promise of another great night at Molineux.

The Wolves Review

MATCH 46 • ENDSLEIGH LEAGUE DIVISION 1

Wednesday 15th March 1995 • The Hawthorns • 7.45pm

WEST BROMWICH ALBION 2 WOLVES 0

Half-time 1-0 • Attendance 20,661

Referee John BRANDWOOD (Lichfield) †

Linesmen T.A. ATKINSON and P.M. ROBERTS †44

Blue and White Striped Shirts, White Shorts	Goals	Gold Shirts with Black Trim, Black Shorts	Goals
1 Stuart NAYLOR		1 Mike STOWELL	
2 Daryl BURGESS		2 James SMITH ■	
3 Paul AGNEW		3 Andy THOMPSON	
4 Mike PHELAN†		4 Mark RANKINE ❑	
5 Paul MARDON		5 Brian LAW	
6 Paul RAVEN		6 Peter SHIRTLIFF	
7 Kevin DONOVAN		7 Don GOODMAN	
8 Lee ASHCROFT ❑	6	8 David KELLY	
9 Bob TAYLOR	48	9 Steve BULL ‡	
10 Andy HUNT		10 Gordon COWANS†	
11 Ian HAMILTON		11 Robbie DENNISON	
Substitutes		*Substitutes*	
12 Tony REES		12 Neil EMBLEN †46	
14 Kieran O'REGAN †67		14 Jermaine WRIGHT ‡78	
gk Tony LANGE		gk Paul JONES	

BEFORE		P	W	D	L	F	A	pts	AFTER		P	W	D	L	F	A	pts
4	Wolves	33	18	5	10	58	43	59	4	Wolves	34	18	5	11	58	45	59
19	Albion	35	11	8	16	32	44	41	15	Albion	36	12	8	16	34	44	44

FACTFILE *Glamour semi-final in prospect... Wolves plan double dealing derby... Albion's relegation problems... Wanderer Goodman returns... Jamie Smith sent off after running battle with Lee Ashcroft... defeat hits local pride – plus prospects for automatic promotion*

96   *The Wolves Review*

DERBY DEFEAT FOR THE TEN MEN

Cowans injury shock

After Saturday's FA Cup heroics in South London, Wolves not only have a sixth round replay to savour but also – if they beat Crystal Palace – the prospect of a glamour semi-final against mighty Manchester United.

In the meantime, thoughts switch back to the League and a Black Country derby in which passions will run every bit as high as in any Cup semi-final.

Having beaten Albion comprehensively at Molineux in August, Wolves are aiming to complete a double which would boost their chances of automatic promotion – and at the same time push the Baggies one step closer to the second division.

The Hawthorns has been riddled with relegation fears all season despite a change of management in October, when Grimsby Town's former Walsall boss Alan Buckley was recruited to take over from the sacked Keith Burkinshaw.

The guaranteed white hot atmosphere of the derby encounter could be warmed up even further through the addition to the Molineux ranks of one-time Hawthorns favourite Don Goodman, who returns to his old stamping ground for the first time in the gold and black of his new club.

The £1.1 million striker brings the Wolves complement of ex-Baggie boys to four – and all of them will figure in an unchanged team this evening. "There's no way the Albion fans will want to see their team lose to a Wolves side with me and Steve Bull in it", says Goodman with a classic touch of understatement. "It's going to be a hard, roll-up-your-sleeves battle."

So, let battle commence – and it's Albion who make the early forays to draw first blood after just six minutes. Kevin Donovan's cross clears Jamie Smith for the waiting Lee Ashcroft to direct a neat header into the top corner.

The running feud which ensues between full back Smith and winger Ashcroft proves the most crucial factor in a fiercely fought derby scrap.

Ashcroft is booked for a 10th minute challenge on his marker, who himself receives a caution for taking retribution on the Albion man eight minutes later.

Wolves gradually force their way into the match and Albion goalkeeper Stuart Naylor has to save well-struck efforts from Mark Rankine, Andy Thompson and David Kelly as the visitors control the latter stages of the first half.

But an injury to Gordon Cowans, who is replaced by substitute Neil Emblen at half time, robs Wolves of their most influential player on the night.

And when Albion increase their lead three minutes after the break, Wolves have a Black Country mountain to climb.

The ill-fated Smith loses control of the ball near the touchline, allowing Ashcroft to race clear and cross for Bob Taylor to score with a brilliant diving header.

Smith's night of woe is ended on the hour, when he is sent off for a crude challenge on his tormentor Ashcroft. As the Wolves youngster tearfully leaves the field, his team's hopes of saving the match effectively leave with him.

Mike Stowell saves a cheeky chip by Ashcroft to prevent a heavier defeat, but the damage inflicted on Wolves could not be much more severe to either egos or automatic promotion prospects.

As the pride-stung fans begin their sad trek home, manager Graham Taylor offers a few (but probably indigestible) crumbs of comfort: "We had a lot of the game and I don't think the gods smiled too kindly on us. But we won three games on the trot after we were beaten by Middlesbrough, so who knows? We've just got to keep battling on."

The Wolves Review 1995

MATCH 47 • ENDSLEIGH LEAGUE DIVISION 1

Saturday 18th March 1995 • Molineux • 3.00pm

WOLVES 1 WATFORD 1

Half-time 1-0 • Attendance 24,380

Referee Ken LUPTON (Stockton-on-Tees)
Linesmen D.J. ADCOCK and P.J. GRIGGS

Gold Shirts with Black Trim, Black Shorts		Goals	Blue and White Striped Shirts, White Shorts		Goals
1	Mike STOWELL		1	Kevin MILLER	
2	Paul BLADES		2	Gerard LAVIN	
3	Andy THOMPSON		3	Nigel GIBBS ‡	
4	Tom BENNETT ❏		4	David HOLDSWORTH	
5	Brian LAW		5	Keith MILLEN	
6	Peter SHIRTLIFF		6	Craig RAMAGE	
7	Mark RANKINE ‡		7	Andy HESSENTHALER	
8	Geoff THOMAS †	23	8	Derek PAYNE	
9	David KELLY		9	Mick QUINN †	
10	Don GOODMAN		10	Gary PORTER	
11	Robbie DENNISON		11	Kevin PHILLIPS	90
	Substitutes			*Substitutes*	
12	Mark VENUS †61		12	Richard JOHNSON ‡75	
14	Jermaine WRIGHT ‡78		14	Peter BEADLE †71	
gk	Paul JONES		gk	Perry DIGWEED	

BEFORE		P	W	D	L	F	A	pts	AFTER		P	W	D	L	F	A	pts
4	Wolves	34	18	5	11	58	45	59	4	Wolves	35	18	6	11	59	46	60
9	Watford	34	13	11	10	38	35	50	10	Watford	35	13	12	10	39	36	51

FACTFILE

Injury and suspension problems add to post-Hawthorns depression... fixture backlog increasing... Smith dropped... Thomas back with a goal – then another injury blow... Shirtliff error sets up horror ending, as mis-kick lets in Phillips for last minute equaliser.

CHANCE TO CATCH LEADERS THROWN AWAY

Late strike stunner

As if post-Hawthorns depression wasn't enough, Wolves' seemingly unending injury problems have piled up even further by the time the team is announced for this afternoon's game against Watford.

Gordon Cowans, substituted at half time against Albion, will be out for at least three weeks with a medial knee ligament injury. And Steve Bull misses today's match due to a 'dead leg' which forced him to limp out of the action in the last few minutes on Wednesday.

Geoff Thomas, happily over his own injury worries, makes only his second start in 20 games as Cowans' replacement. Don Goodman switches forward to take over from Bull, with Tom Bennett slotting into midfield.

At right back the experienced Paul Blades is preferred to young Jamie Smith, who has been taken out of the firing line following his traumatic evening at the Hawthorns.

Smith's sending-off means that – like Peter Shirtliff – he will be unavailable through suspension for the forthcoming match at Southend. With Darren Ferguson also about to start a two-match ban, Wolves have suddenly got disciplinary as well as injury problems.

Against this background, the club's Cup-induced backlog of fixtures could pose a serious threat to the all-important aim of promotion to the Premiership.

With next Wednesday's sixth round Cup replay leading to the postponement of the scheduled midweek

Tragedy for Peter Shirtliff

League trip to Tranmere, it is vital today that Wolves beat Watford and keep themselves in touch with the top spot.

Graham Taylor's men give no early indication that they can overcome the visitors, but a dull game is brought to life when Thomas puts Wolves in front after 23 minutes. Robbie Dennison's left wing cross is flicked on by David Kelly and, when Mark Rankine heads the ball back across goal, Thomas is there to nod in his first goal of the season.

Watford quickly hit back, but after on-loan Coventry striker Mick Quinn fluffs an easy close range chance Andy Porter fires a dipping shot just over the bar. Towards half time Wolves get well on top and Dennison, Goodman and Rankine all go close to increasing the lead.

Straight after the break a Brian Law mistake lets in Craig Ramage for a shot which Mike Stowell has to save; but seconds later Kelly misses a good opportunity at the other end after Goodman has headed the ball down – then Kelly creates a fine chance which is wasted by Goodman, who shoots straight at goalkeeper Kevin Miller.

Just after the hour Thomas, who has not looked 100 per cent fit, sadly has to leave the action. And 12 minutes from time Rankine, another injury victim, also has to be substituted. In the meantime Dennison has brought a fine save from Miller, who also produces a good stop from substitute Mark Venus.

In injury time, however, tragedy strikes. Shirtliff – 25 yards from his own goal line and under no pressure – completely misses his kick, leaving Watford striker Kevin Phillips to move in and strike a devastating equaliser.

Two precious points have been tossed away, as has the chance to steal a march on the top two teams – Tranmere and Middlesbrough have both lost. And with play-off contenders Sheffield United, Reading and Barnsley all winning, the pressure around fourth-in-the-table Wolves is mounting considerably.

The Wolves Review 1995

MATCH 48 • FA CUP SIXTH ROUND REPLAY

Wednesday 22nd March 1995 • Molineux • 7.45pm

WOLVES 1 CRYSTAL PALACE 4

Half-time 1-3 • Attendance 27,548

Referee Gary WILLARD (Worthing)
Linesmen W.M. JORDAN and J.P. ROBINSON

Gold Shirts with Black Trim, Black Shorts	Goals	Red Shirts with Blue Stripes, Red Shorts	Goals
1 Mike STOWELL		1 Nigel MARTYN	
2 Mark RANKINE ❑		22 Darren PATTERSON	
3 Andy THOMPSON		14 Richard SHAW ❑	
4 Tom BENNETT †		5 Eric YOUNG	
5 Brian LAW		6 Chris COLEMAN	
6 Peter SHIRTLIFF ❑		4 Gareth SOUTHGATE	
7 Don GOODMAN ❑		16 Darren PITCHER	45
8 David KELLY ❑	34	11 John SALAKO	
9 Steve BULL ❑		21 Ian COX †	
10 Mark VENUS		9 Chris ARMSTRONG ‡	32, 67
11 Robbie DENNISON		8 Iain DOWIE	37
Substitutes		Substitutes	
12 Neil EMBLEN †21		23 Ricky NEWMAN †78	
14 Jermaine WRIGHT		10 Bruce DYER ‡88	
gk Paul JONES		gk Rhys WILMOT	

FACTFILE

United here we come?... Thomas makes ten – injury list proves too much of a handicap... Bully back – so is Chris Armstrong to bag a brace of goals... Palace on fire... Wolves have no answer... Wembley dream turns to Molineux nightmare... now for the premiership.

Goodman, Bull and Kelly celebrate Wolves' goal

The Wolves Review 1995

END OF THE ROAD TO WEMBLEY

Injury crisis deepens

A Villa Park semi-final against the most charismatic club in English football awaits Wolves if they can beat Palace. Manchester United are clear favourites to win the Cup and so retain the trophy they won last year with a convincing Wembley win against Chelsea – the quarter final conquerors of Wolves.

The Molineux men have already gone a little further than they did last season by forcing a quarter final replay against Premiership opponents. Now they aim to finish the job and stride into the semis, though for the umpteenth time manager Graham Taylor is forced to re-shuffle his team because of injuries.

Geoff Thomas, who suffered so badly last season, is about to miss the rest of the current campaign after limping out of Saturday's match. He has subsequently had a knee operation, thus bringing to double figures the number of Wolves players to undergo surgery this season.

With John de Wolf having preceded Thomas on to the operating table by a week or so, the first team squad is now down to only 16 fit players. But for tonight's game manager Taylor can at least call on two – Mark Rankine and Andy Thompson – who were injured against Watford but have thankfully recovered.

Taylor is also able to bring back Steve Bull, whose dead-leg problem has cleared. But just as Wolves' main striker has returned, so Palace welcome back Chris Armstrong.

The £4 million rated front man is back after a drugs-related ban kept him out of the Selhurst Park clash with Wolves. Traces of marijuana were allegedly found in a routine test sample which followed a training session. But now Armstrong is back in match action and aiming to send Wolves' FA Cup hopes to pot.

And, sadly for the Molineux men and their fans, his aim is true. Armstrong's first strike arrives in the 32nd minute, a spectacular bicycle-kick zooming into the net after John Salako's long throw has fallen on the edge of the six yard box.

Wolves have already been dealt one blow, Tom Bennett having to be taken off injured following a crunching tackle for which Darren Pitcher was lucky not to receive at least a caution.

Spirits are fleetingly raised when, within two minutes of Armstrong's opener, Rankine's right wing cross deflects off Pitcher and David Kelly stoops to head the equaliser.

But after just three further minutes, another Salako throw-in leads to panic in the Wolves defence and Iain Dowie is allowed the time and room to volley the visitors back into the lead.

Even worse follows on the stroke of half-time, Rankine heading an intended clearance only as far as Pitcher and – from 30 yards – the Palace midfielder thundering an unstoppable shot into the top of the net.

The second half fails to bring a reprieve for Wolves, who cannot find the spark they had shown in the early stages of the match. Frustratingly, bookings – five in all – rather than goals are all they can muster.

When it comes to finding the net, Palace are far more proficient and they wrap up victory in the 67th minute. Armstrong skips past Brian Law to hit an angled, rising shot with such power that the ball wedges in the stanchion bars.

The closing stages are played out in near silence as a stunned crowd comes to an inevitable conclusion – on this evidence, Wolves are simply not good enough to compete at Premiership level.

Palace may be in the top division's relegation zone and the lowest scorers in the entire League – but they have been too good for Wolves. The Cup dream is dead. What now of Premiership ambitions?

The Wolves Review 1995

MATCH 49 • ENDSLEIGH LEAGUE DIVISION 1

Friday 24th March 1995 • Molineux • 7.45pm

WOLVES 2 BURNLEY 0

Half-time 1-0 • Attendance 25,703

Referee Peter FOAKES (Clacton)

Linesmen J.B. GOULDING and E.J. WALSH

Gold Shirts with Black Trim, Black Shorts	Goals	Claret and Blue Shirts, White Shorts	Goals
1 Mike STOWELL		1 Wayne RUSSELL	
2 Paul BLADES		2 Gerry HARRISON ‡	
3 Mark VENUS ❏		3 Mark WINSTANLEY	
4 Mark RANKINE		4 Steve DAVIS	
5 Brian LAW		5 Chris VINNICOMBE	
6 Peter SHIRTLIFF		6 Adrian RANDALL	
7 Don GOODMAN		7 Jamie HOYLAND	
8 David KELLY		8 Steve THOMPSON	
9 Steve BULL	10	9 Kurt NOGAN	
10 Neil EMBLEN	58	10 Liam ROBINSON †	
11 Robbie DENNISON		11 David EYRES	
Substitutes		*Substitutes*	
12 James SMITH		12 Paul SHAW †46	
14 Jermaine WRIGHT		14 Chris BRASS ‡67	
gk Paul JONES		gk Marlon BERESFORD	

BEFORE		P	W	D	L	F	A	pts	AFTER		P	W	D	L	F	A	pts
6	Wolves	35	18	6	11	59	46	60	4	Wolves	36	19	6	11	61	46	63
23	Burnley	36	8	11	17	35	58	35	23	Burnley	37	8	11	18	35	60	35

FACTFILE

Fourth match in 10 days... struggling Burnley must be beaten... Taylor programmes a warning... on-loan Richards watches from the bench... Bully starts it, Emblen finishes it, Mexican Wave celebrates it – Wolves are back on the victory trail.

BACK IN CONTENTION

One more for Bully's 200

Less than 48 hours after going out of the FA Cup in demoralising fashion, Wolves step back out at Molineux in search of a winning end to a punishing schedule of four matches in 10 days.

The sequence has so far brought only disappointment, Wednesday's crushing Cup exit having followed a morale-denting defeat at Albion and the frustration of throwing away two points in Saturday's match against Watford.

Tonight bottom-but-one club Burnley are the visitors for a match which, quite simply, has to be won. Anything less would leave Wolves just outside the play-off positions and exposed to the challenge of improving promotion contenders Derby and Barnsley.

In his match-day programme column, prepared after the Cup disaster against Crystal Palace, Graham Taylor spells out a pointed warning to the players charged with the task of taking Wolves into the Premiership.

The manager notes: "I have been here one year now – not five or six like a lot of players – which is enough time to realise this is a big club that needs big players with big hearts and all-out commitment. I hope the players know me well enough by now and that I have not come here to be an also-ran."

In the little time he has had since the Palace match, Taylor has brought Bradford City central defender Dean Richards to the club. The 20-year-old defender, tracked by several Premiership clubs including Manchester United, signed on loan during yesterday's transfer deadline day.

The loan extends to the end of the season, when a permanent £1.5 million deal could be completed.

Richards, on stand-by for next week's England Under-21 international against Eire, signed too late to play tonight but is watching from the dug-out as Wolves start the match with an early goal.

David Kelly lobs up a ball which goalkeeper Wayne Russell fluffs and Steve Bull, after missing an attempted header and falling over in the process, regains his balance to push the ball into the unguarded net.

Bully's 199th League goal is not one of his best, but it serves as a great booster to a team whose confidence lay in tatters just a couple of nights ago.

More injuries have not helped – Tom Bennett and Andy Thompson have both been forced to miss tonight's game, with the desperately unlucky Bennett seemingly set for a long spell out through a knee injury sustained against Palace.

His replacement tonight, Neil Emblen, plays an increasingly important role as Wolves threaten at times to take the vistors apart.

There are a few bad moments too, particularly straight after the interval when a 20-yard shot from David Eyres slithers through Mike Stowell's grasp and bounces off the post before the goalkeeper can make a frantic goal-line save.

But any remaining Wolves' nerves are calmed in the 58th minute, when Emblen hits a 25-yard shot which deceives Russell to land re-assuringly in the Burnley net.

Stowell has to save from Eyres and Kurt Nogan as Burnley produce an occasional threat, but at the other end both Bull and Kelly have efforts well saved as a Mexican Wave sweeps round the stands in celebration of an impending and important victory.

It is Wolves first win in five attempts, putting them back up into the play-off places and also in good spirits for a daunting run-in – seven of the remaining 10 matches are away from home.

The Wolves Review 1995

MATCH 50 • ENDSLEIGH LEAGUE DIVISION 1

Saturday 1st April 1995 • Roots Hall • 3.00pm

SOUTHEND UNITED 0 WOLVES 1

Half-time 0-0 • Attendance 8,522

Referee Mick PIERCE (Portsmouth)

Linesmen C.T. FINCH and P.J. GRIFFIN

Blue Shirts with Red Trim, Blue Shorts	Goals	Gold Shirts with Black Trim, Black Shorts	Goals
1 Simon ROYCE		1 Mike STOWELL	
2 Mark HONE †		2 Paul BLADES	
3 Chris POWELL		3 Neil MASTERS	
4 Ronnie WHELAN		4 Neil EMBLEN	
5 Mick BODLEY		5 Brian LAW	
6 Andy EDWARDS		6 Dean RICHARDS	
7 Gary JONES		7 Don GOODMAN	
8 Andy SUSSEX		8 David KELLY	
9 Julian HAILS ‡		9 Steve BULL	83
10 Steve TILSON		10 Mark VENUS	
11 Keith DUBLIN		11 Robbie DENNISON	
Substitutes		*Substitutes*	
12 Tony BATTERSBY †46		12 Paul BIRCH	
14 Phil GRIDELET ‡80		14 James KELLY	
gk Paul SANSOME		gk Paul JONES	

BEFORE	P	W	D	L	F	A	pts	AFTER	P	W	D	L	F	A	pts
4 Wolves	36	19	6	11	61	46	63	3 Wolves	37	20	6	11	62	46	66
16 Southend	39	13	8	18	42	66	47	16 Southend	40	13	8	19	42	67	47

FACTFILE

Rare break after mad-March schedule… away report – must do better… depleted squad "down to the bare bones", says Taylor… Richards and Masters drafted in… 200 up for captain Bully… Another clean for Stowell keeps the Shrimpers at bay… Taylor's title target.

104   *The Wolves Review 1995*

AWAY PERFORMANCES HOLD THE KEY

Bully hits his two hundredth

After a hectic March schedule of seven games in 20 days, Wolves have had the rare pleasure of an eight-day break between their home win against Burnley and today's visit to Southend United.

The seaside outfit were hammered 5-0 at Molineux back in September, Wolves' most clear-cut win of the season starting their two-month spell as first division leaders.

But completing the double, let alone repeating the magnitude of their home victory, looks a much taller order for a team who have won only once away in the League since the turn of the year.

As Graham Taylor concedes: "Our promotion hopes depend on us winning some games away from Molineux. We have been scoring away, but we have also conceded far too many goals."

Whether or not the manager would have contemplated team changes, his hand has been forced yet again by injury and suspension problems. This time they have hit a new peak – the team coach to the South Coast contains the only 17 players Taylor has at his command.

Two of them, David Kelly and Brian Law, only re-joined the squad on Friday after returning from midweek international duty with Eire and Wales respectively.

That has left precious little time for Law to work on his new central defensive partnership with Dean Richards, last week's loan signing who is pitched into today's side in place of the suspended Peter Shirtliff.

With Mark Rankine failing a morning fitness test, left back Neil Masters gets his first start for 13 months – and after hopefully ending his long injury nightmare.

In the absence of Shirtliff, Steve Bull is made captain four days after his 30th birthday and on the afternoon he goes looking for his 200th League goal.

The early stages show that Bully's task will not be an easy one, though. Southend are unbeaten in five outings and, despite their lowly placing in the table, they take the game confidently to the visitors.

Mike Stowell has to make saves from Julian Hails and Ronnie Whelan, then Paul Blades is called on to clear a Hails header off the line as Southend probe for an opening goal.

Wolves begin to find some rhythm midway through the first half, but apart from a 39th minute Bull effort – saved by Simon Royce – they rarely threaten the home goal.

As the second half progresses Southend still look the more likely scorers, though both Steve Tilson and Gary Jones fire chances over the bar.

But in the final quarter Wolves find more urgency and are rewarded seven minutes from time, when Bull gets his landmark goal. Latching on to a long Brian Law pass which David Kelly has flicked on, Bull races into the penalty area to efficiently despatch the ball past Royce and into the Southend net.

Fittingly, it is a goal which carries the no-nonsense hallmark stamped on so many of the striker's goals in a still-glittering career. It also earns Wolves a precious victory which takes them up to third place, six points behind leaders Middlesbrough with two games in hand.

With six of the nine remaining matches away from home, winning the championship is going to be a mighty tough task. But manager Taylor, encouraged by two successive wins (and two clean sheets), nevertheless sets his men a title target.

"We may well have to win four away games and all of the ones at home", he says. "But we are still in with a shout after today – these were three big points for us."

MATCH 51 • ENDSLEIGH LEAGUE DIVISION 1

Tuesday 4th April 1995 • Kenilworth Road • 7.45pm

LUTON TOWN 3 WOLVES 3

Half-time 2-0 • Attendance 9,651

Referee Graham POOLEY (Bishops Stortford)
Linesmen S.G. CLINGO and M. TINGEY

White Shirts with Blue Trim, White Shorts	Goals	Gold Shirts with Black Trim, Black Shorts	Goals
1 Kelvin DAVIS		1 Mike STOWELL	
2 Julian JAMES		2 Paul BLADES	
3 Marvin JOHNSON		3 Neil MASTERS †	
4 Gary WADDOCK		4 Neil EMBLEN	90
5 Richard HARVEY		5 Brian LAW	
6 Trevor PEAKE		6 Dean RICHARDS	
7 Paul TELFER	6, 11	7 Paul BIRCH ‡	
8 Scott OAKES		8 Don GOODMAN	
9 John TAYLOR	51	9 Steve BULL	
10 David PREECE		10 Gordon COWANS	
11 Dwight MARSHALL †		11 Mark VENUS	
Substitutes		*Substitutes*	
12 Rob MATTHEWS		12 David KELLY ‡46	48, 59
14 Jamie WOODSFORD †89		14 Robbie DENNISON †34	
gk Juergen SOMMER		gk Paul JONES	

BEFORE	P	W	D	L	F	A	pts	AFTER	P	W	D	L	F	A	pts
3 Wolves	37	20	6	11	62	46	66	3 Wolves	38	20	7	11	65	49	67
12 Luton	38	14	10	14	52	53	52	12 Luton	39	14	11	14	55	56	53

FACTFILE

Chance to pile on the promotion pressure... selection shock – Kelly and Dennison dropped... Luton's lightning start... super-sub leads the fightback – Kelly comes on to score twice... Emblen's injury time face-saver... title dream ended? Play-offs look the best bet now.

INJURY TIME LIFE SAVER

Super sub Kelly hits two

A trip to Luton gives Wolves the chance to use up one of their games in hand and put pressure on leaders Middlesbrough in the race for the championship and automatic promotion.

Victory over David Pleat's team would not only push Graham Taylor's men into second place in the table for the first time since mid-February, but would also put them just three points behind Boro – and still with a game to spare.

After Saturday at Southend, where Taylor had 11 players unavailable due to either injury or suspension, the manager has a much wider selection choice at Kenilworth Road.

He decides to leave well alone in defence, meaning Dean Richards keeps his place in the centre and Peter Shirtliff – having served his one match suspension – has to wait for a recall.

But Taylor switches around his midfield and attack to produce two surprise omissions. David Kelly and Robbie Dennison are dropped to the substitutes' bench, Dennison after 21 successive appearances and Kelly after 18.

Fit-again former Villa colleagues Gordon Cowans and Paul Birch are the players brought in, Birch taking over on the right side of midfield and enabling Don Goodman to switch into the middle of the attack alongside Steve Bull.

The re-jigged line-up gets an early pasting, Luton racing into a two goal lead inside the first 11 minutes. Both strikes come from winger Paul Telfer, the first after Gary Waddock has beaten the offside trap down the left and the second following Dwight Marshall's delivery from the right.

Completely outwitted by Luton's lively, inventive play, Wolves look likely to shed more goals before substitutions are made either side of half time. Dennison takes over from Masters 11 minutes before the break and, crucially, Kelly is sent on immediately after the interval in place of Birch.

With almost his first touch Kelly puts Wolves back into the game, stooping to head home in the 48th minute after Richards has flicked on Cowans' corner.

The goal sparks Wolves into attacking mode but, just as they are getting on top, Luton are handed a third goal when poor marking allows Telfer and Marvin Johnson to provide the chance for John Taylor to head past Mike Stowell.

Refusing to buckle despite what might have been a killer blow, Wolves storm back for Kelly to net a deserved second goal just before the hour. Meeting a Neil Emblen pull-back from the right, Kelly sweeps in a fine shot to record his 19th goal of the season.

The visitors are now looking irresistable, but inexplicably they go right off the boil and Luton re-gain total control. It seems only a matter of time before a fourth goal arrives, Stowell saving well from Taylor and Telfer as the home side continually carve a way through.

But in the fourth minute of injury time, Wolves amazingly conjure up an equaliser. Emblen runs at the defence from midfield, squeezing past two opponents to get in a shot which – with the help of an 'assist' from Scott Oakes – rolls into the net off a post.

The improbable point-saver has kept Wolves well in contention for a play-off place, though automatic promotion by taking the title now looks beyond them.

Indeed, manager Taylor seems to have lowered his sights when he reckons: "Wins in our next two matches should see us into the play-offs, but we've got Barnsley and Derby – two teams on the coat-tails of play-off places – and beating them is going to be very hard."

The Wolves Review 1995

MATCH 52 • ENDSLEIGH LEAGUE DIVISION 1

Saturday 8th April 1995 • Molineux • 3.00pm

WOLVES 0 BARNSLEY 0

Half-time 0-0 • Attendance 26,385

Referee Paul HARRISON (Oldham)

Linesmen P.I. HARRIS and B.T. MILLERSHIP

Gold Shirts with Black Trim, Black Shorts	Goals	Red Shirts with Black and White Trim, White Shorts	Goals
1 Mike STOWELL		1 David WATSON	
2 Mark RANKINE		2 Nicky EADEN	
3 Neil MASTERS		3 Gary FLEMING	
4 Neil EMBLEN ‡		4 Danny WILSON ■	
5 Brian LAW ❑		5 Gerry TAGGART	
6 Dean RICHARDS		6 Malcolm SHOTTON	
7 Don GOODMAN		7 Brendan O'CONNELL	
8 David KELLY		8 Martin BULLOCK	
9 Steve BULL		9 Andy PAYTON ❑	
10 Gordon COWANS		10 Andy LIDDELL †	
11 Robbie DENNISON †		11 Darren SHERIDAN	
Substitutes		*Substitutes*	
12 Peter SHIRTLIFF ‡67		12 Neil REDFEARN †89	
14 Darren FERGUSON †57		14 Andy RAMMELL	
gk Paul JONES		gk Lee BUTLER	

BEFORE	P	W	D	L	F	A	pts	AFTER	P	W	D	L	F	A	pts
3 Wolves	38	20	7	11	65	49	67	4 Wolves	39	20	8	11	65	49	68
7 Barnsley	38	18	8	12	57	45	62	6 Barnsley	39	18	9	12	57	45	63

FACTFILE *Super-sub back in the starting line-up... Returns for Robbie Dennison and Mark Rankine... Emblen injury blow... Fergie back in the fold... Stowell saves the day... Wilson sent-off in penalty drama... Kelly steps up, but Watson saves... Two more points go begging.*

108   The Wolves Review 1995

STOWELL TO THE RESCUE

Kelly's late penalty miss

After his two-goal 'super-sub' appearance at Luton on Tuesday, David Kelly's return to the starting line-up for today's visit of promotion hopefuls Barnsley is perhaps the most predictable team change of the season.

As far as Graham Taylor is concerned, Kelly's match-turning double strike at Kenilworth Road was a dividend from dropping him to the substitutes' bench. "Sometimes players need a kick up the back-side", reckons the manager. "That's what happened to David on Tuesday, and he responded in the right way."

With the Eire international back in the side, Don Goodman reverts to the right wing in place of Paul Birch.

On the left wing Robbie Dennison, dropped along with Kelly on Tuesday, replaces the suspended Mark Venus. And at right back fit-again Mark Rankine takes over from calf strain victim Paul Blades.

There is also a return to the fold for Darren Ferguson, out of contention since Boxing Day's disastrous 4-1 defeat at Oldham, but back today as substitute.

Wolves start the match well, winning a couple of early corners and Steve Bull having a header saved by goalkeeper David Watson. But Barnsley almost take the lead from their first attack.

Dean Richards – on his home debut – misplaces a pass straight to the feet of Martin Bullock, whose long range effort slips through the grasp of Mike Stowell but drops wide of the post. Stowell does much better in the 24th minute, diving to make a fine stop from Danny Wilson's well struck 25 yard shot.

Three minutes later Dennison has a goal ruled out for offside, then Goodman and Bull both miss the target from 20 yards before Goodman has a 44th minute close range effort well saved by Watson.

For a hectic 10 minutes after the interval all the goalmouth action is at the Wolves end, Stowell having to save from Malcolm Shotton, Brendan O'Connell, Andy Payton and Andy Liddell.

But in the 56th minute, Neil Emblen runs through the opposition ranks to fire in a 20 yard shot which is brilliantly saved at full stretch by Watson.

It is a rare moment to savour for the Wolves fans, however, as the visitors quickly regain the upper hand. And the pressure is stepped up still further after the unfortunate departure of Emblen through a knee injury.

Stowell has to save from Wilson and Bullock as Barnsley look for what would be a deserved winner. But in the last minute, ragged Wolves are dramatically given the chance to wrap up the points.

As a ruck of players goes up for Gordon Cowans' cross, the ball strikes Shotton on the back of the arm and referee Paul Harrison – to the massive annoyance of the visitors – awards a penalty.

Harrison is quickly surrounded by the whole of the Barnsley team, whose player-manager Danny Wilson leads the protests and is sent off for allegedly pushing the ref during the melee.

Wilson is watching from the touchline as Kelly, a surprise penalty-taker in the absence of Andy Thompson, strikes the spot-kick against the legs of the diving Watson.

After wasting a golden opportunity to win the match, Wolves almost lose it in injury time – Bullock races through and Stowell has to pull off an excellent save from the one-on-one situation.

"The penalty was a get-out clause we didn't take, but we owe our point to Mike Stowell", says disappointed manager Taylor after a match which has further weakened Wolves' chances of automatic promotion.

MATCH 53 • ENDSLEIGH LEAGUE DIVISION 1

Wednesday 12th April 1995 • The Baseball Ground • 7.45pm

DERBY COUNTY 3 WOLVES 3

Half-time 1-1 • *Attendance* 16,040

Referee John HOLBROOK (Ludlow)

Linesmen P. ROBERTS and G. SHAW

White Shirts with Black Trim, Black Shorts	Goals	Gold Shirts with Black Trim, Gold Shorts	Goals
1 Russell HOULT		1 Mike STOWELL	
2 Jason KAVANAGH ❏		2 Dean RICHARDS	75, 90
3 Darren WASSALL ❏		3 James SMITH	
4 Paul TROLLOPE		4 Mark RANKINE	
5 Craig SHORT		5 Brian LAW ❏	
6 Paul WILLIAMS		6 Peter SHIRTLIFF	
7 John HARKES		7 Don GOODMAN	11
8 Mark PEMBRIDGE		8 David KELLY	
9 Lee MILLS		9 Steve BULL	
10 Marco GABBIADINI ❏	52	10 Gordon COWANS †	
11 Paul SIMPSON	35pen, 64	11 Mark VENUS ❏	
Substitutes		*Substitutes*	
12 Wayne SUTTON		12 Paul BLADES	
14 Darren WRACK		14 Jermaine WRIGHT †87	
gk Steve SUTTON		gk Paul JONES	

BEFORE	P	W	D	L	F	A	pts	AFTER	P	W	D	L	F	A	pts
4 Wolves	39	20	8	11	65	49	68	4 Wolves	40	20	9	11	68	52	69
8 Derby	40	17	10	13	55	41	61	8 Derby	41	17	11	13	58	44	62

FACTFILE *Injury crisis drags on... challenge to the fit 15... change of formation... ex-Wanderer Mills out for Wolves' blood... sweet and sour - and sweet again... Richards the villain, then the hero... another high-scoring draw... manager Taylor aging fast after another last gasp point.*

The Wolves Review 1995

RAMS ROCKED BY RICHARDS

Defender is villain and hero

Wolves' season-long injury crisis shows no sign of abating as a difficult match at in-form Derby approaches. Tests on Neil Emblen, injured on Saturday, have revealed knee ligament damage which could keep him out for the rest of the season. And a back problem could do likewise for Neil Masters just three games after his return from injury.

"We don't deal in minor knocks here", complains Graham Taylor. "Wolves players don't limp off and come back for the next game – when they come off, they stay off!"

Partly because of the injury situation, the manager has decided to change the team's formation tonight. A five-man back line will include three central defenders, Peter Shirtliff coming back into the side in place of midfielder Emblen. Jamie Smith replaces Masters at left back, while the re-shaped midfield is not only reduced to a trio but sees Mark Venus replacing Robbie Dennison.

Forced changes or not, Taylor still refuses to use injuries as any kind of excuse. Instead he throws down a challenge to his dwindling band of available players: "We still have 15 fit men – and this is their opportunity to win us promotion to the Premiership."

An opportunity it may be, but it is an increasingly difficult one. Five of the remaining seven games are away and include visits to promotion chasing Sheffield United and Tranmere as well as tonight's trip to the Baseball Ground.

Derby have won six of their last eight matches, taking them to within five points of the play-off places. And in striker Lee Mills, scorer of five goals in his first eight games after his recent move from Molineux, they have a player with the utmost desire to put one over Taylor and his team.

But it is Wolves' Don Goodman who calls the shots during the early exchanges. After thumping a 20 yard effort against the woodwork, Goodman opens the scoring from 15 yards when David Kelly's driven shot rebounds into his path.

Revelling in his attacking midfield role, Goodman goes close again when he flashes a shot into the side netting. But in the 35th minute things start to turn sour for Wolves.

Brian Law is very harshly adjudged to have handled the ball in the penalty area and Paul Simpson, given the same spot-kick chance that Kelly wasted for Wolves on Saturday, makes no mistake.

After 52 minutes Dean Richards fails to stop Marco Gabbiadini getting in a 20 yard shot which the flailing Mike Stowell cannot keep out of the net.

And bad goes to worse in the 64th minute, Richards allowing a Gabbiadini flick to reach Simpson for the winger to score Derby's third goal.

Two disastrous errors are partly atoned for in the 75th minute by Richards, who steers home a Smith cross to put Wolves back in the game.

But Derby roar back – only for Mills to miss a great chance to ensure victory when, two minutes from time, he blasts the ball over the bar from eight yards.

Cue Richards, whose earlier mistakes are forgotten as he beats marker Mills to a Venus free-kick and powers home the equaliser with an injury time header.

It's deja vu from Wolves' comeback at Luton last week, though unlike the Kenilworth Road nail-biter this point was truly deserved.

It has done nothing, however, for the constitution of manager Taylor. Last Saturday he prefaced his programme notes with a 'health warning' about watching Wolves. Tonight, after the latest Great Escape, he utters: "I'm 50 years old – what are they doing to me?".

He is jesting, of course – but thousands of nerve-wracked Wolves fans know exactly what he means.

The Wolves Review 1995

MATCH 54 • ENDSLEIGH LEAGUE DIVISION 1

Saturday 15th April 1995 • The Valley • 3.00pm

CHARLTON ATHLETIC 3 WOLVES 2

Half-time 1-1 • Attendance 10,922

Referee Andy D'URSO (Billericay)

Linesmen B.C. FISH and R.J. ZIPFEL

Red Shirts with White Trim, White Shorts		Goals	Gold Shirts with Black Trim, Black Shorts		Goals
1	Mike AMMANN		1	Mike STOWELL	
2	Steve BROWN ◻		2	Dean RICHARDS	
3	Jamie STUART		3	James SMITH ‡	
4	Colin WALSH ◻	55	4	Mark RANKINE	
5	Richard RUFUS		5	Brian LAW ◻	
6	Stuart BALMER		6	Peter SHIRTLIFF †	
7	Mark ROBSON †		7	Don GOODMAN ◻	
8	Carl LEABURN		8	David KELLY	
9	Alan PARDEW		9	Steve BULL	43, 67
10	David WHYTE	12	10	Gordon COWANS	
11	Paul MORTIMER	61	11	Mark VENUS ◻	
	Substitutes			Substitutes	
12	Paul LINGER		12	Paul BLADES ‡77	
14	Shaun NEWTON †90		14	Jermaine WRIGHT †46	
gk	Andy PETTERSON		gk	Paul JONES	

BEFORE	P	W	D	L	F	A	pts	AFTER	P	W	D	L	F	A	pts
4 Wolves	40	20	9	11	68	52	69	4 Wolves	41	20	9	12	70	55	69
14 Charlton	40	14	10	16	51	57	52	14 Charlton	41	15	10	16	54	59	55

FACTFILE *Wanted – a victory at the Valley... unchanged Wolves... early shock... Steve Bull's 200th Wolves League goal after double disaster... a mountain too far... Gordon Cowans pledges that everyone will give their all to achieve a play-off place for the club.*

112   The Wolves Review 1995

DEFENSIVE FRAILTIES COST WOLVES DEAR

Bully's brace not enough

Victory at the Valley is essential if Wolves are to retain any hope of automatic promotion. Three successive draws have left them six points behind leaders Middlesbrough with only one game in hand – and a dwindling number of matches left in which to overtake Bryan Robson's team for the championship.

On the eve of Wolves' clash with a Charlton side still not safe from relegation, Graham Taylor has admitted: "Because we keep taking only a third of the loaf, automatic promotion is no longer in our hands.

"It's been an incredible season of expectation and the tension has taken it's toll on everybody. We've got six games left and anything can happen – but to put pressure on the other clubs we must get three points at Charlton."

After the stirring fightback which earned a deserved point at Derby, the Wolves manager sticks to the same line-up. Charlton's side, meanwhile, is depleted by having three midfielders missing through suspension.

But, chasing the one victory which manager Alan Curbishley says they need to ensure first division survival, they get a great start with a 12th minute goal. Mark Robson sends over a free-kick and Wolves' static defence is punished as David Whyte volleys the ball home.

A minute later Colin Walsh strikes the bar with a ferocious 20 yard shot, then Mike Stowell has to brilliantly save another fine effort by Walsh as Charlton keep up the early pressure.

But Wolves gradually force their way into the game and two minutes from half time, Steve Bull powerfully heads the equaliser from a Gordon Cowans cross.

After the break Wolves step out with a changed line-up, substitute Jermaine Wright replacing Peter Shirtliff and the formation reverting to 4-4-2.

A short spell of pressure looks promising for the re-shaped visitors, but they are rocked on their heels when Walsh finishes off a 55th minute move to regain Charlton's lead.

And six minutes later poor defending allows Paul Mortimer to move forward from the centre circle to beat Stowell with a tremendous 18 yard shot.

For the third time in three away games, Wolves are facing a 3-1 deficit. True to form though, they mount a fightback which this time starts with Bull's 200th League goal for the club.

From a 67th minute Cowans corner, Bull sends a header in off the crossbar to set up the possibility of yet another miraculous escape.

Three minutes from time the escape route is invitingly clear for Wright as Charlton goalkeeper Mike Ammann drops the ball at his feet – only for the substitute to miss the glaring net from six yards.

Another 3-3 scoreline was perhaps too much to ask for, Taylor reckoning: "This was one mountain we couldn't climb." But the manager, not for the first time, is highly critical of his team's defending. "Giving away silly goals is costing us dear", he says. "Our defending has been naive all season."

Middlesbrough's point at bottom club Notts County has stretched their lead at the top, while sixth-placed Reading's home draw with Port Vale has put them just two points behind Wolves. Suddenly, there is a question mark against Wolves' finishing in the play-offs, let alone clinching automatic promotion.

But the experienced Cowans, despite his disappointment of the moment, sums up the resolve of the players."We can still make it through to the play-offs", he says, "and every one of us is absolutely determined to do it."

MATCH 55 • ENDSLEIGH LEAGUE DIVISION 1

Monday 17th April 1995 • Molineux • 3.00pm

WOLVES 2 OLDHAM ATHLETIC 1

Half-time 1-1 • Attendance 25,840

Referee Clive WILKES (Gloucester)

Linesmen R.M. DAVIS and M.A. WILLIAMS

Gold Shirts with Black Trim, Black Shorts	Goals	Blues Shirts with Red and White Trim, White Shorts	Goals
1 Mike STOWELL		1 Paul GERRARD	
2 Dean RICHARDS		2 Ian SNODIN ❏	
3 Mark VENUS		3 Neil POINTON ‡	
4 Mark RANKINE ❏		4 Nick HENRY	
5 Brian LAW		5 Simon WEBSTER	
6 Peter SHIRTLIFF		6 Steve REDMOND	
7 Don GOODMAN		7 Gunnar HALLE	
8 David KELLY	33, 82	8 Paul BERNARD ❏	37
9 Steve BULL		9 Sean McCARTHY	
10 Gordon COWANS		10 Andy RITCHIE †	
11 Robbie DENNISON		11 Mark BRENNAN	
Substitutes		*Substitutes*	
12 Paul BLADES		12 Richard GRAHAM †73	
14 Jermaine WRIGHT		14 Nicky BANGER ‡78	
gk Paul JONES		gk Jon HALLWORTH	

BEFORE	P	W	D	L	F	A	pts	AFTER	P	W	D	L	F	A	pts
4 Wolves	41	20	9	12	70	55	69	4 Wolves	42	21	9	12	72	56	72
13 Oldham	41	15	11	15	54	54	56	13 Oldham	42	15	11	16	55	56	56

FACTFILE

Revenge win a must... defensive deficiencies still in evidence despite shake-up... Dean Richards in the thick of the action... two-goal Kelly passes the 20-mark... play-offs a safe bet after first win in five matches – but title still on, claims Kelly, as Middlesbrough slip up.

The Wolves Review 1995

GOOD WIN CLOSES GAP AT THE TOP

Disputed goal beats Latics

With no wins and only three points from their last four games, Wolves need an Easter Monday revenge victory over Oldham to put some space between themselves and the teams chasing them for a promotion play-off place.

Memories are still painfully fresh of Boxing Day's 4-1 pounding at Boundary Park – a reversal of that scoreline would certainly boost Wolves' Premiership prospects!

After conceding six goals in the last two matches, the defence gets a shake-up in formation and personnel. Saturday's half-time switch from 5-3-2 to 4-4-2 is repeated from the start this afternoon, Dean Richards moving out of the centre to occupy the right back position.

Mark Rankine is pushed forward to make the extra man in midfield, where Robbie Dennison returns to the wide-left berth while Mark Venus drops into the back four in place of left back Jamie Smith.

The new-look side makes a bright start, though after Steve Bull has gone close with an early effort David Kelly shoots wastefully wide from an excellent opportunity created by Richards.

Richards almost opens the scoring himself when he heads goalwards from a Dennison free-kick, but Neil Pointon is on the line to clear.

Wolves' defensive deficiencies, exposed so ruthlessly in the last couple of matches, are in evidence once more as Sean McCarthy frees Gunnar Halle for a shot which the Norwegian puts wide.

Then McCarthy, again given too much room, smacks in a shot which deflects off Brian Law's chest onto the post but, luckily, falls for Mike Stowell to collect.

The let-off acts as a spur as well as a warning for Wolves, who push forward to take the lead in the 33rd minute. Richards is once more the provider and Kelly, latching on to a Dennison knock-down from the full back's cross, makes amends for his earlier miss by scoring from six yards.

But within four minutes the visitors are level, McCarthy again splitting the defence and Paul Bernard striking a good cross-shot into the far corner.

If play-off hopes are beginning to fade away at this point, they are revived after half-time as Wolves get well on top. In one spell of intense pressure Kelly, Goodman and Bull all go desperately close to regaining the lead.

Anxious fans have to wait until eight minutes from time for the deserved winner – and when it does arrive it is in controversial circumstances.

When a half-cleared Gordon Cowans corner lands back in the danger area, Kelly volleys in a goal which is allowed to stand despite Oldham protests that Richards had impeded goalkeeper Paul Gerrard.

The visitors are still complaining as the final whistle blows, but a delighted Kelly celebrates his 20th and 21st goals of the season by claiming: "We can still win automatic promotion – if we win our last four games I'm confident we will be champions."

That's a tall order, though Middlesbrough's failure to beat Sheffield United this afternoon has seen Wolves close the gap on the leaders to five points with a game in hand.

The play-offs are still the more realistic target, however, and that has come closer to fruition thanks to Grimsby beating Barnsley. It has left the Yorkshire side one place outside the play-off positions but five points behind Wolves – and that means Graham Taylor's team now looks a safe bet to finish in the top five.

The Wolves Review 1995

MATCH 56 • ENDSLEIGH LEAGUE DIVISION 1

Saturday 22nd April 1995 • Bramall Lane • 3.00pm

SHEFFIELD UNITED 3 WOLVES 3

Half-time 1-0 • Attendance 16,714

Referee Neale BARRY (Scunthorpe)
Linesmen B. BELLO and E. TAYLOR

Red and White Striped Shirts with Black Trim, Black Shorts	Goals	Gold Shirts with Black Trim, Gold Shorts	Goals
1 Alan KELLY		1 Mike STOWELL	
2 Paul BEESLEY		2 Paul BLADES †	
3 Roger NILSEN		3 Mark VENUS	
4 Dane WHITEHOUSE † 16pen		4 Mark RANKINE	
5 David TUTTLE ❏		5 Dean RICHARDS	
6 Mark FORAN	73	6 Peter SHIRTLIFF	
7 Paul ROGERS		7 Don GOODMAN ❏	58
8 Carl VEART ‡		8 David KELLY	83
9 Andy SCOTT		9 Steve BULL	65
10 Glyn HODGES ❏		10 Gordon COWANS	
11 Nathan BLAKE		11 Robbie DENNISON	
Substitutes		*Substitutes*	
12 Jostein FLO ‡73	90	12 Andy THOMPSON †79	
14 Kingsley BLACK †52		14 Jermaine WRIGHT	
gk Simon TRACEY		gk Paul JONES	

BEFORE	P	W	D	L	F	A	pts	AFTER	P	W	D	L	F	A	pts
5 Wolves	42	21	9	12	72	56	72	4 Wolves	43	21	10	12	75	59	73
8 Sheffield Utd	43	16	16	11	67	49	64	8 Sheffield Utd	44	16	17	11	70	52	65

FACTFILE

Topsy-turvy promotion race, Tranmere and Bolton lose, Reading move up... Wolves on top after slow start... powerful attacking sets up victory chance... Yet another 3-3 draw... Wolves anger at injury-time equaliser... Spitting incident outrages Taylor – fan will be banned promises Bassett.

LAST MINUTE DRAMA INFURIATES PLAYERS

Another high scoring draw

The first division promotion race is continuing in topsy-turvy style as Wolves travel to Bramall Lane. Last night third placed Tranmere lost to lowly Southend, while second-in-the-table Bolton were beaten at Reading – whose win leapfrogged them over Wolves into fourth place.

With leaders Middlesbrough facing a tough match at Barnsley this afternoon, a win for Wolves would not only take them up to second position but also leave them perfectly placed to take advantage of any late slips by Boro.

Having seen his team somehow conjure up two late-late goals to draw 2-2 with United at Molineux in January, Graham Taylor is hoping for a less stressful afternoon in Sheffield as he sends out a slightly changed side from Monday's victory over Oldham.

With central defender Brian Law suspended, Taylor has moved Dean Richards into the middle and brought in Paul Blades to fill the right back spot. Andy Thompson, recovered from his ankle injury, is on the substitutes' bench.

A combative afternoon is signalled when United full back Dave Tuttle scythes down Robbie Dennison and is booked, then when scuffles break out between Nathan Blake and Peter Shirtliff – then between Mark Rankine and Paul Rogers.

In the circumstances it is no surprise when United's 16th minute opening goal comes from a penalty, conceded by Mark Venus and converted by Dane Whitehouse.

The signs do not look good for Wolves, who lost each of their previous three visits to Bramall Lane. But a determined effort brings them into the game and, by half time, they are well on top.

Midway through the second period, victory is on the cards following Don Goodman's half-hit equaliser from a Dean Richards cross and Steve Bull's vollied goal courtesy a Richards-Mark Rankine build-up.

Though the Blades draw level through Mark Foran's header from a 73rd minute corner, Wolves – attacking now with tremendous power – regain the advantage when David Kelly finishes a five man move with a stooping header seven minutes from time.

Kelly's 22nd goal of the season sets the visiting fans off on a roll of victory chants which continue until deep into injury time. But the jubilation is ended when substitute Jostein Flo heads in a dramatic equaliser, the goal leading to referee Neale Barry being surrounded by Wolves players angrily protesting that too much injury time has been played.

It is an ugly scene, but far worse follows as Graham Taylor ushers his bitterly frustrated players off the pitch when the final whistle confirms the loss of two vital points.

As the Wolves contingent enters the players' tunnel, Dean Richards and Taylor are spat on by spectators. The Wolves manager, totally incensed, wades into the crowd but is unable to apprehend the foul-mouthed United fan.

"I tried to make what you might call a citizen's arrest", says Taylor. "The phlegm was running down my face, but when I asked a steward if he was going to do anything about it he didn't appear to want to know.

"So I went in and grabbed the fellow, but he was surrounded by his mates and broke away." The so-called supporter is apparently ejected by stewards, but not handed over to the police.

However, United boss Dave Bassett confirms: "We know who he is, he's been identified – we've got him bang to rights. The scumbag will be banned from United games for the rest of his life."

Sadly but inevitably, the unsavoury incident has overshadowed another cliff-hanging Wolves encounter in a season of never-ending high drama.

MATCH 57 • ENDSLEIGH LEAGUE DIVISION 1

Saturday 29th April 1995 • Blundell Park • 3.00pm

GRIMSBY TOWN 0 WOLVES 0

Half-time 0-0 • Attendance 10,112

Referee Richard POULAIN (Huddersfield)

Linesmen D.S. BABSKI and M. CARRINGTON

Black and White Striped Shirts, Black Shorts	Goals	Gold Shirts with Black Trim, Gold Shorts	Goals
1 Jason PEARCEY		1 Mike STOWELL	
2 Brian LAWS †		2 Andy THOMPSON	
3 Kevin JOBLING		3 Mark VENUS	
4 Mark LEVER ■		4 Mark RANKINE	
5 Graham RODGER		5 Dean RICHARDS	
6 Paul GROVES		6 Peter SHIRTLIFF	
7 Gary CROFT		7 Don GOODMAN	
8 Jim DOBBIN ❑		8 David KELLY	
9 Neil WOODS		9 Steve BULL	
10 Steve LIVINGSTONE		10 Gordon COWANS	
11 Dave GILBERT		11 Robbie DENNISON	
Substitutes		*Substitutes*	
12 Gary CHILDS †74		12 Paul BLADES	
14 Jamie FORRESTER		14 Jermaine WRIGHT	
gk Paul CRICHTON		gk Paul JONES	

BEFORE	P	W	D	L	F	A	pts	AFTER	P	W	D	L	F	A	pts
5 Wolves	43	21	10	12	75	59	73	4 Wolves	44	21	11	12	75	59	74
9 Grimsby	44	17	13	14	61	53	64	9 Grimsby	45	17	14	14	61	53	65

FACTFILE

Spit sensation still in the headlines, Mr Taylor presses charges... Dean Richards and Steve Bull OK, Thompson back... slender title hopes hang on a thread... rookie keeper denies Wolves – so does a linesman!... Lever off for professional foul... automatic promotion – the final goodbye?

CHAMPIONSHIP HOPES DASHED

Rookie keeper halts Wolves

Despite Wolves building up to a critical match at Blundell Park, it has been the Bramall Lane spitting incident which has dominated the week's headlines.

On Monday Graham Taylor was interviewed by South Yorkshire Police about pressing charges, while the FA announced they would be mounting their own inquiry.

On Wednesday a man was arrested in connection with the incident after he had walked into a Sheffield police station and been interviewed. He is due to appear in court next week.

When the media's attention was fully refocussed on the playing side of Wolves' affairs, the good news was reported that injury victims Dean Richards and Steve Bull would both be fit to face Grimsby.

Richards had recovered from an ankle injury which, sadly, cost him his first international call-up when he had to be withdrawn from the England Under-21 party for Tuesday's game in Latvia.

Bull missed training early in the week due to a knee problem, but he was fully fit by the time the players made their Friday journey to the East coast.

That meant there were no last minute problems for manager Taylor, who this afternoon has made just one change from last week's team. Andy Thompson, a substitute at Bramall Lane after recovering from an ankle injury, has been brought back into the starting line-up in place of Paul Blades.

Wolves go into the match knowing their slender hopes of winning the title will disappear completely if they fail to beat Grimsby, then Middlesbrough win their Sunday game at home to Luton.

But beating the Mariners looks well with the visitors' capabilities as they take control of the first half. Though Steve Livingstone fires an early 18 yard effort narrowly wide of Mike Stowell's goal, the Wolves keeper spends most of the first period admiring the work of his opposite number Jason Pearcey.

The 23 year old rookie, a £10,000 signing from Mansfield in December, is making his home debut and only his second senior appearance.

But there is no sign of nerves as first he dives to palm away Don Goodman's 28th minute header, then changes direction to somehow keep out a deflected 36th minute shot by Mark Rankine.

The more Wolves throw at him the better Pearcey becomes, tipping aside Thompson's 40th minute piledriver then turning a David Kelly shot over the bar seconds before half-time.

Grimsby come more into game after the interval and almost take the lead after a Stowell slip in the 66th minute. The keeper's mistake leads to a Neil Woods lob for goal, but Richards clears from in front of the empty net.

Four minutes later a linesman denies Wolves the lead. A Kelly shot is blocked by Pearcey, Goodman follows up to put the ball in the net – but the flag goes up for offside against Bull.

It looks a dubious decision, but it stands – and almost takes on greater ramifications in Grimsby's next attack, when Woods breaks clear but Stowell does well to block the striker's shot.

Five minutes from time Grimsby defender Mark Lever is sent off for a professional foul on Rankine, who was bursting through for a shot at goal.

But Wolves are unable to take advantage of the free kick or of their extra man in the final few minutes. They have to settle instead for a fourth draw in their last five away matches.

It means they can almost certainly kiss a final goodbye to automatic promotion – but one win from their last two matches will assure them of a play-off place.

MATCH 58 • ENDSLEIGH LEAGUE DIVISION 1

Wednesday 3rd May 1995 • Prenton Park • 7.30pm

TRANMERE ROVERS 1   WOLVES 1

Half-time 1-0 • Atendance 12,306

Referee John LLOYD (Wrexham)

Linesmen A.S. BRECKELL and G. EDGELEY

White Shirts with Green and Blue Trim, White Shorts — Goals

1	Eric NIXON	
2	Gary STEVENS	
3	Tony THOMAS	
4	John McGREAL	
5	Shaun GARNETT	
6	Liam O'BRIEN	
7	Ged BRANNAN	
8	John ALDRIDGE	34
9	Chris MALKIN	
10	Kenny IRONS	
11	Pat NEVIN	

Substitutes

12	Gary JONES
14	Jon KENWORTHY
gk	Danny COYNE

Gold Shirts with Black Trim, Black Shorts — Goals

1	Mike STOWELL	
2	Andy THOMPSON	
3	Mark VENUS	
4	Mark RANKINE	
5	DEAN RICHARDS	
6	Peter SHIRTLIFF	
7	Don GOODMAN	
8	David KELLY	
9	Steve BULL	73
10	Gordon COWANS	
11	Robbie DENNISON	

Substitutes

12	Paul BLADES
14	Jermaine WRIGHT
gk	Paul JONES

BEFORE	P	W	D	L	F	A	pts
4 Wolves	44	21	11	12	75	59	74
5 Tranmere	44	22	8	14	65	56	74

AFTER	P	W	D	L	F	A	pts
4 Wolves	45	21	12	12	76	60	75
5 Tranmere	45	22	9	14	66	57	75

FACTFILE

Middlesbrough set for championship... play-offs one point away for Wolves... promotion still on, insists Taylor... spit verdict "a joke"... Aldo opener fires Wolves... Bully's 250th goal clinches play-off spot... goal hero's promotion promise.

The Wolves Review 1995

GOOD PERFORMANCE ENSURES PLAY-OFF PLACE

Bully's 250th goal for Wolves

The fluctuations of the promotion race have left Wolves needing only a draw from tonight's match at Prenton Park to clinch a place in the play-offs.

Middlesbrough beat Luton on Sunday and are set to go up as champions. But when Barnsley could only draw with Oldham last night, it eased the pressure on both Wolves and Tranmere.

A point this evening will almost certainly ensure Rovers a place in the play-offs. With just one game left for everyone it would leave them, like Wolves, on 75 points – three ahead of Barnsley, whose goals-for column lags three behind the Prenton Park outfit and an unbreechable 13 behind Wolves.

Though Tranmere have home advantage this evening, Wolves are in the more buoyant mood. While the desired results have not been forthcoming of late, Graham Taylor's men have been playing well. But Rovers have had a poor run, culminating in Sunday's 5-1 trouncing by Albion.

As manager Taylor prepares to send out an unchanged team from Saturday's goalless draw at Grimsby, he has mixed feelings about the impending climax to a volatile season for Wolves. "Despite all our problems, we still had enough about us to have gone up as champions", he says. "So I'm very disappointed about not making that automatic promotion place. But if we approach our final games positively, we can still go up via the play-offs."

Taylor heard yesterday that Robert Hollister, the Sheffield United fan who spat in his face at Bramall Lane, had been fined £50 and banned from the Blades' ground for 12 months.

The punishment, handed out by Sheffield magistrates, was thought by many to be far too lenient – indeed the League Managers Association described it as "a joke". But Taylor's thoughts are trained on Prenton Park, not Bramall Lane, as his team sets out to keep alive their promotion dream.

The match starts with a near disaster, John Aldridge intercepting a weak back-header by Dean Richards but the Eire striker putting his shot over the bar.

The mistake is quickly forgotten by Richards, the on-loan Bradford defender recovering to have a fine match. The team in general is looking a little edgy, but Wolves gradually get on top.

When half-chances arrive, Don Goodman heads against the woodwork from an Andy Thompson throw and Steve Bull goes close with a couple of snap shots.

But the opening goal comes at the other end, Aldridge finding space to head in a 34th minute cross from Kenny Irons. That simply fires Wolves to even greater efforts in the second half, however.

Mark Venus, Robbie Dennison, Don Goodman and David Kelly all have efforts well saved by Eric Nixon before Steve Bull grabs a well deserved 73rd minute equaliser from Peter Shirtliff's deflected pass.

Coolly taking the ball on his thigh just inside the penalty area, Bull bends his shot round Nixon and into the far corner for his 18th goal of the season – and his 250th for Wolves.

Though both sides go close to winning the game in the last five minutes – Goodman and Kelly for Wolves, Liam O'Brien for Tranmere – it is fitting that Bull's milestone goal should earn the point that gives Wolves their promotion chance through the play-offs.

"For Steve to do that was just perfect", says Taylor. "If he can go on now to get the winner in the play-off final at Wembley, it would be absolutely ideal."

Bully will drink to that! Playing for Wolves in the top flight is the one ambition which has so far eluded him – but not for much longer, he reckons. "I'm sure we'll get promotion", he says.

"It's time I was making my mark in the Premiership, and we'll be with the big boys next year – our marvellous fans can take my word for that."

The Wolves Review 1995   *121*

MATCH 59 • ENDSLEIGH LEAGUE DIVISION 1

Sunday 7th May 1995 • Molineux • 3.00pm

WOLVES 1   SWINDON TOWN 1

Half-time 1-1 • Attendance 26,245

Referee John WATSON (Whitley Bay)
Linesmen R. INGHAM and K. THOMPSON

Gold Shirts with Black Trim, Black Shorts	Goals	Red Shirts with White Trim, White Shorts	Goals
1 Mike STOWELL		1 Fraser DIGBY	
2 Andy THOMPSON	36pen	2 Wayne O'SULLIVAN	
3 Mark VENUS		3 Kevin HORLOCK ■	
4 Mark RANKINE		4 Mark ROBINSON	
5 Dean RICHARDS		5 Luc NIJHOLT ❑	
6 Peter SHIRTLIFF		6 Shaun TAYLOR	
7 Don GOODMAN		7 Jamie PITMAN †	
8 David KELLY ❑		8 Ben WORRALL ❑	
9 Steve BULL		9 Peter THORNE	39
10 Gordon COWANS		10 Chris HAMON ‡	
11 Robbie DENNISON †		11 Joey BEAUCHAMP	
Substitutes		*Substitutes*	
12 Brian LAW		12 Martin LING †76	
14 Jermaine WRIGHT †46		14 Eddie MURRAY ‡76	
gk Paul JONES		gk Nicky HAMMOND	

BEFORE	P	W	D	L	F	A	pts	AFTER	P	W	D	L	F	A	pts
4 Wolves	45	21	12	12	76	60	75	4 Wolves	46	21	13	12	77	61	76
21 Swindon	45	12	11	22	53	72	47	21 Swindon	46	12	12	22	54	73	48

FACTFILE

Play-off conundrum to be settled... red card for Horlock's hand-ball offence... a perfect nine for Thommo... second half chances go begging... fouth successive draw... fourth place finish... it's Bolton in the play-off semi-final, with the first leg at Molineux.

The Wolves Review 1995

GOAL-SHY WOLVES DROP POINTS

Ten-man Robins hold out

A televised last match of the League season will have no bearing on the promotion or relegation issues. Swindon, just 12 months after dropping out of the Premiership, are already doomed to a second successive relegation.

Wolves' play-off place is assured, though today's result will have a bearing on who they meet in the two-leg semi-final. It will also determine whether they play their first leg at home or away.

If they finish second or third behind champions Middlesbrough, they will have the benefit of playing the second leg at Molineux. They must beat Swindon, however, then hope that one of the two teams currently above them – Bolton and Reading – fail to win this afternoon.

Wolves are once more unchanged and start promisingly against a young Swindon side. After Gordon Cowans, David Kelly and Steve Bull have all produced early goal attempts, Bull is denied a 25th minute opener when Fraser Digby dives to save his 20-yard shot.

But Wolves take the lead 11 minutes later, with Swindon having a player sent off in the same incident. Kelly's shot from a Mark Venus cross is goalbound but hand-balled away by left back Kevin Horlock, who is immediately shown the red card by refree John Watson.

Wolves have a one-man advantage – and seconds later they have a one goal advantage too, Andy Thompson stepping up to score his ninth League penalty of the season from nine attempts.

Any thoughts that Wolves might now stroll to a comfortable victory are rudely interrupted within three minutes of Thompson's spot-kick. Chris Hamon crosses from the Swindon left and Peter Thorne heads in the equaliser.

Don Goodman and Kelly both have goalbound efforts cleared as Wolves try to quickly regain the lead, but two minutes after the interval they are lucky not to go behind.

A defensive mix-up between Mark Venus, Peter Shirtliff and Dean Richards gives Thorne the chance to advance into the penalty area and hammer a drive which Mike Stowell brilliantly tips over the bar.

The scare over, Wolves settle down to run 10-man Swindon ragged. But although any number of scoring opportunities are created, they just cannot find the net.

Bull has a 20 yard drive saved by Digby then, in the 66th minute, sees a header from Goodman's cross unluckily strike the bar. Two minutes later Kelly has a 12 yard shot stopped by Digby, then Wolves' top scorer shoots hopelessly wide from a good position.

Bull goes close again with a well struck shot, but in the 84th minute he balloons a far post volley yards over the bar. And when Kelly gets a good header on target three minutes from time, the outstanding Digby pushes the ball over the top to ensure the game will end in stalemate.

It is Wolves' fourth successive draw in the run-in to the end of their League campaign. Performances have been good, but the goals have dried up – only two have been scored in the final three games, following a goal-count of 10 in the previous four outings.

The draw also means Wolves have finished fourth in the table and will meet Bolton in the play-off semi-final. Like Wolves, Bolton could only draw 1-1 at home to a relegated side, Burnley, this afternoon.

But Bolton's third place finish means the first leg will take place at Molineux. Wolves would have preferred it the other way round, but Graham Taylor says:"You have got to take what's given you. We've played well away from home recently, so we shouldn't be afraid of going to Bolton for the second leg."

The Wolves Review 1995

MATCH 60 • ENDSLEIGH LEAGUE DIVISION 1 PLAY-OFF SEMI-FINAL, 1ST LEG

Sunday 14th May 1995 • Molineux • 3.00pm

WOLVES 2 BOLTON WANDERERS 1

Half-time 1-0 • Attendance 26,153
Referee Clive Wilkes (Gloucester)
Linesmen M. CARRINGTON and K.J. HAWKES

Gold Shirts with Black Trim, Black Shorts	Goals	White Shirts with Black Trim, White Shorts	Goals
1 Mike STOWELL		1 Peter SHILTON	
2 Andy THOMPSON		2 Scott GREEN	
3 Mark VENUS	51	3 Jimmy PHILLIPS ❑	
4 Mark RANKINE		4 Jason McATEER	46
5 Dean RICHARDS		5 Gudni BERGSSON	
6 Peter SHIRTLIFF		6 Alan STUBBS	
7 Don GOODMAN		7 Neil McDONALD ■	
8 David KELLY		8 John DREYER	
9 Steve BULL	44	9 Mixu PAATELAINEN	
10 Gordon COWANS		10 John McGINLAY †	
11 Robbie DENNISON		11 Alan THOMPSON	
Substitutes		*Substitutes*	
12 Brian LAW		12 David LEE	
14 Jermaine WRIGHT		14 Owen COYLE †71	
gk Paul JONES		gk Aidan DAVISON	

FACTFILE

Promotion depending on cup-tie football... Taylor rallying call... Bolton favourites... veteran Shilton – 997 today!... opponent sent off in second successive game... Wolves on the rampage, inspired performance deserves more... will slender lead be enough for the second leg?

Graham Taylor – happy to have a first-leg lead

The Wolves Review 1995

SCORELINE FLATTERS BOLTON

Strikers fail to capitalise

After nine months of slogging for League points, Wolves must turn to the Cup-tie format and atmosphere of the play-offs as their route to the Premiership.

"It's brilliant for the fans but brutal for the players", says the experienced Gordon Cowans, who has battled through to Wembley play-off finals with both Blackburn (won) and Derby (lost).

As Cowans and Co prepare to meet Bolton in the first leg of the semi-final, Graham Taylor calls for one last concerted effort to achieve Wolves' aim of getting back into the top flight for the first time in 11 years.

"We need a steady nerve, a disciplined approach and a thoroughly professional attitude", says the manager. "It's cup football and a bit of a lottery in some ways, but we've got to live with that."

Cup specialists Bolton are generally acknowledged as favourites, particularly after this season's Coca-Cola Cup run which took them to Wembley via a two-leg semi-final. They can also look back on a 5-1 home win against Wolves in February, though at Molineux in October Taylor's team won 3-1.

This afternoon unchanged Wolves are looking for a win to at least equal their autumn home success against a Bolton side which today shows a notable goalkeeping switch.

With Keith Branagan injured, recent signing Peter Shilton is brought in for his first League appearance in 19 months – but, staggeringly, the 997th senior outing of the 45-year-old former England keeper's glittering playing career.

And with Bolton adopting a cautious approach aimed at away-leg damage limitation, all of Shilton's guile is needed as Wolves attack from the start.

The keeper expertly turns aside a sixth minute David Kelly shot, but he can do nothing as Steve Bull and Mark Rankine narrowly miss the target, or when Don Goodman's 18th minute header glances off the angle of post and crossbar.

An excellent diving stop keeps out a 15 yard Bull shot, but – after Alan Thompson has had a breakaway drive blocked by Mike Stowell at the other end – Shilton is finally beaten when Bull powers in a near post header from Robbie Dennison's 44th minute cross.

Wolves' joy at their opener lasts only until the first minute of the second half, when the unmarked Jason McAteer mis-hits a 20 yard shot – straight into the top corner of Stowell's net!

It is a cruel equaliser, but the Wolves fans are soon cheering again as Goodman climbs high to head Cowans' 51st minute corner back across goal for Mark Venus to glance home a well-timed header.

A third goal agonisingly fails to materialise in the 78th minute, when Goodman bangs in a superb 20 yard shot which rattles against the bar.

The game reaches boiling point a minute later as Bolton midfielder Neil McDonald, already booked for a first half foul on Rankine, is sent off for bundling over the same player.

But the controversial incident does not distract Wolves from their sole objective – bagging further goals which could prove crucial in the second leg.

Bull has a looping header cleared off the line by Gudni Bergsson, then two minutes from time Cowans hits a 30 yard drive which the diving Shilton just manages to touch round the post.

The final, narrow 2-1 scoreline is no justice to Wolves' superiority. But boss Taylor insists: "I'm happy to be taking any kind of lead into the second leg."

And striker Goodman, so unlucky not to get on the scoresheet, says: "Bolton didn't deserve what they got away with, but that should make us all the more determined to finish the job at Burnden Park – we are 2-1 up and 90 minutes from Wembley."

MATCH 61 • ENDSLEIGH LEAGUE DIVISION 1 PLAY-OFF SEMI-FINAL, 2ND LEG

Wednesday 17th May 1995 • Burnden Park • 7.30pm

BOLTON WANDERERS 2   WOLVES 0

(aet – 90 minutes, 1-0). Aggregate score 3-2 • Half-time 1-0 • Attendance 20,041

Referee Steve DUNN (Bristol)
Linesmen M.J. DOUGLAS and P. DOWD

White Shirts with Black Trim, Black Shorts	Goals	Gold Shirts with Black Trim, Gold Shorts	Goals
1 Keith BRANAGAN		1 Mike STOWELL	
2 Scott GREEN		2 Andy THOMPSON	
3 Jimmy PHILLIPS		3 Mark VENUS	
4 Jason McATEER		4 Mark RANKINE ❑	
5 Gudni BERGSSON		5 Dean RICHARDS ❑	
6 Alan STUBBS ‡		6 Peter SHIRTLIFF	
7 David LEE †		7 Don GOODMAN	
8 Owen COYLE		8 David KELLY ❑	
9 Mixu PAATELAINEN		9 Steve BULL	
10 John McGINLAY ❑	44, 109	10 Gordon COWANS	
11 Alan THOMPSON		11 Robbie DENNISON †	
Substitutes		*Substitutes*	
12 Fabian deFREITAS †60		12 Brian LAW	
14 John DREYER ‡70		14 Jermaine WRIGHT †100	
gk Peter SHILTON		gk Paul JONES	

FACTFILE

Emotional night in store... Wolves fans at Burnden – and Molineux... final permutations... Bolton dominate following Bull miss... two-goal John McGinlay the Bolton hero after narrowly escaping a red card... We're not going to Wembley – it's another season in Division One for Wolves.

David Kelly – floored by John McGinlay, which earned the Bolton striker only a yellow card

126   *The Wolves Review 1995*

EXTRA TIME DRAMA HARD ON WOLVES

Time to start planning ahead

A tense and emotional evening is in store as 4,000 Wolves supporters make their way up the M6 for the play-off semi-final second leg.

While Burnden Park will be packed with its first 20,000 crowd of the season, Molineux will house a further 8,000 Wolves fans watching the game on the giant video wall or closed-circuit TV.

Unless Wolves are beaten by two clear goals they are in the Wembley final. But if they lose by one goal, the game will go into extra time. If the scores are still level at that stage, away goals will count double. The final permutation is if Bolton are winning 2-1 after extra time, leaving the aggregate score at 3-3, then it's all down to a penalty shoot-out. There's drama in store!

Wolves are unchanged for the fifth game in succession – easily the season's longest sequence in which the same line-up has figured.

Bolton bring goalkeeper Keith Branagan back as Peter Shilton suffered a groin injury on Sunday, while midfielder Neil McDonald is suspended following his sending off at Molineux.

Bruce Rioch's team also switch their formation, from a negatively applied 5-3-2 to an attacking 4-4-2. But that will make little difference to Wolves' tactics. "We won't set out to defend because we can't defend", Graham Taylor has noted wryly before the game.

But Mark Rankine, a recent revelation in midfield, does his best to prove the manager wrong by clearing a 10th minute Mixu Paatelainen header off the line.

Four minutes later Steve Bull misses a fine chance, dragging his shot wide after Don Goodman has headed down Andy Thompson's free-kick. It would have been Bull's 20th goal of the season.

But the miss signals a long spell of Bolton pressure and a deserved goal just before half time, when Jason McAteer cleverly chips a pass over the defence for John McGinlay to lob the ball home.

Spurred on by a frenzied crowd, Bolton take even more of a grip after the break. Paatelainen has a 54th minute header hooked off the line by Peter Shirtliff, then nine minutes later McGinlay vollies narrowly wide.

Though Bull has a 65th minute shot blocked, Wolves rarely look like getting the goal they need as the game goes into extra time.

The flashpoint of the night arrives two minutes into added time, when a penalty area tusssle ends with McGinlay flooring David Kelly with a left hook. Amazingly McGinlay is allowed to stay on the field by referee Steve Dunn, who simply books both players.

With cruel predictability, McGinlay then delivers the killer blow by scoring from close range following a 109th minute mistake by the otherwise outstanding Shirtliff.

The game is up, the dream is over for a Wolves team who battle to the end but never threaten to come back. Supporters are in tears at the final whistle as Taylor leads his crestfallen players in a tribute to their followers.

"We probably only needed one goal, but I just couldn't see it coming", admits Taylor after congratulating Bolton on reaching the final. They will meet Reading, 3-1 aggregate winners against Tranmere in the other semi.

Tomorrow Taylor will start preparing for another season in Division One. But tonight the thoughts of the fans are summed up by chairman Jonathan Hayward, who with father Sir Jack has done so much to drag Wolves out of the doldrums and to the brink of the Premiership.

As he steps into his car for a long, sad drive home, he says: "There are more important things in life than football – it's just that right now, I can't think of any..."

The Wolves Review 1995

BILLY WRIGHT
6th February 1924 – 3rd September 1994

The announcement of Billy Wright's retirement in 1959 hit me like a thunderbolt. As a Wolves-mad schoolboy, the contemplation of our captain (England's too, by the way) hanging up his boots was beyond me. It would have shocked me less if the Queen had abdicated or, closer to my own world, if Roy Race had missed a last minute penalty to cost Melchester Rovers the championship.

When I heard of Billy's death last September I was similarly stunned, even though I knew he had been ill for some time. Like Billy Wright the player, you see, Billy Wright the man was somehow always going to be there.

Though he was never one of my big footballing heroes – Peter Broadbent headed that small and exclusive list – I knew that Billy was the greatest Wolves player of all time. But, strangely perhaps, that knowledge led not to idolatry but to an almost taking-for-granted of this most wonderful of footballers.

Oh, I could reel off the statistics – Billy Wright, captain of England 90 times, 105 caps in all; captain of three Wolves championship winning teams, plus the side which won the FA Cup in 1949; Footballer of the Year in 1951-52; an incredibly consistent performer – he missed only 31 Wolves games in nine seasons during the 1950's and, indisputably, was the rock on which the monumental success of the club's glory years was built.

But he was also part of the Molineux furniture – and didn't seem to mind one bit. As magnificent a player as he was, he never sought adulation and was always happy to be seen as part of the team.

Quite simply, he was a nice bloke. And that's how he stayed. I never got to know him until his final years, but I still – always will – value the too few moments I spent with him.

On the day Billy died there were countless tributes paid to him from all over the football world. But it was a few words from close to home which said it all for me.

Wolves president Sir Jack Hayward – on whose invitation Billy became a Wolves director in 1990 – said; "He was just a wonderful person, England's finest player and gentleman. We shall never see his like again."

Tony Leighton

PRE-SEASON TOUR MATCH

Tuesday 19th July 1994
Hvidovre Stadium • 7.00pm

HVIDOVRE 1 WOLVES 2

Half-time 0-2 • *Referee* Lars GERNER

Linesmen C. NORUP and A. HANSEN

Gold Shirts with Black Trim, Gold Shorts — Goals

1 Paul JONES §
2 Andy THOMPSON
3 Mark VENUS
4 Mark RANKINE †
5 Paul BLADES ‡‡
6 Peter SHIRTLIFF
7 Kevin KEEN #
8 Paul COOK ‡
9 Steve BULL ## — 40, 42
10 Lee MILLS ■
11 Steve FROGGATT ††

Substitutes

James SMITH †33 ■
Darren FERGUSON ‡33
Darren SIMKIN #46
Robbie DENNISON ††46
Neil EMBLEN ‡‡66
Tony DALEY ##66
gk Mike STOWELL §46

FACTFILE

Copenhagen first stop on pre-season Scandinavian tour... leading Danish team the hosts... new boys Tony Daley, Steve Froggatt and Neil Emblen on display... Hividovre goal scored by Michael Manniche (67 min).

PRE-SEASON TOUR MATCH

Wednesday 20th July 1994
Solvesborgs Idrottsplats • 7.00pm

SOLVE 1 WOLVES 6

Half-time 0-3

Referee Lars JONSSON

Blue Shirts with Black and Gold Trim, Blue Shorts — Goals

1	Mike STOWELL †	
2	Mark RANKINE ‡	
3	James SMITH	
4	Kevin KEEN #	
5	Paul BLADES	
6	Neil EMBLEN	
7	Robbie DENNISON	47, 75
8	Geoff THOMAS §	
9	Tony DALEY	11, 52
10	Lee MILLS	20
11	Steve FROGGATT ††	45

Substitutes

Mark VENUS ‡46
Chris MARSDEN #46
Paul COOK §46
Darren FERGUSON ††46
gk Paul JONES †46

FACTFILE

The long awaited comeback for Geoff Thomas... Tony Daley and Steve Froggatt net their first goals for Wolves... Robbie Dennison hits a double... Neil Emblen concedes penalty, but Swedish fourth division side hammered by a much superior Wolves side... Solve's goalscorer was Walton Ssen (71 pen).

PRE-SEASON TOUR MATCH

Saturday 23rd July 1994
Tingbyskans • 4.00pm

SMEDBY BOIK 0
WOLVES 9

Half-time 0-4

Referee Berne LUNDSTROM

Gold Shirts with Black Trim, Gold Shorts — Goals

1	Paul JONES	
2	Mark RANKINE †	
3	Andy THOMPSON	29
4	Darren FERGUSON	
5	Peter SHIRTLIFF	
6	Neil EMBLEN	
7	Kevin KEEN	
8	Geoff THOMAS	
9	Steve BULL	22, 51, 58, 67, 81
10	Lee MILLS	9, 42, 88
11	Paul COOK	

Substitutes

Darren SIMKIN †46
James SMITH
Tony DALEY
Paul BLADES
Robbie DENNISON
Mark VENUS
gk Mike STOWELL

FACTFILE

Sun shines, but goals rain on Swedish third division side... nap hand for Bully... Lee Mills' first Wolves hat-trick... subs in half-time kick-volleyball match – Wolves win 11-5... Thomas finishes first 90 minutes since late 1993.

The Wolves Review 1995

PRE-SEASON TOUR MATCH

Monday 25th July 1994

KRISTIANSTADS FF 0
WOLVES 2

Half-time 0-1 • Referee Gert JONSSON

Gold Shirts with Black Trim, Black Shorts — Goals

1	Mike STOWELL	
2	Darren SIMKIN ‡	
3	Andy THOMPSON	
4	Darren FERGUSON †	
5	Paul BLADES	
6	Mark VENUS	
7	Tony DALEY	75
8	Paul COOK	
9	Steve BULL	34
10	Lee MILLS #	
11	Robbie DENNISON	

Substitutes
Kevin KEEN †54
James SMITH ‡67
Mark RANKINE #73
Peter SHIRTLIFF
gk Paul JONES

FACTFILE: Steve Bull bags his eighth goal of the tour... explosive Tony Daley hits a cracker... Wolves are stretched but an impressive Swedish second division side fail to score past Mike Stowell and his men... an impressive cameo performance from young substitute Jamie Smith.

PRE-SEASON TOUR MATCH

Wednesday 27th July 1994
Asarums Idrottsplats

ASARUMS IF FK 1
WOLVES 3

Half-time 0-0

Gold Shirts with Black Trim, Black Shorts — Goals

1	Mike STOWELL	
2	James SMITH	
3	Andy THOMPSON	
4	Darren FERGUSON †	
5	Paul BLADES	
6	Peter SHIRTLIFF	
7	Kevin KEEN	
8	Geoff THOMAS	
9	Steve BULL	
10	Lee MILLS	65, 78, 81
11	Steve FROGGATT	

Substitutes
Darren SIMKIN
Robbie DENNISON †46
Mark RANKINE
Tony DALEY
gk Paul JONES

FACTFILE: Sweden's fourth division leaders prove stubborn opponents... Mills breaks them with 16 minute hat-trick – his second treble in five days... Andy Thompson and Steve Froggatt outstanding... successful tour ends with five straight wins, 22 goals scored and just three conceded... Asarums goal scored by Nilsson Johannes (89 min).

PRE-SEASON FRIENDLY MATCH

Wednesday 3rd August 1994 • Molineux • 7.45pm

WOLVES 1 MANCHESTER UNITED 2

Half-time 1-0 • Attendance 28,145
Referee Terry HOLBROOK (Wolverhampton)
Linesmen B. JEAVONS and M. WARREN

Gold Shirts with Black Trim, Black Shorts	Goals	Red Shirts with Black and White Trim, White Shorts	Goals
1 Mike STOWELL ‡		1 Peter SCHMEICHEL	
2 James SMITH #		2 David MAY	
3 Andy THOMPSON		3 Lee SHARPE †	
4 Darren FERGUSON §		4 Steve BRUCE ‡	
5 Paul BLADES	62 og	5 Keith GILLESPIE #	
6 Peter SHIRTLIFF		6 Gary PALLISTER	
7 Kevin KEEN		7 Eric CANTONA	
8 Geoff THOMAS ††		8 Paul INCE	53
9 Steve BULL	9	9 Brian McCLAIR	
10 Lee MILLS †		10 Mark HUGHES §	
11 Steve FROGGATT		11 Ryan GIGGS	
Substitutes		*Substitutes*	
12 Paul COOK §72		12 Nicky BUTT #65	
14 David KELLY †46		14 Dion DUBLIN §77	
15 Mark VENUS ††72		15 David BECKHAM	
16 Darren SIMKIN #72		16 Simon DAVIES ‡65	
gk Paul JONES ‡72		17 Graeme TOMLINSON	
		18 Chris CASPER †46	

FACTFILE *Record crowd for all-seater Molineux... club all-time record receipts of £228,000... rookie Smith takes on Giggs – and the boy Jamie does good... Steve Bull on target, but Reds hit back... sub David Kelly's first outing since Eire international duty at World Cup finals in USA.*

The Wolves Review 1995 131

PRE-SEASON FRIENDLY MATCH

Saturday 6th August 1994 • Molineux • 3.00pm

WOLVES 2 COVENTRY CITY 1

Half-time 1-1 • Attendance 8,171

Referee Terry HOLBROOK (Wolverhampton)
Linesmen M. FLETCHER and A. SHEFFIELD

Gold Shirts with Black Trim, Black Shorts	Goals	Sky Blue Shirts with White Trim, Sky Blue Shorts	Goals
1 Mike STOWELL		1 Steve OGRIZOVIC	
2 James SMITH		2 Brian BORROWS	
3 Andy THOMPSON		3 Steve MORGAN	
4 Darren FERGUSON ‡		4 Willie BOLAND †	
5 Paul BLADES		5 David BUSST	
6 Peter SHIRTLIFF		6 Phil BABB ‡	
7 Kevin KEEN		7 Sean FLYNN ††	
8 Geoff THOMAS #		8 Julian DARBY	
9 Steve BULL †	21	9 David RENNIE	
10 Lee MILLS		10 Mick QUINN #	43 pen
11 Steve FROGGATT		11 Leigh JENKINSON §	
Substitutes		*Substitutes*	
12 Paul COOK ‡63		12 John WILLIAMS §65	
14 David KELLY †22	50	14 Sandy ROBERTSON ††75	
15 Mark VENUS #73		15 Ally PICKERING	
16 Neil EMBLEN		16 Mick HARFORD #55	
gk Paul JONES		17 Paul WILLIAMS ‡46	
		18 Roy WEGERLE †46	
		gk Jonathan GOULD	

FACTFILE

Bully goal joy cut short through hamstring injury... Mick Quinn scores from the spot for the Sky Blues... but Kelly's eye for goal proves to be a winner... Premiership scalp for impressive Wolves.

PRE-SEASON FRIENDLY MATCH

Monday 8th August 1994 • Dens Park • 7.30pm

DUNDEE 1   WOLVES 4

Half-time 0-2 • Attendance 2,248

Referee M. POCOCK (Aberdeen)
Linesmen W. MILLER and J.C. LYON

Blue Shirts, White Shorts	Goals	Gold Shirts with Black Trim, Black Shorts	Goals
1 Michael PAGEAU		1 Paul JONES	
2 John McQUILLAN		2 Mark RANKINE	
3 Mike TEASDALE ‡		3 Andy THOMPSON	
4 Gary McKEOWN		4 Mark VENUS	
5 Noel BLAKE	19og	5 Neil EMBLEN	
6 Ray FARNINGHAM ❏ †		6 Peter SHIRTLIFF	
7 George SHAW		7 Kevin KEEN	
8 Dusan VRTO		8 Paul COOK	84
9 Morten WIEGHORST §		9 Lee MILLS ❏ †	
10 Gerry BRITTON #	58	10 David KELLY ❏ ‡	31
11 Neil McCANN		11 Steve FROGGATT	87
Substitutes		*Substitutes*	
Iain ANDERSON †46		Paul BLADES †46	
Craig TULLY ‡62 ❏		Geoff THOMAS ‡46	
Paul TOSH #70		Darren FERGUSON	
Alan DINNIE §78		gk Mike STOWELL	

FACTFILE

Last pre-season friendly brings Wolves best performance... own goal by ex-Birmingham City defender Noel Blake starts the ball rolling... goalkeeper Paul Jones in fine form... 'Ned' Kelly on target again... Paul Cook scores one, sets one up to complete emphatic victory.

The Wolves Review 1995

OPENING OF REYNOLDS STAND

Monday 10th October 1994 • Aggborough • 7.30pm

KIDDERMINSTER HARRIERS 2 WOLVES 2

Half-time 1-1 • Attendance 3,622

Referee Terry HOLBROOK (Wolverhampton)
Linesmen G.S. HASLEWOOD and S. CARTWRIGHT

Red and White Halved Shirts, Red Shorts	Goals	Gold Shirts with Black Trim, Black Shorts	Goals
1 Kevin ROSE †		1 Paul JONES †	
2 Simeon HODSON		2 Darren SIMKIN §§	
3 Jay POWELL ‡		3 Stuart GRAY ‡	
4 Mark YATES ††		4 Mark RANKINE	
5 Chris BRINDLEY		5 Peter SHIRTLIFF #	
6 Richard FORSYTH #		6 Tom BENNETT §	
7 Paul WEBB		7 Tony DALEY ††	
8 Paul GRAINGER		8 Darren FERGUSON ‡‡	
9 Delwyn HUMPHRIES		9 Steve BULL	9, 68
10 Paul DAVIES §	25, 62	10 Lee MILLS ##	
11 Lee HUGHES		11 Mark WALTERS	
Substitutes		*Substitutes*	
12 John DEAKIN ‡57		12 Jason BARNETT ‡46	
14 Mark DEARLOVE ††86		14 Paul BLADES #46	
15 Neil CARTWRIGHT #75		15 Chris WESTWOOD §46	
16 Les PALMER §84		16 Paul BIRCH ††46	
gk Darren STEADMAN †13		17 Chris MARSDEN ‡‡46	
		18 Scott VOICE ##46	
		19 Quentin TOWNSEND §§84	
		gk Mike STOWELL †46	

FACTFILE
Kidder open new Reynolds Stand... Daley outstanding in first Wolves appearance in England... Marsden also back from long injury lay-off... two goals apiece for Bull and Davies (over 500 goals between them for Wolves and Kidder).

The Wolves Review 1995

ARTHUR ROWLEY BENEFIT MATCH

Tuesday 9th May 1995 • Gay Meadow • 7.30pm

SHREWSBURY TOWN 1   WOLVES 3

Half-time 1-1 • *Attendance* 2,240

Referee Terry HOLBROOK (Wolverhampton)

Linesmen N. PRICE and T. DAVIES

Blue Shirts, Blue Shorts	Goals	Gold Shirts with Black Trim, Black Shorts	Goals
1 Tim CLARKE †		1 Paul JONES	
2 Darren SIMKIN ‡	44	2 James SMITH	
3 Chris WITHE		3 Andy THOMPSON †	
4 Paul EVANS		4 Mark RANKINE ‡	
5 Mark HUGHES ††		5 Chris WESTWOOD	
6 Kevin SEABURY		6 Brian LAW	
7 Roy WOODS		7 Paul BIRCH §	
8 Wayne CLARKE #		8 Don GOODMAN	47
9 Dean SPINK *		9 Steve BULL #	29
10 Richard SCOTT		10 Darren FERGUSON	
11 Ian REED §*		11 Robbie DENNISON	
Substitutes		*Substitutes*	
12 Mark WILLIAMS ††60		2 Dean RICHARDS	
14 Nathan KING #46		3 Mark VENUS §68	
15 Lee MARTIN ‡46		4 James KELLY ‡46	
16 Sean WRAY §46		6 Peter SHIRTLIFF	
gk Paul EDWARDS †46		7 Jason BARNETT †46	
		8 David KELLY #46	66
		10 Gordon COWANS	
		gk Mike STOWELL	

FACTFILE

Fund raising match in aid of Shrewsbury goalscoring legend Arthur Rowley... ex-Wanderer Darren Simkin bags equaliser... Bull, Goodman and Kelly wrap it up for Wolves... first team debuts for Chris Westwood and Jason Barnett.

* *Ian Reed returned as a substitute for Dean Spink after 60 minutes.*

The Wolves Review 1995   135

THE MANAGEMENT TEAM

Graham Taylor had no intention of retreating quietly into retirement when his three-and-a-half-year stint as England manager ended unhappily towards the end of 1993.

After his failure to guide the national team to the 1994 World Cup finals in America, he undertook a period of recuperation and self-analysis as he departed to the sunshine to gather his thoughts.

But he quickly returned to job-seek – and Wolves came calling in March of last year. It was an appointment that, at a stroke, lifted the Molineux profile by several notches.

Camera crews and reporters followed Taylor's every move back into the club environment he had handled so superbly at Lincoln City, Watford and Villa.

There was sniping from those opposition fans who were still amused by England-connected vegetable analogies propogated by the lower end of the tabloid market. But Taylor was ready for them and took it in good part.

There was even questioning from some quarters of his very right to manage again. In his first few months at Molineux he asked a dozen times or more: "Why are people surprised I've returned? Do they think I should have run away because I'm a former England manager?"

If others had forgotten, Taylor had still-fresh memories of how – in the space of three years – he had taken a "shambles" of a Villa team up by the bootlaces and guided them to the runners-up spot in the top flight.

He wanted to repeat that kind of achievement at another club of vast potential – and that has been his aim since he walked into Molineux six weeks before the end of last season.

His management has been bold, no-nonsense and attack-minded. His players may have had an edge of uncertainty about them at times, but they have found Molineux under Taylor a demanding and exhilarating place to work.

They have trained longer and harder than ever before, and they have become fitter for it. And despite the disappointment of their failure to win promotion through the play-offs, they have been a more successful Wolves team than any other since the club returned from the lower divisions six years ago.

In assembling his backroom team, Taylor brought a distinctive Villa Park feel to Molineux by recruiting several of his trusted former aides.

He quickly recruited **Bobby Downes** as assistant manager, handing the locally-born ex-Albion reserve player the joint duties of scouting, administration and coaching.

Downes, who was tempted down the M6 after helping John Rudge steer Port Vale to promotion into the First Division, has rarely been seen by the Molineux masses.

The dug-out place alongside Taylor on match-days belongs to first team coach **Steve Harrison**, who previously worked with Taylor at Watford, Villa and for England. On his appointment at Molineux, the wise-cracking coach quickly became the ideal buffer between manager and players.

While Harrison is a track-suited figure at the training ground, Downes is usually to be found at his desk. But for a spell he did take an increasing role in coaching the second string after yet another ex-Villa man, **Stuart Gray**, had departed his post as reserve team coach barely three months into the season.

Ian Miller, a quietly spoken Scot whose playing career took him to Blackburn Rovers and Port Vale among other clubs, was Taylor's choice as the replacement for Gray. And, following his appointment, the reserves' season took off in spectacular fashion.

Taylor made one other off-field personnel change, bringing in physiotherapist **Barry Holmes** who – due to the club's horrendous injury problems – had a hectic first season at Molineux.

While the manager also drastically revamped the scouting system, he was happy on the youth side of the club to retain two of the staff he had inherited from previous boss Graham Turner.

Proud Welshman **Chris Evans** is Molineux's volubly enthusiastic youth coach, while **Robert Kelly** – a former Wolves player whose career was ended by a back injury – is its dedicated youth development officer.

The Wolves Review 1995

TOM BENNETT

Born Falkirk
12th December 1969
Joined Wolves 5th July 1988 from Aston Villa, free transfer
Wolves' debut v Southend United, Lge (h), 5/11/88

Finished the 1992-93 season in possession of the number four shirt but, mainly through injury, Bennett was no more than a fringe member of the 1994-95 first team squad.

He started only four League games but also played in all three of the FA Cup ties against Premiership opponents.

Bennett's season was ended through a knee injury sustained in the sixth round Cup replay against Crystal Palace on March 22nd. He was transferred to Stockport County for £75,000 in early June.

Career Record:

Season	Club	League Apps Gls	Cups Apps Gls
87-88	Aston Villa	- -	- -
88-89	Wolves	-(2) -	-(1) -
89-90	Wolves	30 -	4 -
90-91	Wolves	24(2) -	3(1) -
91-92	Wolves	37(1) 2	5 -
92-93	Wolves	-(1) -	- -
93-94	Wolves	8(2) -	- -
94-95	Wolves	4(3) -	3(1) -
Wolves' Record		103(11) 2	15(3) -
TOTAL		103(11) 2	15(3) -

★ *Signed on a free transfer from Aston Villa when Graham Taylor was Villa manager.*

★ *Longest run of appearances (7) last season came after Taylor's arrival at Molineux.*

( ) indicates appearances as a used substitute.
Cup figures include FA Cup, League Cup, League Play-Offs, Full Members' Cup, Associate Members' Cup, Mercantile Credit Centenary Trophy, Screen Sport Super Cup, FA Charity Shield, European Champions' Cup, European Cup Winners' Cup, UEFA Cup, European Super Cup and World Club Championship.

The Wolves Review 1995

PAUL BIRCH

Born West Bromwich
20th November 1962
Joined Wolves 1st February 1991 from Aston Villa, £400,000
Wolves' debut v West Ham Utd, Lge (h) (scored in 2-1 win) 2/2/91

Though he seemed destined to spend the season as understudy to summer signing Tony Daley, Birch was a semi-regular during the first half of the season after his former Villa wing colleague suffered a long-term injury problem.

Birch made only one appearance after being injured against Sheffield Wednesday in the drawn FA Cup fourth round match at Hillsborough on January 30th.

He scored a fine goal against Nottingham Forest in the 3-2 Coca-Cola Cup defeat at Molineux on October 26th. Transfer-listed at the end of the season.

Career Record:

Season	Club	League Apps Gls	Cups Apps Gls
80-81	Aston Villa	- -	- -
81-82	Aston Villa	- -	- -
82-83	Aston Villa	- -	0(1) -
83-84	Aston Villa	22 2	4 -
84-85	Aston Villa	24(1) 3	4 -
85-86	Aston Villa	25(2) 2	11(1) 3
86-87	Aston Villa	26(3) 3	6(1) 1
87-88	Aston Villa	38 5	7 1
88-89	Aston Villa	6(6) -	- -
89-90	Aston Villa	6(6) -	3(3) 3
90-91	Aston Villa	6(2) -	4(5) -
90-91	Wolves	20 2	- -
91-92	Wolves	43(2) 8	5 2
92-93	Wolves	27(1) 3	4(1) 1
93-94	Wolves	25(7) 1	3 -
94-95	Wolves	8(2) 1	7(1) 1
Wolves' Record		123(12)15	19(2) 4
TOTAL		456(32)30	58(13)12

137

PAUL BLADES

Born Peterborough
5th January 1965
Joined Wolves 14th August 1992
from Norwich City, £325,000
Wolves' debut v Brentford
Lge (a) 15/8/92

Ended the season out of favour and on the transfer list after long spells in the centre of defence and at right back.

As a central defender, Blades was a virtual ever-present in the second half of the 1993-94 season and through the early stages of 1994-95. He lost his place, however, after the signings of John de Wolf and Brian Law in December.

But he then made 16 appearances in the number two shirt before making way for the Andy Thompson/Mark Venus full back pairing which played out the last five matches.

Career Record:

Season	Club	League Apps	Gls	Cups Apps	Gls
81-82	Derby Co	-	-	-	-
82-83	Derby Co	6	-	1	-
83-84	Derby Co	4	-	-	-
84-85	Derby Co	21 (1)	-	1 (1)	-
85-86	Derby Co	24 (6)	-	9 (2)	-
86-87	Derby Co	16	-	-	-
87-88	Derby Co	30 (1)	-	4 (1)	-
88-89	Derby Co	38	1	9	-
89-90	Derby Co	18 (1)	-	5 (1)	-
90-91	Norwich C	21	-	8	-
91-92	Norwich C	26	-	7	-
92-93	Wolves	38 (2)	1	2	-
93-94	Wolves	35	1	8	1
94-95	Wolves	30 (2)	-	-	-
Wolves' Record		103 (4)	2	10	1
TOTAL		307 (7)	3	54 (5)	1

★ *England Youth international.*

★ *Won a Division Two championship medal with Derby County in 1986-87.*

STEVE BULL

Born Tipton
28th March 1965
Joined Wolves 21st November 1986
from West Bromwich Albion, £65,000
Wolves' debut v Wrexham
Lge (h) 22/11/86

Knocked off his perch as leading scorer in 1994-95 for the first time in his eight years at Molineux. In an injury-hit season though, Bully kept up an excellent strike rate – 19 goals in 39 appearances.

He equalled his personal record of scoring in five successive matches, in a spell before and after a December achilles operation which cost him two months of action.

His 250th goal for the club, at Tranmere on May 3rd, clinched a promotion play-off spot for Wolves.

Career Record:

Season	Club	League Apps	Gls	Cups Apps	Gls
85-86	West Brom	1	-	3	-
86-87	West Brom	1 (1)	2	2	1
86-87	Wolves	30	15	7	4
87-88	Wolves	44	34	14	18
88-89	Wolves	45	37	10	13
89-90	Wolves	42	24	6	3
90-91	Wolves	43	26	5	1
91-92	Wolves	43	20	4	3
92-93	Wolves	36	16	6	3
93-94	Wolves	27	14	2 (1)	1
94-95	Wolves	31	16	8	3
Wolves' Record		341	202	62 (1)	49
TOTAL		343 (1)	204	67 (1)	50

★ *Wolves' all-time leading goalscorer.*

★ *Won the last of his 13 England caps during Graham Taylor's reign as national manager.*

★ *Collected winners medals with Wolves in Division Four, Division Three and the Sherpa Van Trophy.*

GORDON COWANS

Born Durham
27th October 1958
Joined Wolves 27th December 1994 from Derby County
Wolves' debut v Charlton Athletic
Lge (h) 28/12/94

Signed just before Christmas as midfield cover and to work with the reserves, veteran 'Sid' Cowans nevertheless made a first team place his own after a Boxing Day debut at Oldham.

His 28 appearances were broken only by a four-game absence which followed a sad night at the Hawthorns, when his half-time withdrawal through injury was a contributory factor in a morale-denting defeat by Albion.

One of the games he was forced to miss was the FA Cup quarter final replay against Crystal Palace – a replay he had set up with a memorable equaliser at Selhurst Park.

Career Record:

Season	Club	League Apps	Gls	Cups Apps	Gls
75-76	Aston Villa	- (1)	-	-	-
76-77	Aston Villa	15 (3)	3	6 (2)	-
77-78	Aston Villa	30 (5)	7	5 (3)	-
78-79	Aston Villa	34	4	2 (1)	-
79-80	Aston Villa	42	6	10	1
80-81	Aston Villa	42	5	4	-
81-82	Aston Villa	42	6	19	5
82-83	Aston Villa	42	10	15	3
83-84	Aston Villa	-	-	-	-
84-85	Aston Villa	29 (1)	1	4	-
85-88	Bari, Italy				
88-89	Aston Villa	31 (1)	2	9	-
89-90	Aston Villa	34	4	13	-
90-91	Aston Villa	38	1	11	-
91-92	Aston Villa	10 (2)	-	2 (1)	-
91-92	Blackburn R	29	2	2	1
92-93	Blackburn R	23 (1)	1	7	-
93-94	Aston Villa	9 (2)	-	6	-
93-94	Derby Co	22	1	-	-
94-95	Derby Co	17	-	5 (1)	-
94-95	Wolves	21	-	7	-
TOTAL		510 (16)	53	127 (7)	11

TONY DALEY

Born Birmingham
18th October 1967
Joined Wolves 6th June 1994 from Aston Villa, £1,250,000
Wolves' debut v Millwall
Lge (h) (as substitute) 22/10/94

The England winger endured a couple of injury-plagued seasons during his 11 years at Aston Villa – but nothing to match the annus horribilis which saw him play just 14 minutes of competitive football in his first Molineux season.

A record £1.3m signing in the summer of 1994, Daley made a bright impression during the pre-season Swedish tour before a knee problem sidelined him until his brief substitute appearance against Millwall on October 22nd.

Reaction to his injury led to a cruciate ligaments operation in November and a long period of convalescence – hopefully to be ended with a full and fruitful 1995-96 campaign.

Career Record:

Season	Club	League Apps	Gls	Cups Apps	Gls
85-86	Aston Villa	16 (7)	2	2 (1)	-
86-87	Aston Villa	25 (7)	3	6 (1)	2
87-88	Aston Villa	10 (4)	3	1	-
88-89	Aston Villa	25 (4)	5	8 (1)	1
89-90	Aston Villa	31 (1)	6	11 (1)	2
90-91	Aston Villa	22 (1)	2	8	2
91-92	Aston Villa	29 (5)	7	7	-
92-93	Aston Villa	8 (5)	2	-	-
93-94	Aston Villa	19 (8)	1	9 (1)	-
94-95	Wolves	- (1)	-	-	-
TOTAL		185 (43)	31	52 (5)	7

★ Capped at Youth, 'B' and full international levels – seven full caps

★ Coca-Cola Cup winner with Villa in 1994.

The Wolves Review 1995

ROBBIE DENNISON

Born Bainbridge, N. Ireland
30th April 1963
Joined Wolves 13th March 1987
from West Bromwich Albion, £20,000
Wolves' debut v Swansea
Lge (h) 14/3/87

The long-serving winger's Molineux days seemed numbered following the close season signing of Steve Froggatt. But, following Froggatt's season-ending injury at Reading on December 18th, Northern Ireland international Dennison came back with a bang.

He hit five goals in his first 10 full appearances, though despite a further 18 outings in the number 11 shirt he failed to find the target again. The crowd favourite did, however, earn himself a new contract – only to find himself transfer-listed at the end of the season.

Career Record:

Season	Club	League Apps Gls	Cups Apps Gls
85-86	West Brom	7 (5) 1	3 -
86-87	West Brom	2 (2) -	- -
86-87	Wolves	10 3	- -
87-88	Wolves	43 3	15 7
88-89	Wolves	41 (2) 8	10 2
89-90	Wolves	46 8	6 1
90-91	Wolves	41 (1) 6	4 (1) -
91-92	Wolves	12 (10) 1	2 (1) -
92-93	Wolves	31 (6) 5	2 (3) -
93-94	Wolves	10 (4) 2	2 (1) -
94-95	Wolves	21 (1) 4	8 (1) 1
Wolves' Record		255 (24) 40	49 (7) 11
TOTAL		264 (31) 41	52 (7) 11

★ Capped 17 times by Northern Ireland.

★ Followed Steve Bull and Andy Thompson from Albion to Wolves.

★ Integral part of Wolves teams which won Division Four, Division Three and the Sherpa Van Trophy.

ANDY DE BONT

Born Wolverhampton
7th February 1974
Joined Wolves (apprentice) 1990, (professional) 7th July 1992
Wolves' debut Has yet to make a senior debut

A highly promising local-born goal-keeper, de Bont has suffered from a chronic lack of competitive match action due to the ruling on goalkeeping substitutes.

As well as being restricted to only two appearances on the first team substitutes' bench, he has rarely been given the chance of a full reserve outing because either Paul Jones or Mike Stowell – the main contestants for the first team shirt – has been between the sticks in order to keep in trim.

Like so many young keepers at present, de Bont's progress is being held back through an artificial situation – how will he gain the experience to one day be thrust into first team action?

★ Product of Wolves' youth scheme.

The Wolves Review 1995

JOHN DE WOLF

Born Schiedam, Holland
10th December 1962
Joined Wolves 8th December 1994
Wolves' debut v Notts County
Lge (h) 10/12/94

Adorned with trademark long hair, beard and earrings, de Wolf gained instant cult hero status following his December arrival at Molineux.

But the powerful Dutch international made only 17 appearances before a serious knee injury ruled him out of the last two months of the season.

He bagged a historic hat-trick in the 4-2 win at Port Vale on February 25th – it was the first treble by a Wolves defender for 93 years.

Career Record:

Played for Sparta of Rotterdam (58 apps, 4 goals) FC Groningen (112 (1) apps, 5 goals) Feyenoord (99 (1) apps, 9 goals) before joining Wolves.

Season	Club	League Apps	Gls	Cups Apps	Gls
94/95	Wolves	13	4	4	-

★ Won 11 caps for Holland.

★ Scored 2 goals in six internationals for Holland (1987-94).

★ Captained Feyenoord to their Dutch Cup triumph in 1993-94.

★ One of the scorers in the FA Cup penalty shoot-out success against Sheffield Wednesday.

★ Played 4 games in the Olympics.

NEIL EMBLEN

Born Bromley
19th June 1971
Joined Wolves 14th July 1994
from Millwall, £600,000
Wolves' debut v Reading
Lge (h) 13/8/94

Signed as a central defender, Emblen was quickly and successfully switched to midfield after a disappointing debut against Reading on the opening day of the season.

Though he hit some scorching goals, his most crucial were injury time equalisers against Sheffield United (home) in January and Luton Town (away) in April.

He missed the end of the season after sustaining knee ligaments damage against Barnsley at Molineux on April 8th.

Career Record:

Season	Club	League Apps	Gls	Cups Apps	Gls
93-94	Millwall	12	-	1	-
94-95	Wolves	23 (4)	7	6 (4)	-
TOTAL		35 (4)	7	7 (4)	-

★ Played non-League for Sittingbourne before Millwall took him into the professional game.

★ Scored in both the last game of 1994 and the first of 1995.

The Wolves Review 1995

DARREN FERGUSON

Born Glasgow
9th February 1972
Joined Wolves 13th January 1994
from Manchester United, £250,000
Wolves' debut v Crystal Palace
Lge (h) 15/1/94

A neat midfielder signed by previous manager Graham Turner, Ferguson was involved in every game of the 1994-95 campaign until losing his place to Gordon Cowans just after Christmas.

His only appearance in the second half of the season was as substitute against Barnsley on April 8th.

Birmingham City are reputedly among the clubs interested in signing him if Graham Taylor decides to put him on the 'open to offers' list.

Career Record:

Season	Club	League Apps	Gls	Cups Apps	Gls
90-91	Man Utd	2 (3)	-	-	-
91-92	Man Utd	2 (2)	-	-	-
92-93	Man Utd	15	-	1	-
93-94	Man Utd	1 (2)	-	1 (1)	-
93-94	Wolves	12 (2)	-	4	-
94-95	Wolves	22 (2)	-	7	-
Wolves' Record		34 (4)	-	11	-
Total		54 (11)	-	13 (1)	-

★ Capped by Scotland at Youth and Under-21 levels.

★ Won Premiership championship medal with Manchester United, 1992-93.

STEVE FROGGATT

Born Lincoln
9th March 1973
Joined Wolves 11th July 1994
from Aston Villa, £1 million
Wolves' debut v Reading
Lge (h) (scored in 1-0 win) 13/8/94

Signed shortly after ex-Villa colleague Tony Daley last summer, Froggatt had a dream debut for Wolves with the winning goal against Reading on the opening day of the season.

His surging left wing runs and pinged-in crosses gave the fans plenty of exciting moments during the first half of the season.

But after being stretchered off with ankle ligaments damage at Reading on December 18th, he had to undergo surgery and took no further active part in the season.

Career Record:

Season	Club	League Apps	Gls	Cups Apps	Gls
90-91	Aston Villa	-	-	-	-
91-92	Aston Villa	6 (3)	-	2 (1)	-
92-93	Aston Villa	16 (1)	1	3 (1)	-
93-94	Aston Villa	8 (1)	1	1 (1)	-
94-95	Wolves	19	2	5	1
Total		49 (5)	4	11 (3)	1

★ Became an England Under-21 international in 1992 – after being wanted by Eire boss Jack Charlton on the strength of a family connection.

★ Played on opposite wing to Tony Daley at Villa.

DON GOODMAN

Born Leeds
9th May 1966
Joined Wolves 8th December 1994
from Sunderland, £1.1 million
Wolves' debut v Notts County
Lge (h) 10/12/94

Joined Wolves at the same time as John de Wolf and made his debut in the same match, against Notts County on December 10th.

Goodman was then involved in every game apart from the home fixture with Stoke in January, when a calf strain kept him out.

Scored only three goals but also clinched the FA Cup penalty shoot-out victory over Sheffield Wednesday with the final, dramatic spot-kick.

Career Record:

Season	Club	League Apps Gls	Cups Apps Gls
83-84	Bradford C	- (2) -	- -
84-85	Bradford C	23 (2) 5	1 (2) 4
85-86	Bradford C	19 (1) 4	1 (2) 1
86-87	Bradford C	23 5	7 (1) 3
86-87	West Brom	10 2	- -
87-88	West Brom	34 (6) 7	4 -
88-89	West Brom	30 (6) 15	5 1
89-90	West Brom	39 21	8 -
90-91	West Brom	16 (6) 8	2 -
91-92	West Brom	11 7	4 2
91-92	Sunderland	20 (2) 11	- -
92-93	Sunderland	41 16	3 1
93-94	Sunderland	34 (1) 10	9 6
94-95	Sunderland	17 (1) 3	2 -
94-95	Wolves	24 3	7 (1) -
TOTAL		341 (27) 117	53 (6) 18

★ The fourth ex-Albion player (Bull, Dennison and Thompson are the others) currently at Molineux.

PAUL JONES

Born Chirk
18th April 1967
Joined Wolves 23rd July 1991
from Kidderminster Harriers, £40,000
Wolves' debut v Peterborough Utd
Anglo-Italian Cup (h) 30/9/92

The number two goalkeeper had his first international call-ups this season – as standby for Wales – and also enjoyed a 13 match spell as Wolves' first choice midway through the campaign.

He captured the national headlines with a penalty save at Sheffield Wednesday to force a fourth round FA Cup replay – then with two further spot-kick stops in the incredible replay shoot-out which Wolves won.

Career Record:

Season	Club	League Apps Gls	Cups Apps Gls
90-91	Kidd Harriers	- -	5 -
91-92	Wolves	- -	- -
92-93	Wolves	16 -	2 -
93-94	Wolves	- -	- -
94-95	Wolves	9 -	7 -
Wolves' Record		25 -	9 -
TOTAL		25 -	14 -

★ As well as his penalty-saves in Cup matches, Jones kept out spot-kicks against both Charlton and Middlesbrough in the League.

★ Chicken farmer and part-time footballer before joining Wolves.

The Wolves Review 1995

KEVIN KEEN

Born Amersham
25th February 1967
Joined Wolves 7th July 1993
from West Ham United, £900,000
Wolves' debut v Bristol City
Lge (h) 14/8/93

A regular in 1993-94 after signing from West Ham, Keen was transferred to Stoke City last October after failing to break into the side on a regular basis under Graham Taylor.

The winger never started a Wolves League match after the opening day of the current campaign, but he was quickly in action for his new club – he made his home debut against Wolves on October 30th, scoring the opening goal in the 1-1 draw.

Career Record:

Season	Club	League Apps	Gls	Cups Apps	Gls
84/85	West Ham U	-	-	-	-
85/86	West Ham U	-	-	-	-
86/87	West Ham U	7 (6)	-	4 (1)	1
87/88	West Ham U	19 (4)	1	1 (1)	1
88/89	West Ham U	16 (8)	3	3 (6)	1
89/90	West Ham U	43 (1)	10	13	3
90/91	West Ham U	36 (4)	-	10 (1)	2
91/92	West Ham U	20 (9)	-	10	1
92/93	West Ham U	46	7	9 (1)	-
93/94	Wolves	36 (5)	7	9	2
94/95	Wolves	1	-	2 (1)	-
Wolves' Record		37 (5)	7	11 (1)	2
TOTAL		224 (37)	28	61 (11)	11

★ Son of former QPR player Mike Keen.

★ England Youth and Schoolboy international

DAVID KELLY

Born Birmingham
25th November 1965
Joined Wolves 23rd June 1993
from Newcastle United, £750,000
Wolves' debut v Bristol City
Lge (h) (1 goal scored) 14/8/93

First player since Steve Bull joined Wolves to top the goal charts ahead of Bully. Kelly's 22 goals helped earn him the Official Supporters Club's 'Player of the Year' award.

The Eire striker hit his first Wolves hat-trick at Bristol in November, plus a strong contender for Goal of the Season with his superb match-winner against Leicester in the fifth round of the FA Cup.

His unhappiest night of the season came at Lansdowne Road in February, when he scored the only goal of the Eire v. England match which was tragically abandoned through the loutish behaviour of England 'fans'.

Career Record:

Season	Club	League Apps	Gls	Cups Apps	Gls
83-84	Walsall	5 (1)	3	- (1)	-
84-85	Walsall	22 (10)	7	8 (1)	4
85-86	Walsall	7 (21)	10	1 (4)	-
86-87	Walsall	42	23	13	3
87-88	Walsall	39	20	15	10
88-89	West Ham U	21 (4)	6	13 (1)	5
89-90	West Ham U	8 (8)	1	6 (3)	2
89-90	Leicester C	10	7	-	-
90-91	Leicester C	41 (3)	14	4	1
91-92	Leicester C	12	1	5	2
91-92	Newcastle U	25	11	1	-
92-93	Newcastle U	45	24	12	4
93-94	Wolves	35 (1)	11	8	3
94-95	Wolves	38 (4)	15	12	7
Wolves' Record		73 (5)	26	20	10
TOTAL		350 (56)	153	98 (10)	41

★ Republic of Ireland international – 19 caps.

JIMMY KELLY

Born Liverpool, 14th February 1973
Joined Wolves 21st February 1992
from Wrexham, player-exchange deal involving John Paskin
Wolves' debut v Newcastle United
Lge (h) (as substitute) 31/3/92

Involvement in a murder inquiry ruled Kelly out of the early season reckoning and he never subsequently played a first team game.

His only appearance in the senior squad was as an unused substitute at Southend United on April 1st.

The Liverpudlian midfielder has not had a regular berth in the side since a five-match spell in October 1993.

Career Record:

Season	Club	League Apps	Gls	Cups Apps	Gls
90-91	Wrexham	2 (10)	-	- (2)	-
91-92	Wrexham	9	-	4	-
91-92	Wolves	- (3)	-	-	-
92-93	Wolves	-	-	-	-
(loan)	Walsall	7 (3)	2	2	-
93-94	Wolves	4	-	1	-
(loan)	Wrexham	9	-	-	-
94-95	Wolves	-	-	-	-
Wolves' Record		4 (3)	-	1	-
TOTAL		31 (16)	2	7 (2)	-

★ Played on loan for Walsall in both legs of their losing third division play-off semi-final against Crewe in 1993.

BRIAN LAW

Born Merthyr Tydfil
1st January 1970
Joined Wolves 10th January 1994
from QPR, £250,000
Wolves' debut v Oldham Athletic
Lge (a) 26/12/94

Made a fairy-tale comeback to the game after being forced into premature retirement through a foot injury sustained at his previous club QPR.

A spell of back-packing round the world cured the problem and, after a successful trial spell, Welshman Law was signed by Wolves and quickly pitched into first team action.

The central defender variously partnered John de Wolf, Peter Shirtliff and Dean Richards before missing out on the final six games of the season.

Career Record:

Season	Club	League Apps	Gls	Cups Apps	Gls
87-88	QPR	- (1)	-	-	-
88-89	QPR	6	-	4	-
89-90	QPR	10	-	-	-
90-91	QPR	3	-	2 (1)	-
91-92	QPR	-	-	-	-
92-93	Premature retirement				
93-94	Premature retirement				
94-95	Wolves	17	-	6	-
TOTAL		36 (1)	-	12 (1)	-

★ Won full and Under-21 international caps for Wales.

★ Sent off in the destiny-shaping crunch match against Middlesbrough at Molineux in February.

NEIL MASTERS

Born Lisburn, Northern Ireland
25th May 1972
Joined Wolves 22nd December 1993
from Bournemouth, £600,000
Wolves' debut v Tranmere Rovers
Lge (a) 27/12/93

The talented left back has spent more time in the treatment room than on the pitch in his injury-plagued 18 months at Molineux.

After a couple of substitute appearances during December, the Irishman made three consecutive first team starts (his longest run for Wolves) before a mid-April injury consigned him once more to the sidelines.

He was transfer-listed at the end of the season.

Career Record:

Season	Club	League Apps Gls	Cups Apps Gls
91-92	Bournemouth	- -	- -
92-93	Bournemouth	19 (1) -	4 (2) -
93-94	Bournemouth	18 2	6 2
93-94	Wolves	4 -	- -
94-95	Wolves	3 (2) -	- -
Wolves' Record		7 (2) -	- -
TOTAL		44 (3) 2	10 (2) 2

★ Played for Ballymena before joining Bournemouth.

★ His four appearances in 1993-94 included local derbies against Albion and Birmingham.

LEE MILLS

Born Mexborough
10th July 1970
Joined Wolves professional:
9th December 1992
Wolves' debut v Watford
Lge (a) (as substitute) 7/10/94

A surprise transfer to Derby ended Mills' Wolves career after just over two years at Molineux.

The 24-year-old striker progressed quite well after joining Wolves from non-league Stocksbridge, but he never claimed a regular first team place.

His best run of 1994-95 was a six-match sequence in the number nine shirt while Steve Bull was recovering from an achilles operation.

Career Record:

Season	Club	League Apps Gls	Cups Apps Gls
92/93	Wolves	- -	- -
93-94	Wolves	6 (8) 1	3 2
94-95	Wolves	7 (3) 1	4 (1) 2
TOTAL		13 (11) 2	7 (1) 4

★ Local Government officer in Barnsley before moving into professional football with Wolves.

★ Hit five goals in his first seven games for Derby – but failed to find the net in the 3-3 draw with Wolves on April 12th.

FANS ROLL CALL FOR 1996

If you wish to have your name, or that of a family member or friend, recorded in the next edition of The Wolves Review (1996), then simply write to Sports Projects Ltd. at the address below, with your name, address, telephone number and name to be included in the
Fans' Roll Call.

Closing date for the 1996 edition is Friday 31st May 1996.

Sports Projects Ltd, 188 Lightwoods Hill, Smethwick, Warley, West Midlands B67 5EH
Telephone: 0121 632 5518   Fax: 0121 633 4628

MARK RANKINE

Born Doncaster
30th September 1969
Joined Wolves 31st January 1992 from Doncaster Rovers, £70,000
Wolves' debut v Leicester City
Lge (h) (as substitute) 1/2/92

Came to prominence during the end of season run-in, when he was playing in his favourite central midfield position and produced arguably the best form of his Wolves career.

Beforehand Molineux's Mr Versatile had usually played either at right back or on the right side of midfield, though in the early stages of the season he played a couple of games in the number nine shirt deputising for Steve Bull.

Career Record:

Season	Club	League Apps Gls	Cups Apps Gls
87-88	Doncaster R	14 (4) 2	1 (1) -
88-89	Doncaster R	46 11	7 1
89-90	Doncaster R	36 2	9 1
90-91	Doncaster R	40 2	7 1
91-92	Doncaster R	24 3	6 2
91-92	Wolves	10 (5) 1	- -
92-93	Wolves	23 (4) -	5 -
93-94	Wolves	28 (3) -	8 -
94-95	Wolves	24 (3) -	8 (4) -
Wolves' Record		85 (15) 1	21 (4) -
TOTAL		245 (19) 21	51 (5) 5

★ Was on Manchester United's books as an associated schoolboy.

★ Played in every outfield position for his first club Doncaster Rovers.

DEAN RICHARDS

Born Bradford
9th June 1974
Joined Wolves (initially on loan) from Bradford City, 23rd March 1995
Wolves' debut v Southend Utd
Lge (a) 1/4/95

Brought to Molineux on loan from Bradford City on transfer deadline day, Richards impressed so much that he became Wolves' record signing a week after the end of the season.

The fee, which could stack up to £1.95m through add-ons such as appearances and international caps, was also a record for a player from the lower divisions.

Manchester United were among the clubs also chasing the signature of the 21-year-old central defender.

Career Record:

Season	Club	League Apps Gls	Cups Apps Gls
91-92	Bradford C	5 (2) 1	2 -
92-93	Bradford C	1 (2) -	- (2) -
93-94	Bradford C	46 2	7 -
94-95	Bradford C	28 1	6 1
94-95	Wolves	10 2	2 -
TOTAL		90 (4) 6	17 (2) 1

★ Hit two late goals to snatch a 3-3 draw at Derby on April 12th.

★ Gained his first international recognition with a place in the England Under-21 squad for this summer's Toulon tournament.

PETER SHIRTLIFF

Born Hoyland
6th April 1961
Joined Wolves 18th August 1993
from Sheffield Wednesday, £250,000
Wolves' debut v Birmingham City
Lge (a) 22/8/93

The club captain lost four months of the season due to an achilles injury which required surgery.

But he came back to re-claim the number six shirt and was in the starting line-up for all but three of the last 20 matches of the campaign.

Played alongside John de Wolf, his rival for the captain's armband, only three times before injury ended the Dutchman's season.

Career Record:

Season	Club	League Apps	Gls	Cups Apps	Gls
77-78	Sheff Wed	-	-	-	-
78-79	Sheff Wed	26	1	2	-
79-80	Sheff Wed	3	-	-	-
80-81	Sheff Wed	28	-	1	-
81-82	Sheff Wed	31	2	3	-
82-83	Sheff Wed	8	-	2 (1)	-
83-84	Sheff Wed	36	1	11	2
84-85	Sheff Wed	35	-	7 (1)	-
85-86	Sheff Wed	21	-	7	-
86-87	Charlton A	33	-	9	2
87-88	Charlton A	36	2	6	-
88-89	Charlton A	33 (1)	2	7	-
89-90	Sheff Wed	33	2	7	1
90-91	Sheff Wed	39	2	15	2
91-92	Sheff Wed	12	-	-	-
92-93	Sheff Wed	20	-	9	-
93-94	Wolves	39	-	8	-
94-95	Wolves	26 (2)	-	8	-
Wolves' Record		65 (2)	-	16	-
Total		459 (3)	12	102 (2)	7

★ *Won a League Cup winners medal and promotion with Sheffield Wednesday in 1990-91.*

JAMES SMITH

Born Birmingham
17th September 1974
Joined Wolves 30th June 1992 from school as trainee; professional 7th June 1993
Wolves' debut v Reading
Lge (h) 13/8/94

First player for a decade to come through the Molineux youth ranks and claim a regular first team place.

An impressive pre-season earned Smith his chance in the senior side, where his performances quickly gained him international recognition – he was selected for the England Under-21 squad after just 10 first team appearances.

The 20-year-old full back also played in the Football League Under-21 representative team which beat the Italian Serie B Under 21's 3-2 in February.

Career Record:

Season	Club	League Apps	Gls	Cups Apps	Gls
93-94	Wolves	-	-	-	-
94-95	Wolves	24 (1)	-	6	-
Total		24 (1)	-	6	-

★ *Played alongside Dean Richards in the Football League Under-21 side.*

★ *Sent off in the 2-0 defeat at Albion on March 15th.*

PAUL STEWART

Born Manchester
7th October 1964
Joined Wolves on loan 28th October 1994 from Liverpool
Wolves' debut v Stoke City
Lge (a) (as substitute) 30/10/94

Though he was signed on loan with a view to a permanent £1m transfer, Stewart returned to Liverpool after an injury-hit three months at Molineux.

The striker's loan spell started well but, after being injured while scoring against Tranmere in the 2-0 Molineux victory on September 10th, he failed to impress sufficiently in his final six appearances (two as substitute).

His temporary stay ended on a sad note – he was booed off when substituted in the 2-0 home defeat by Derby on November 27th.

Career Record:

Season	Club	League Apps	Gls	Cups Apps	Gls
80-81	Blackpool	-	-	-	-
81-82	Blackpool	9 (5)	3	-	-
82-83	Blackpool	34 (4)	7	3	1
83-84	Blackpool	40 (4)	10	5	2
84-85	Blackpool	31	7	5	1
85-86	Blackpool	42	8	5	1
86-87	Blackpool	32	21	5	1
86-87	Man City	11	2	-	-
87-88	Man City	40	24	12	4
88-89	Tottenham	29 (1)	12	5	1
89-90	Tottenham	24 (4)	8	7	1
90-91	Tottenham	35	3	11	6
91-92	Tottenham	38	5	18	1
92-93	Liverpool	21 (3)	1	7	2
93-94	Liverpool	7 (1)	-	3	-
(loan)	Crystal Pal	18	3	-	-
94-95	Liverpool	-	-	-	-
(loan)	Wolves	5 (3)	2	2	-
TOTAL		416 (25)	116	88	21

MIKE STOWELL

Born Preston
19th April 1965
Joined Wolves 28th June 1990 from Everton, £250,000
Wolves' debut v Bury
Lge (h) (won 4-0) 18/3/89

Started and ended the season as first choice keeper, but lost the jersey to Paul Jones for a 13 match sequence between Boxing Day and the beginning of March.

It was the first time in his five seasons at Wolves that Stowell had been dropped, though injuries prevented him from being an ever-present in all but the 1991-92 and 1993-94 campaigns.

Career Record:

Season	Club	League Apps	Gls	Cups Apps	Gls
85-86	PNE	-	-	-	-
85-86	Everton	-	-	1	-
86-87	Chester (loan)	14	-	2	-
87-88	Man City (loan)	14	-	1	-
88-89	Port Vale (loan)	7	-	1	-
88-89	Wolves (loan)	7	-	-	-
89-90	PNE (loan)	2	-	-	-
90-91	Wolves	39	-	5	-
91-92	Wolves	46	-	5	-
92-93	Wolves	26	-	3	-
93-94	Wolves	46	-	9	-
94-95	Wolves	37	-	8	-
Wolves' Record		194	-	30	-
TOTAL		238	-	35	-

★ Had loan spells at six clubs (including Wolves) during his four and a half years as Neville Southall's understudy at Everton.

★ Never played a first team match in a major competition for Everton.

The Wolves Review 1995

GEOFF THOMAS

Born Manchester
5th August 1964
Joined Wolves 18th June 1993 from
Crystal Palace, £800,000
Wolves' debut v Bristol City
Lge (h) 14/8/93

Just as in the 1993-94 campaign, which was his first at Molineux, Thomas was ruled out of the vast majority of the season through injury.

Apart from the opening month and a nine-match run in the Autumn, the former England midfielder was restricted to a virtual spectator's role as his injury problems confined him to playing in barely a quarter of the first team's matches.

Scored his only goal of the season in his final appearance – the 1-1 draw with Watford on March 18th.

Career Record:

Season	Club	League Apps	Gls	Cups Apps	Gls
81-82	Rochdale	-	-	-	-
82-83	Rochdale	- (1)	-	-	-
83-84	Rochdale	10	1	- (1)	-
83-84	Crewe A	5 (3)	1	-	-
84-85	Crewe A	38 (2)	4	4 (1)	-
85-86	Crewe A	37	6	5	-
86-87	Crewe A	40	10	3	-
87-88	Crystal P	41	6	5	-
88-89	Crystal P	22	5	6	1
89-90	Crystal P	33 (2)	1	14 (2)	3
90-91	Crystal P	38	6	14	2
91-92	Crystal P	30	6	8	3
92-93	Crystal P	28	2	6	1
93-94	Wolves	8	4	2	-
94-95	Wolves	13 (1)	1	3	-
Wolves' Record		21 (1)	5	5	-
Total		343 (9)	53	70 (4)	10

★ Won nine England caps, all of them under Graham Taylor's management.

ANDY THOMPSON

Born Cannock
9th November 1967
Joined Wolves 21st November 1986 from
West Bromwich Albion, £35,000
Wolves' debut v Wrexham
Lge (h) 22/11/86

A Molineux favourite for over eight years, Thompson produced yet another season of outstanding consistency – and not only in his performances at full back. He also scored nine League penalties from nine attempts.

His only missed spot-kick proved inconsequential – it came in the successful FA Cup penalty shoot-out against Sheffield Wednesday.

He was forced out of action for two spells during the season, the first through a hernia operation and the second through an ankle injury.

Career Record:

Season	Club	League Apps	Gls	Cups Apps	Gls
85-86	West Brom	13 (2)	1	3	-
86-87	West Brom	5 (4)	-	-	-
86-87	Wolves	28 (1)	8	5	-
87-88	Wolves	41 (1)	2	14	-
88-89	Wolves	46	6	10	1
89-90	Wolves	31 (2)	4	3	-
90-91	Wolves	43 (1)	3	5	-
91-92	Wolves	15 (2)	-	2	-
92-93	Wolves	15 (5)	-	1	-
93-94	Wolves	36 (1)	3	7	1
94-95	Wolves	30 (1)	9	14	-
Wolves' Record		285 (14)	35	61	2
TOTAL		303 (20)	36	64	2

★ Wolves' joint-longest serving player - arrived from Albion on the same day as Steve Bull in November 1986.

★ Important member of the Wolves team which, in successive seasons, won divisions Four and Three plus the Sherpa Van Trophy.

MARK VENUS

Born Hartlepool
6th April 1967
Joined Wolves 21st March 1988, from Leicester City, £40,000
Wolves' debut v Peterborough Utd
Lge (h) 22/3/88

A surprise end-of-season transfer listing after playing in most of the first team's 1994-95 fixtures.

Proved his versatility during the campaign by playing at left back, in the centre of defence and both as a wide and central midfielder.

He also bagged some important goals, including the winner against Bolton in the first leg of the play-off semi-final.

Career Record:

Season	Club	League Apps	Gls	Cups Apps	Gls
84-85	Hartlepool U	4	-	-(1)	-
85-86	Hartlepool U	-	-	-	-
85-86	Leicester C	1	-	-	-
86-87	Leicester C	38(1)	-	4	-
87-88	Leicester C	19(2)	1	3(1)	-
87-88	Wolves	4	-	-	-
88-89	Wolves	31(4)	-	8(1)	-
89-90	Wolves	44	2	6	-
90-91	Wolves	6	-	-	-
91-92	Wolves	46	1	5	-
92-93	Wolves	12	-	1	-
93-94	Wolves	38(1)	1	8	-
94-95	Wolves	35(4)	3	12(1)	2
Wolves' Record		216(9)	7	40(2)	2
TOTAL		278(12)	8	47(4)	2

★ Won a Division Three championship medal in 1988-89 – his first season with Wolves.

★ Apart from the number nine, played in every outfield shirt (including 12 and 14) during 1994-95.

MARK WALTERS

Born Birmingham
2nd June 1964
Joined Wolves on loan from Liverpool, 6th September 1994
Wolves' debut v Tranmere Rovers
Lge (h) 10/9/94

The former Villa and Glasgow Rangers winger marked his two-month loan spell with three goals, two of them spectacular efforts in September victories over Southend and Portsmouth.

Though he proved a more effective loan player than his Liverpool colleague Paul Stewart, Walters was never considered seriously by Graham Taylor as a permanent signing.

Career Record:

Season	Club	League Apps	Gls	Cups Apps	Gls
81-82	Aston Villa	-(1)	-	-	-
82/83	Aston Villa	18(4)	1	3(3)	3
83-84	Aston Villa	33(4)	8	10(1)	2
84-85	Aston Villa	35(1)	10	3	-
85-86	Aston Villa	40	10	13	3
86-87	Aston Villa	18(3)	3	6(1)	1
87-88	Aston Villa	24	7	4	-
Dec 87- Aug 91	Rangers	101(5)	32	37	19
91-92	Liverpool	18(7)	3	11(1)	3
92-93	Liverpool	26(8)	11	10	2
93-94	Liverpool	7(10)	-	1(2)	-
(loan)	Stoke City	9	2	-	-
94-95	Liverpool	-	-	-	-
(loan)	Wolves	11	3	-	-
TOTAL		340(43)	88	100(8)	33

★ Sold to Rangers during Graham Taylor's managerial reign at Aston Villa.

★ Won three successive Scottish League championships with Rangers – also a Scottish League Cup winner in 1989 and 1991.

JERMAINE WRIGHT

Born Greenwich
21st October 1975
Joined Wolves 21st December 1994 from Millwall, £50,000
Wolves' debut v Sunderland
Lge (h) (as substitute) 8/3/95

Signed from Millwall just before Christmas – and before he had a single League game under his belt – rookie Wright showed his potential in a handful of substitute appearances towards the end of the season.

With the more established Paul Birch and Robbie Dennison both transfer-listed, 19-year-old Wright looks destined to become Wolves' first choice wide-man behind wingers Tony Daley and Steve Froggatt.

Career Record:

Season	Club	League Apps Gls	Cups Apps Gls
Wolves 94-95		- (6) -	- (1) -

★ On trial at Bolton before Wolves stepped in to snap up the teenager.

★ Scored on his home debut for the Reserves, a 1-0 win against Blackburn Rovers on 16th January.

LEAGUE ATTENDANCES

	Average	Highest	Lowest
Wolves	26,001	28,298	22,768
Middlesbrough	18,641	23,903	14,878
Sunderland	15,388	19,758	11,661
West Bromwich A	15,217	21,071	11,782
Sheffield United	14,408	20,693	11,568
Derby County	13,588	16,839	10,585
Bolton Wanderers	13,029	18,370	9,519
Stoke City	12,918	20,429	9,111
Burnley	12,008	17,766	9,655
Charlton Athletic	10,189	13,638	8,169
Swindon Town	9,407	14,036	6,553
Reading	9,350	13,223	6,921
Port Vale	9,214	19,510	7,141
Tranmere Rovers	8,908	16,377	5,480
Watford	8,124	10,108	6,024
Bristol City	7,989	11,127	6,030
Millwall	7,680	12,289	5,260
Luton Town	7,352	9,651	5,764
Notts County	7,202	11,102	4,703
Barnsley	6,525	11,711	3,659
Oldham Athletic	6,439	11,962	5,465
Portsmouth	6,269	13,466	5,272
Grimsby Town	5,921	10,112	3,216
Southend United	5,154	8,522	3,619

Leage matches only – not including the play-offs.

★ Wolves average gate for the season, excluding the play-offs, is 7,360 above that of their nearest rivals, Middlesbrough.
★ Wolves had a staggering 20 home gates higher than Middlesbrough's highest of the season.
★ West Brom, third in the highest gate of the season league, had a best attendance lower than Wolves' lowest of the season.
★ Eight clubs had their highest gate of the season against Wolves.

FIRST TEAM APPEARANCES & GOALSCORERS

	LEAGUE Apps	LEAGUE Gls	PLAY-OFFS Apps	PLAY-OFFS Gls	FA CUP Apps	FA CUP Gls	LGE CUP Apps	LGE CUP Gls	ANGLO-ITALIAN Apps	ANGLO-ITALIAN Gls
Tom BENNETT	4 (3)	-	-	-	2 (1)	-	-	-	1	-
Paul BIRCH	8 (2)	1	-	-	1	-	3	1	3 (1)	-
Paul BLADES	30 (2)	-	-	-	3	-	2 (1)	-	4	-
Steve BULL	31	16	2	1	2	-	3	2	1	-
Gordon COWANS	21	-	2	-	5	1	-	-	-	-
Tony DALEY	- (1)	-	-	-	-	-	-	-	-	-
Robbie DENNISON	21 (1)	4	2	-	6	1	-	-	- (1)	-
John De WOLF	13	4	-	-	4	-	-	-	-	-
Neil EMBLEN	23 (4)	7	-	-	3 (2)	-	1 (1)	-	2 (1)	-
Darren FERGUSON	22 (2)	-	-	-	-	-	3	-	4	-
Steve FROGGATT	19	2	-	-	-	-	3	1	2	-
Don GOODMAN	24	3	2	-	5 (1)	-	-	-	-	-
Paul JONES	9	-	-	-	4	-	-	-	3	-
Kevin KEEN	1	-	-	-	-	-	- (1)	-	2	-
David KELLY	38 (4)	15	2	-	6	4	3	2	1	1
Brian LAW	17	-	-	-	6	-	-	-	-	-
Neil MASTERS	3 (2)	-	-	-	-	-	-	-	-	-
Lee MILLS	7 (3)	1	-	-	2 (1)	1	-	-	2	1
Mark RANKINE	24 (3)	-	2	-	4 (1)	-	- (1)	-	2 (2)	-
Dean RICHARDS	10	2	2	-	-	-	-	-	-	-
Peter SHIRTLIFF	26 (2)	-	2	-	2	-	2	-	2	-
James SMITH	24 (1)	-	-	-	1	-	3	-	2	-
Paul STEWART	5 (3)	2	-	-	-	-	-	-	2	-
Mike STOWELL	37	-	2	-	2	-	3	-	1	-
Geoff THOMAS	13 (1)	1	-	-	-	-	1	-	2	-
Andy THOMPSON	30 (1)	9	2	-	5	-	3	-	4	-
Mark VENUS	35 (4)	3	2	1	3 (1)	-	3	-	4	1
Mark WALTERS	11	3	-	-	-	-	-	-	-	-
Jermaine WRIGHT	(6)	-	- (1)	-	-	-	-	-	-	-
Own Goals	-	4	-	-	-	-	-	-	-	-

Unused Substitutes:
Paul Jones 45, Mike Stowell 14, Jermaine Wright 10, Tom Bennett 9, Mark Rankine 8, Paul Birch 7, Paul Blades 6, Lee Mills 6, James Smith 5, Kevin Keen 3, Brian Law 3, Geoff Thomas 3, Robbie Dennison 2, Andy de Bont 1, Neil Emblen 1, James Kelly 1, Steven Piearce 1, Peter Shirtliff 1, Mark Venus 1, Mark Walters 1.

Goalscorers in friendly games:
Steve Bull 13, Lee Mills 7, Tony Daley 3, David Kelly 3, Robbie Dennison 2, Steve Froggatt 2, Paul Cook 1, Don Goodman 1, Andy Thompson 1, own goal 1.

The Wolves Review 1995

ENDSLEIGH LEAGUE DIVISION 1 STATISTICS 1994-95

FINAL TABLE

		Pl	W	D	L	F	A	W	D	L	F	A	W	D	L	F	A	Pts
1	Middlesbrough	46	15	4	4	41	19	8	9	6	26	21	23	13	10	67	40	82
2	Reading	46	12	7	4	34	21	11	3	9	24	23	23	10	13	58	44	79
3	Bolton Wanderers	46	16	6	1	43	13	5	8	10	24	32	21	14	11	67	45	77
4	Wolves	46	15	5	3	39	18	6	8	9	38	43	21	13	12	77	61	77
5	Tranmere Rovers	46	17	4	2	51	23	5	6	12	16	35	22	10	14	67	58	76
6	Barnsley	46	15	6	2	42	19	5	6	12	21	33	20	12	14	63	52	72
7	Watford	46	14	6	3	33	17	5	7	11	19	29	19	13	14	52	46	70
8	Sheffield United	46	12	9	2	41	21	5	8	10	33	34	17	17	12	74	55	68
9	Derby County	46	12	6	5	44	23	6	6	11	22	28	18	12	16	66	51	66
10	Grimsby Town	46	12	7	4	36	19	5	7	11	26	37	17	14	15	62	56	65
11	Stoke City	46	10	7	6	31	21	6	8	9	19	32	16	15	15	50	53	63
12	Millwall	46	11	8	4	36	22	5	6	12	24	38	16	14	16	60	60	62
13	Southend United	46	13	2	8	33	25	5	6	12	21	48	18	8	20	54	73	62
14	Oldham Athletic	46	12	7	4	34	21	4	6	13	26	39	16	13	17	60	60	61
15	Charlton Athletic	46	11	6	6	33	25	5	5	13	25	41	16	11	19	58	66	59
16	Luton Town	46	8	6	9	35	30	7	7	9	26	34	15	13	18	61	64	58
17	Port Vale	46	11	5	7	30	24	4	8	11	28	40	15	13	18	58	64	58
18	Portsmouth	46	9	8	6	31	28	6	5	12	22	35	15	13	18	53	63	58
19	West Bromwich A.	46	13	3	7	33	24	3	7	13	18	33	16	10	20	51	57	58
20	Sunderland	46	5	12	6	22	22	7	6	10	19	23	12	18	16	41	45	54
21	Swindon Town	46	9	6	8	28	27	3	6	14	26	46	12	12	22	54	73	48
22	Burnley	46	8	7	8	36	33	3	6	14	13	41	11	13	22	49	74	46
23	Bristol City	46	8	8	7	26	28	3	4	16	16	35	11	12	23	42	63	45
24	Notts County	46	7	8	8	26	28	2	5	16	19	38	9	13	24	45	66	40

PLAY-OFFS

SEMI FINALS
Wolves 2 Bolton Wanderers 1
Bolton Wanderers 2 Wolves 0
Bolton Wanderers win 3-2 on aggregate

Tranmere Rovers 1 Reading 3
Reading 0 Tranmere Rovers 0
Reading win 3-1 on aggregate

FINAL (at Wembley)
Bolton Wanderers 4 Reading 3
After extra time. Bolton Wanderers gain promotion to the Premier League.

ROLL OF HONOUR
Division One Champions: Middlesbrough
Also promoted (Through the play-offs): Bolton Wanderers
FA Cup winners: Everton
Coca-Cola Cup winners: Liverpool

FACTS AND FIGURES
Most goals: 77, Wolves
Most home goals: 51, Tranmere Rovers
Most away goals: 38, Wolves
Least goals: 41, Sunderland
Least home goals: 22, Sunderland
Least away goals: 13, Burnley
Least goals conceded: 40, Middlesbrough
Least home goals conceded: 13, Bolton W
Least away goals conceded: 21, Middlesbro'
Most goals conceded: 74, Burnley
Most home goals conceded: 33, Burnley
Most away goals conceded: 48, Southend U
Best home record: 55pts, Tranmere Rovers
Best away record: 36pts, Reading
Worst home record: 27pts, Sunderland
Worst away record: 11pts, Notts County

WOLVES LEADING SCORERS
(including league and cup games)

22	David Kelly
19	Steve Bull
9	Andy Thompson
7	Neil Emblen
5	Robbie Dennison
5	Mark Venus
4	John De Wolf

154   *The Wolves Review 1995*

RESERVE AND YOUTH ROUND-UP

Injury-hit season affects all teams

After looking relegation certainties following a disastrous opening to their Pontins Legaue season, the Reserves finished in a respectable mid-table position.

Just three of the first 11 games ended in victories. But, following the appointment of Ian Miller as Reserve team coach in place of the departed Stuart Gray, the second string climbed off the bottom of the table and lost only three of their final 23 outings.

The Youth team enjoyed a run in the FA Youth Cup before succumbing to the eventual losing finalists Tottenham Hotspur.

They looked to be heading for a top six finish in the Purity League but, in the closing stages, were drained of resources when several players were moved up to the Reserves in the wake of the club's horrendous injury problems.

Importantly, however, this meant that several schoolboy triallists were given the opportunity of playing at Youth team level.

Five of the Youth team - Carl Robinson, Gavin Mahon, Quentin Townsend, Matthew Bytheway and Chris Westwood - were signed on professional terms at the end of the season.

PONTINS LEAGUE DIVISION ONE

	P	W	D	L	F	A	Pts
Bolton W	34	22	5	7	69	46	71
Leeds United	34	20	4	10	54	36	64
Everton	34	17	10	7	63	32	61
Sheffield United	34	17	8	9	49	36	59
Tranmere Rovers	34	16	9	9	65	53	57
Derby County	34	15	7	12	51	52	52
Notts County	34	15	6	13	46	48	51
WBA	34	13	8	13	53	54	47
Wolves	**34**	**12**	**11**	**11**	**40**	**52**	**47**
Manchester Utd	34	12	9	13	45	45	45
Stoke City	34	12	7	15	46	44	43
Blackburn	34	10	12	12	31	37	42
Liverpool	34	11	9	14	40	48	42
Nottingham F.	34	9	11	14	45	46	38
Sunderland	34	10	8	16	49	56	38
Aston Villa	34	11	4	19	41	53	37
Coventry	34	8	7	19	30	45	31
Rotherham	34	7	5	22	34	67	26

PONTIN'S LEAGUE FIXTURES AND RESULTS

Aug 15	H	WBA	3-1	Bennett, Rankine, Band
Aug 24	A	Bolton W	1-5	Williams
Sep 1	H	Man Utd	0-1	
Sep 6	A	Derby County	0-7	
Sep 19	H	Aston Villa	1-2	Keen
Sep 28	A	Leeds Utd	1-2	Piearce
Oct 3	H	Liverpool	0-1	
Oct 11	A	Rotherham	1-1	Rankine
Oct 19	A	Tranmere R	4-1	Birch 3, Daley
Oct 27	H	Everton	2-5	Emblen 2
Nov 9	A	Sunderland	0-5	
Nov 16	H	Coventry City	1-1	Simkin
Nov 24	A	Nott'm Forest	2-0	Mills, Piearce
Nov 28	H	Tranmere R	1-1	Mills
Dec 7	A	WBA	2-1	Kelly, Mills
Dec 12	H	Bolton W	2-2	Mills, o.g.
Dec 19	H	Stoke City	2-2	Bennett, Voice
Jan 10	A	Sheffield Utd	1-2	Rankine
Jan 16	H	Blackburn R	1-0	Wright
Feb 1	H	Sunderland	2-1	Thomas, Sansam
Feb 6	A	Coventry City	0-0	
Feb 13	H	Nott'm Forest	1-0	Mills
Mar 9	A	Aston Villa	2-1	Piearce 2
Mar 13	H	Leeds Utd	0-1	
Mar 22	A	Man Utd	0-0	
Mar 27	H	Derby County	1-1	Piearce
Apr 6	A	Stoke City	1-0	Foley
Apr 10	H	Notts County	0-0	
Apr 19	A	Blackburn R	0-4	
Apr 24	H	Sheffield Utd	2-0	Rawlins, Westwood
Apr 26	A	Everton	2-1	Bennett, o.g.
May 1	A	Liverpool	2-1	Birch, Foley
May 4	A	Notts County	0-0	
May 8	H	Rotherham	2-2	Townsend, Robinson

BIRMINGHAM SENIOR CUP

Nov 21	A	Hednesford T	2-2	Voice, Mills
Dec 14	A	Hednesford T	0-8	

The Wolves Review 1995

RESERVE TEAM APPEARANCES & GOALSCORERS

	PONTINS LGE Apps	Gls	SENIOR CUP Apps	Gls
Dale BAND	2	1	-	-
Jason BARNETT	17(3)	-	2	-
Tom BENNETT	24(2)	3	1	-
Paul BIRCH	14(1)	4	-	-
Paul BLADES	7	-	-	-
Matthew BYTHEWAY	6(2)	-	1	-
Paul COOK	1	-	-	-
Gordon COWANS	1	-	-	-
Glenn CROWE	-(1)	-	-	-
Tony DALEY	1	1	-	-
Paul DAVIS	-	-	-(1)	-
Andy DE BONT	6(1)	-	2	-
Robbie DENNISON	17	-	-	-
Justin ELLITTS	-(1)	-	-(1)	-
Neil EMBLEN	6(1)	2	-	-
Darren FERGUSON	13	-	-	-
Dominic FOLEY	3	2	-	-
STUART GRAY	2	-	-	-
Michael INNES	1	-	-	-
Paul JONES	23	-	-	-
Kevin KEEN	6	1	-	-
David KELLY	1	1	-	-
Jimmy KELLY	16(1)	-	2	-
Brian LAW	10	-	-	-
Richard LEADBEATER	2	-	-	-
Rob MAAS	2	-	-	-
Andy MacBETH	3(4)	-	2	-
Gavin MAHON	4(3)	-	-	-
Chris MARSDEN	3	-	-	-
Neil MASTERS	7(1)	-	-	-
Joso MATOVAC	3	-	-	-
Lee MILLS	16	5	1	1
David MORRIS	-	-	1	-
Lee NOBLE	1	-	-	-
Mark OWEN	-(2)	-	-	-
Steven PIERCE	22(4)	5	1(1)	-
Mark RANKINE	11	3	-	-
Matt RAWLINS	2	1	-	-
Chris REYNOLDS	5	-	-	-

	PONTINS LGE Apps	Gls	SENIOR Apps	Gls
Dean RICHARDS	1	-	-	-
Carl ROBINSON	5(2)	1	1	-
John ROSS	-	-	1	-
Chris SANSAM	2	1	-	-
Darren SHAW	5	-	2	-
Peter SHIRTLIFF	3	-	-	-
Darren SIMKIN	14	1	1	-
James SMITH	13	-	-	-
Paul STEWART	2	-	-	-
Mike STOWELL	4	-	-	-
Geoff THOMAS	8	1	-	-
Andy THOMPSON	3	-	-	-
Quentin TOWNSEND	7	1	1	-
Mark VENUS	8	-	-	-
Scott VOICE	12(2)	1	2	1
Chris WESTWOOD	17(1)	1	1	-
Gareth WILLIAMS	-(1)	1	-	-
Jermaine WRIGHT	12	1	-	-
OWN GOALS	-	2	-	-

FIRST DIVISION LEADING SCORERS

John Aldridge	Tranmere R	24 (2)
Jan Aage Fjortoft	Swindon Town	16 (10)
David Kelly	**Wolves**	**16 (7)**
John McGinlay	Bolton W	16 (6)
Gerry Creaney	Portsmouth	18 (4)
David Whyte	Charlton A	19 (2)
Martin Foyle	Port Vale	16 (4)
Chris Malkin	Tranmere R	16 (3)
Nathan Blake	Sheffield Utd	17 (1)
Steve Bull	**Wolves**	**15 (3)**
Sean McCarthy	Oldham A	18
John Hendrie	Middlesbrough	15 (2)
Mixu Paatelainen	Bolton W	13 (3)
Phil Gray	Sunderland	12 (3)
Paul Peschisolido	Stoke City	13 (2)
Stuart Lovell	Reading	11 (3)
Neil Woods	Grimsby Town	14

The figure immediately to the right of the club is the number of League goals scored, the figure in brackets is the number of Cup goals scored.

YOUTH TEAM RESULTS

MIDLAND PURITY YOUTH LEAGUE

Aug	13	Notts County	2-1	H	Ellitts, Leadbeater
Aug	20	Birmingham City	1-4	A	Mahon
Aug	27	Nottingham Forest	4-2	H	Mahon, Robinson, Leadbeater, Morris
Sep	10	P'borough United	1-0	H	Leadbeater
Sep	17	Derby County	0-2	A	
Sep	24	Northampton Town	2-0	H	Ellitts, Owen
Oct	1	Grimsby Town	2-1	A	Townsend, Leadbeater
Oct	15	Leicester City	0-4	A	
Oct	29	Lincoln City	4-0	H	Bytheway, Townsend, Robinson, Leadbeater
Nov	5	P'borough United	1-1	A	Nwadike
Nov	19	Mansfield Town	1-1	H	Ellitts
Dec	3	Northampton Town	1-1	A	Davis
Dec	10	Stoke City	3-0	A	Leadbeater, Morris, Cotterill
Dec	17	Aston Villa	1-3	A	Hill
Jan	14	Notts County	1-2	A	Ellitts
Feb	1	Shrewsbury Town	3-0	H	Robinson, Leadbeater (2)
Feb	4	Nottingham Forest	1-0	A	Robinson
Feb	18	Derby County	2-0	H	Ellitts, Owen
Feb	25	Port Vale	4-5	A	Crowe (2), Hill, Smith
Mar	11	Shrewsbury Town	3-0	A	Harper (2), Davis
Mar	15	Walsall	0-1	H	
Mar	18	WBA	6-0	H	Crowe (3), Hill (2), Mahon
Mar	25	Leicester City	3-1	H	Cotterill, Owen, Ross
Mar	29	Grimsby	3-0	H	Leadbeater, Owen (2)
Apr	1	Stoke City	1-4	A	Thomas
Apr	5	Coventry City	3-4	H	Ellitts, Crowe (2)
Apr	8	Lincoln City	1-4	A	Ross
Apr	12	Aston Villa	0-2	H	
Apr	15	Walsall	3-3	A	Cotterill, Willoughby, Friedman
Apr	19	Coventry City	1-3	A	Hill
Apr	22	Mansfield Town	0-1	A	
Apr	26	Port Vale	0-2	H	
Apr	29	WBA	0-6	A	
May	3	Birmingham City	1-1	H	Owen

MIDLAND PURITY YOUTH LEAGUE CUP

Oct	22	Mansfield Town	4-0	H	Ellitts, Mahon, Owen, Cotterill
Mar	8	Aston Villa	2-3	A	Leadbeater, Owen

FA YOUTH CUP

Nov	2	Cambridge United	1-1	H	Ellitts
Nov	9	Cambridge United	6-2	A	Westwood, Ellitts, Leadbeater (2), Morris (2)
Nov	30	Brentford	2-0	H	Leadbeater, Morris
Dec	20	Tottenham Hotspur	2-4	A	Ellitts, Townsend

MIDLAND YOUTH CUP

Aug	29	Stoke City	2-2	A	Ellitts, Mahon
Sep	29	Stoke City	2-3 (aet)	H	Ellitts, Mahon

The Wolves Review 1995

YOUTH TEAM APPEARANCES & GOALSCORERS

	PURITY LEAGUE		PLYC		FAYC	
	Apps	Gls	Apps	Gls	Apps	Gls
Jason ATKINS	1	-	-	-	-	-
Steven BIDDLE	14 (2)	-	-	-	-	-
Mathew BYTHEWAY	21	1	2	-	4	-
Martin CARTER	1	-	-	-	-	-
John COTTERILL	21 (4)	3	1	1	4	-
Glenn CROWE	4	7	-	-	-	-
Paul DAVIS	20 (6)	2	1	-	- (1)	-
Justin ELLITTS	21 (1)	6	2	1	4	3
Gordon FRIEDMAN	2	1	-	-	-	-
Lee HARPER	13 (3)	2	-	-	-	-
Danny HILL	9 (1)	4	-	-	- (2)	-
Paul HILL	1	-	-	-	-	-
Martin HOLMES	14 (3)	-	1	-	-	-
Lee HOOK	6	-	1	-	1	-
Richard LEADBEATER	25 (1)	9	2	1	4	3
Gavin MAHON	19 (3)	3	2	1	4	-
Andy MALE	1	-	-	-	-	-
David MORRIS	10 (4)	2	-	-	4	3
Leroy MURPHY	- (1)	-	-	-	-	-
Sean MURPHY	2	-	-	-	-	-
Emeka NWADIKE	22	1	-	-	-	-
Anthony O'CONNOR	3	-	-	-	-	-
Mark OWEN	18 (6)	6	2	2	- (2)	-
Mark PERRY	- (1)	-	-	-	-	-
Adam PINNEY	1	-	-	-	-	-
Jay PITTERWAY	- (1)	-	-	-	-	-
Carl ROBINSON	20	4	2	-	4	-
Danny ROCHESTER	4	-	-	-	-	-
John ROSS	16	1	2	-	3	-
Robert SAWYERS	9	-	-	-	-	-
Darryl SMITH	5 (2)	1	-	-	-	-
Wyn THOMAS	1	-	-	-	-	-
Quentin TOWNSEND	21	3	2	-	4	1
Chris WESTWOOD	9 (1)	-	1	-	4	1
John WILLOUGHBY	5	1	-	-	-	-
John WILLO	1	-	-	-	-	-
Chris WILSON	10 (2)	-	-	-	1	-
Ian WRIGHT	24	-	1	-	3	-

SUBSCRIBERS' ROLL OF HONOUR

001	Michael Ashmore	058	Lauren Painter	115	Nick Hone
002	Beryl Cooper	059	Alex Painter	116	P. Williams
003	Bob Hotchkiss	060	Nick Mitton	117	A. Richards
004	Pamela James	061	Ron Kendrick	118	Les Hatton
005	Richard White	062	Peter R. Griffiths	119	Richard Finch
006	Paul Reid	063	Nigel Perry	120	Tracey Gilmour
007	Tracey Linforth	064	Gavin Perry	121	Andrew Gilmour
008	Martin Linforth	065	Ian Michael Price	122	A.J. Tyrer
009	Alan Leese	066	Mark Jesic	123	Glyn H. Jones
010	Ian Ferguson	067	Simon Walters	124	Lance Lewin
011	Wayne Harrison	068	Mark Anthony Perry	125	Peter Webb
012	Craig Langston	069	Luke Anthony Perry	126	Raymond Mark Peers
013	Philip Magness	070	Shaun Rickie Perry	127	Ron Stevens
014	Debbie Jones	071	Martin Logue	128	Andy Stevens
015	Jason Smith	072	Gareth Kendrick	129	Georgina Coady
016	Colin Roy Pheasant	073	Steven Boden	130	Sarah Handley
017	Neil Whitehouse	074	Miss Sarah Bushall	131	Barrie Lovewell
018	Jonathan Patrick	075	David Farmer	132	William Danino
019	Carron Patrick	076	Brian Cooper	133	Kate Evans
020	Arthur Patrick	077	Dave Walton	134	Michael Evans
021	Daniel Patrick	078	Grace Rowley	135	Steve English
022	Mark Willis	079	David Haddon	136	Chris Collier
023	Stephen James Price	080	Michael Coldicott	137	John Robinson
024	Desmond Brittain	081	Mrs Joanne Baker	138	Darren Winwood
025	Kelvin Graham	082	Jessica Anne Brittain	139	Miss Lynn Winwood
026	Steve Mohammed	083	Richard Allen	140	Christopher Preece
027	R.J. Pooler	084	Roy Kimbley	141	Andrew M.W. Smith
028	Miss P.A. Pooler	085	Gordon Burcher	142	Peter Duggins
029	Chris Dawson	086	Jason Silver	143	Lee Spencer
030	H. Bradley	087	Albert E. Williams	144	Adam Brachmanski
031	Mrs M.H. Bradley	088	Lee Mitchell	145	Wayne Johnson
032	Don Matthews	089	David C. Chalstrey	146	Andrew George Wells
033	Steve Knowles	090	Mark Rigby	147	Eddie Baker
034	Mark Turvey	091	Haley Rigby	148	Doug Carter
035	Karl Brooks	092	Martin Astley	149	Jean Carter
036	Mark Stagg	093	Neil Chatter	150	Adam Carter
037	Ron Slater	094	Michael Skelding	151	Steven Morris
038	Colin Preece	095	Stephen Street	152	Kevin Wallsgrove
039	Warren Nicholls	096	Graham Harridence	153	Rosanna Wallsgrove
040	Brian Nicholls	097	Aaron Belcher	154	P.A. Simmonds
041	Doreen Nicholls	098	Iain Finch	155	George Millington
042	Derek Turner	099	Richard Crisp	156	Paul John Miller
043	John Game	100	Nick Daniels	157	Danny Walters
044	Jayne Cartwright	101	Graham Partridge	158	Austin Patrick Stack
045	Jonathan Hartland	102	Stephen Carvell	159	Douglas John Pearl
046	Rachel Hartland	103	Peter Carvell	160	David Cook
047	Howard Dean	104	Alan Hayes	161	Alan Cook
048	Matthew Dean	105	S.P. Edgington	162	Craig O'Dea
049	David Richards	106	Richard Letherbarrow	163	Pete O'Dea
050	Thomas Hughes	107	P.J. Megarity	164	Miss Samantha Wright
051	Malcolm Chambers	108	Mrs Carol Megarity	165	Tony Wright
052	Robert Coleman	109	Ben Otto	166	Andrew Dennis Jones
053	Craig Stuart Wood	110	P. Williams	167	Paul D.D. Davis
054	Paul McKenna	111	Dave Howes	168	Louise Cotter
055	Simon Halfpenny	112	Miss M. Steventon	169	Michael Cotter
056	Emma Wright	113	Tim Gibbons	170	Alexandra Jarvis
057	Dave Allden	114	Tom Gibbons	171	Terry Lay

The Wolves Review 1995

SUBSCRIBERS' ROLL OF HONOUR

172 Andrew McCheyne	229 Paul Maskew	286 V.R. Guano
173 Robert Belcher (Darlo Bob)	230 Graham Reed	287 Dennis Noble
174 Mrs Sara Scott	231 Mark D. Burgess	288 Ricky D. Harrison
175 John Adams	232 Miss Anne Viola	289 Michael Ryder
176 David Crowe	233 Christopher Reed	290 John B. Langford
177 Don Cooper	234 Brian Skyrme	291 Graham Rowley
178 Nigel Musgrove	235 Phyllis Skyrme	292 Robert Emery
179 Jonathan Matthews	236 Clifford John Baker	293 Alan Fisher
180 Paul White	237 Christopher John Baker	294 Brian Lockwood
181 Brian Dennis	238 Melanie Francesca Baker	295 Paul Anthony Lloyd
182 David Winchurch	239 Christopher Bale	296 Sarah Hubball
183 Robert (Bob) Gripton	240 Jimmy Jordan	297 John A. Crawford
184 Jason Rhodes	241 Andrew Perry	298 David Lamerton
185 Philip Foster	242 David Dewar	299 Les Smith
186 Kevin Coates	243 Stan West	300 Garry Harris
187 Steven Banfield	244 Miss Gemma Pope	301 Roger Lane
188 Miss P. Dickinson	245 Kevin Blount	302 Paul Stanton
189 Stuart Knight	246 Andy Pope	303 Laura Stanton
190 Bronte Matthews	247 Michael Edward Bonser	304 Rebekah Stanton
191 Ronald Paul Pitt	248 Stuart W. Tomkins	305 Vic Batchelder
192 David Staniland	249 Arthur Campbell	306 David Thomas Jenkins
193 Craig Bailey	250 James Trevitt	307 Neil Ian Jenkins
194 John Harvey	251 Steve Rowley	308 Robert Casson
195 Sharon Louise Harley	252 Per Bjorno	309 Jamie Fleet
196 Spencer Plumb	253 Alan Rogers	310 Jeremy (Jez) Wood
197 Karen Charles	254 Clive Corbett	311 Master Lee Markwick
198 John Alan Chorzempa	255 Keith M. Stanley	312 Mike Whyton
199 Darrel Parker	256 David Tomlinson	313 Sue Gavin
200 John Parker	257 Aled Wyn Jones	314 Mike Lloyd Whyton
201 Steven John Robinson	258 Lee Mansell	315 A. Willetts
202 Ryan Edward Sliz	259 Stephen Mansell	316 Philip Simmonds
203 Edward Sliz	260 Kevin Halligan	317 Arthur Simmonds
204 Allan Gripton	261 Emma Westwood	318 Simon Parry
205 Christopher Gripton	262 Bryan Bridges	319 John Parry
206 Mark Andrew Watts	263 Paul Burden	320 Nicholas Parry
207 Michael Gardener	264 James Muggeridge	321 Samantha Lavender
208 P.J. Butler	265 Rebecca Portman	322 Antony Wayne Yapp
209 D. Dorrance	266 Claire Henderson	323 Christopher Shelton
210 Philip Ruff	267 Simon Powell	324 Andrew Evans
211 Alexander Molloy	268 Morgan Powell	325 June Stretton
212 Bones	269 Graham Cozens	326 John Dobson
213 Clare Watts	270 Keith Greenaway	327 Frank Rowley
214 R.J. Hayward	271 Stevie Smith	328 Peter J. Rowley
215 Roy S. Davies	272 Claire Smith	329 Chris Mountain
216 Emma Ruff	273 Ron Smith	330 Stuart Steer
217 Jean Timmins	274 Clive Smith	331 W.R. Jones
218 Barry Timmins	275 Vinny Coates	332 Ross Neumann
219 Mark Timmins	276 Damian Phelan	333 Andrew Brass
220 Chris Smaje	277 Victor Moore	334 Neil Wallace
221 Neil Stowe	278 Alan Richardson	335 Carl Davies
222 Andrew Icke	279 James Coates	336 Alex J.W. Davies
223 Helen Robinson	280 George Cooper	337 W. Harrison
224 Anthony Redgewell	281 Raynor Stanley	338 P. Harrison
225 Helen Lapper	282 Mark Stanley	339 Graham Burford
226 Emma Cox	283 Robert Williams	340 David Williams
227 Martin Hannaford	284 Steve Smith	341 Colin Cameron
228 Harry Davenhill	285 Bernard Dowler	342 Carl Smith

160   *The Wolves Review 1995*